★★★★★

Average Customer Review, Amazon.co.uk

(16 reviews, 16 five star ratings*)

"Books about football tend to fall into one of several broad categories: the anodyne, air-brushed official club tomes, auto-biographies promising interesting insight and delivering strings of banal, safe comment instead, books which examine football's cultural and societal role, leaving the reader wondering whether the author has in fact ever attended a match, and the books glorifying hooliganism for forty year-old readers who frankly should know better. *Golden Past Red Future*, co-authored by Paul Tomkins and Jonathan Swain, is a refreshing change from the general stultifying pigeon-holing of football titles by the publishing industry, a capable entry in the sub-genre of books about football by club supporters who have nothing to do with trying to assert themselves by behaving as playground bullies on the weekend. Or weeknight, as it were.

Written from the unabashed and unashamed perspective of a Liverpool supporter chronicling the season past, *Golden Past Red Future*'s prose is noteworthy for its attempt to present both the hard-head, club-before-everything-else die-hard supporter perspective interspersed with genuine insight and reflection on both the history and upcoming events at Liverpool football club. Bridging the gap between Constant Fan and detached, Armchair Theoretician is as difficult a task as any in football supporter circles, but Tomkins and Swain weave the magic of the Kop and the role of the passionate Liverpool fan base into a more sober reflection on the tidal wave of change that swept over Anfield this season past with the arrival of Rafael Benitez and the Spanish emigre contingent.

Of course, the book does not neglect the single biggest story of Liverpool's past season, with eyewitness accounts from Tomkins on events in Istanbul. One of the successes of *Golden Past Red Future* is the conveying of the extreme roller-coaster nature of Liverpool's play during the 2004-05 season, the inconsistent performances in the Premiership contrasted with the true-grit, wildly exciting European displays culminating in the Champions League trophy raised above club captain Steven Gerrard's head.

A must-read for Liverpool supporters, particularly those with an open mind for considering issues confronting the club other than which multi-million pound player might be arriving in the next transfer window, *Golden Past Red Future* will appeal to fans of clubs other than Liverpool interested in examining the long, strange saga of a club with tremendous history trying to adjust to the demands of both a modern, financially-centered league competition and a support base firmly in touch with the time when the club swept all before them.

Golden Past Red Future is worth every penny for both committed Liverpool supporters and modern football fans alike."

Bill Urban, Squarefootball

golden past red future

Liverpool FC: Champions of Europe 2005

★★★★★

Paul Tomkins
Jonathan Swain

Website: www.paultomkins.com

Email: gprf@btinternet.com

AnchorPrint
GROUP LIMITED

For my son, William: my little champion.

Dedicated to the memory of my uncle Roy, who passed away in June 2005.

A fair amount of dedications are in order, given the help I received in what was a truly collaborative effort. As the book was self-produced through enduring illness I obviously owe a great debt of gratitude to everyone who has helped and supported me — without which there is no way any of it would have been possible.

First of all, my co-conspirator, Jonathan Swain, whose efforts across a number of tasks connected to production of the book have proved invaluable. If I am the project's Rafa Benítez (if that doesn't sound too immodest!), then Jon is its Pako Ayesteran, supporting in the background. (Of course, we could be the equivalent of Graeme Souness and Phil Boersma . . .)

Second is Matthew Clare, another Red, whose support for the project proved its lifeline. Equal to that has been the constant invaluable support from my family: I am eternally grateful.

A big hand to Sandra Ireland for her marvellous efforts in helping publicise and market the book, and also to Dan Symonds, Garreth Cummins, Chris Hadley and Nikki Murphy.

Next, everyone connected to the websites which have published and championed my work, especially 'Rushian', 'Bob K', Ben, 'Armin', 'Pheeny', Gareth, and everyone else at the now-legendary **redandwhitekop.com**; as well as James and Chris at **shanklygates.com**, Matt and Max at **thisisanfield.com**, Robbie at **talklfc.com,** and all the guys at **ynwa.tv**

Finally, thank you to Andrew Linnett at Anchor, Bill 'the Myth', the 'Elitist Bastards', Adrian Mervyn, Len Mervyn, and 'Nin' for the best home-cooked meals in Liverpool.

More on M.E. can be found at: www.meassociation.org.uk

Jonathan would like to add:
Firstly, thanks to Jane, for putting up with all the hours I spent locked in the study!
For my godson Daniel, a future Red, and all my family.
Dedicated to the memory of Gran and Grampa, and my brother Daniel.

Contents

Preface

The 25th May, 10.40 pm, Istanbul time. AC Milan lead Liverpool by three goals to nil. The dream is in ruins. Liverpool are going to spend the season as losers: runners-up in the Carling Cup; runners-up in the race for the final Champions League spot (5th place being the new 2nd, 4th the new 1st), and now runners-up in the European Cup.

Commenced in the winter of 2004, this book appeared to have seen its chance at documenting something remarkable — rather than 'just' extremely interesting — slip from its grasp. The ending would be one of grim reality — the fairytale evanescing into the cold Turkish night air.

As I sat in the Atatürk stadium, I feared further humiliation in the second half; the result of which would be that, rather than read about Rafael Benítez' attempts to put his stamp on the team, Liverpool fans would sooner pay for a box of sand in which to bury their heads. Still, there remained 45 minutes for the Reds to at least rescue some pride. Milan celebrated at half-time, but made the fatal error of forgetting to book the fat lady to sing. Instead, it was the 40,000 Reds in the stadium who belted out a rousing rendition of *You'll Never Walk Alone*. Whatever the outcome, this confirmed what it was that makes being a Liverpool fan so special.

The game was over. Or was it? As with much of the preceding twelve months, *who could have known?*

My intention was to write a book about a legendary club in transition, fighting to claw its way back to the very top of the game, as, behind the scenes, all manner of changes were taking place. And while that is still ostensibly the case — no one can pretend that the transformation is complete — it also rather unexpectedly turned into a document detailing the Reds' belief-defying charge to the quarter-final, the semi-final, the final, and then — following six crazy minutes and a penalty shoot-out — onto Cloud Nine.

From February onwards, more and more pages were happily dedicated not to what might one day be, but to what was becoming a reality in the here and now. The 'Rafalution' is only just beginning: the rebuilding and restructuring remains necessary. There was just an unexpected early bonus. And some bonus at that . . .

Paul Tomkins
May, 2005

Introduction

There can be little doubt: Liverpool Football Club should have sacked Bill Shankly back in 1961.

If today's technology — coupled with our current vogue for instant judgement — was then in place, a second consecutive failed promotion attempt would have brought that call howling from a myriad newspaper articles and letters pages, internet fora, and radio and TV phone-ins. It was obvious, after two third-placed finishes, that the club was stagnating, and Shankly lacked that extra-special *something* to secure a place in the First Division.

Fast-forward to 1975. It is abundantly clear that Bob Paisley is not fit to follow in the formidable footsteps of Shanks (who, after that unremarkable start, turned out to be a bit of a genius), and there is no way the club will progress under this avuncular and apparently befuddled old man, who muddles and mangles what few words he speaks, and who looks better suited to racing pigeons or tending an allotment. Make no mistake, what Liverpool FC needs is someone with personality, charisma, a figure who is larger than life — just like Shanks, no less — and who preferably wears flashy clothes and a distinctive fedora; someone who *looks* like a modern manager. Malcolm Allison is the answer, and if the board can't see that, they're blind, and need to be sacked forthwith.

The times have changed, football has changed, and this — as you may well already have gathered — is a book about change. Sometimes for the better, often for the worse (*for better and for worse* — the vows of the true football fan), and occasionally neither one way nor the other. Strong opinions on football existed then as now; but the difference, in this disposable, buy-now-pay-later super-quick broadband consumer world, is that reality is not allowed to interfere with the espousing of those opinions. Instant condemnations can be made in this instant world.

Not only have the times changed, but time *itself* has changed; what was once considered a 'reasonably long period of time' is now an eternity. Time is money, and money accelerates time. It's a hire-'em, fire-'em industry, and yet Liverpool still give their managers longer contracts than other clubs, in which time they are allowed to try to develop something. It doesn't guarantee that what they attempt to build will be successful, of course, but very few new managers at any top club have been successful (at least to the standards Liverpool demands) in their first season. Rome wasn't built in a day; Milton Keynes probably was. One of the reasons Rafael Benítez took the Anfield job in 2004 was the five-year contract on offer. Rebuilding the side would not be an overnight task, despite the demands of the most eager fans. Major success tends to first arrive within two-to-five years; rarely sooner, seldom after. (Benítez is one of the exceptions that proves the rule, with his first-season *La Liga* title with Valencia.)

In the modern age, *everyone* has a say. The internet is the world's first truly democratic

medium, allowing every Tom, Dick, Harriet, Rashid and Suki-Yoshiko a public voice
(with internet cafés, you don't even need to own a computer). Meanwhile the 'controlled'
media grow ever-more interested in controversy at the expense of truth; hype and
hyperbole at the expense of sense and sensibility. It's well known that the truth is not
allowed to get in the way of a good story, while falsehoods can form the bedrock of a
thousand bad ones. Even radio phones-ins — open to anyone with a mobile or land
line — appear to have an agenda: call screeners aiming to get only the most outlandish
opinions on air, as it makes for a more 'stimulating' and entertaining show. While that's
true (if you are looking for entertainment, and not insight), it's difficult then to argue that
these are opinions representative of the masses — which often ends up being the case.
(Also, why does it appear to be only those on weekend release from the insane asylums
who call these shows? — are 'real' fans too embarrassed?) While Gérard Houllier's
paranoia with the media grew to almost comical levels (although few Liverpool fans were
laughing in his final two seasons), he did have a point about the number of ex-Liverpool
players writing for the papers and appearing on TV and radio, many of whom were surely
being coaxed into supplying incendiary polemics, which sell papers and enhance ratings.
Sometimes the truth is just too damned *dull*.

The middle of 2004/05 proved the perfect example of the yo-yo effect, and how
modern football is all about the extremes. At the start of February, *BBC Radio Five Live*
ran a special report on the club, with interviews from ex-players, journalists, and an
extensive discussion with Chief Executive, Rick Parry. The context for the show was
'Liverpool in Crisis'.

Yes, *Liverpool in Crisis.*

To almost any other club, Liverpool's 21st Century accomplishments (before the
victory in Istanbul) would be declared a golden period: five cup finals reached, four
trophies won, not to mention the Community Shield and European Super Cup victories
of 2001. Since 2001 there have been three Champions League campaigns — the club's
first since 1985, when it was still known as the European Cup. As notable as these
achievements were, it doesn't mean Liverpool Football Club should accept cup successes
(other than the Champions League) as the height of its ambition — no one at the club
would dare do such a thing. But to read some of the doom-and-gloom assessments of
the club, you would think they referred to Blackpool languishing in the lower divisions;
or, more pertinently, Nottingham Forest — Liverpool's greatest rivals 25 years ago, when
the midlanders won back-to-back European Cups — and who, in 2005, were relegated to
the third tier of English football. Now *that* is a club is crisis.

The reaction to the narrow — but embarrassing — FA Cup defeat at Burnley
(courtesy of a shockingly clumsy own-goal by Djimi Traoré) was indicative of how
criticism can be inconsistent. Liverpool were accused of disrespecting the competition
by fielding a weakened team; and yet almost identical line-ups had won 3-0 at Millwall
in the Carling Cup (the New Den being a far from easy place to play), and beaten a full-
strength Spurs side at White Hart Lane in the same competition. Benítez reasoned that
hungry young fringe players — champing at the bit — would be fit, fresh and eager for
a tough cup battle. He was widely pilloried for selecting these kids at Turf Moor — and
yet such damning assessments came from many of the same sources who had earlier
saluted his bravery and foresight in playing them in the other domestic cup competition,
claiming the kids had proved the previous manager wrong — that they were indeed good
enough for the first team.

Either Benítez should be allowed to use his full squad when he feels the need is there,
or you have to question why the club has a squad at all. Either 'the kids are alright', or
they are not. (Other factors playing their roles in the terrible defeat were Steven Gerrard
being injured, Milan Baros only just returning from a hamstring injury, and new signings

Fernando Morientes and Maurico Pellegrino ruled ineligible for what was a rescheduled game.) Benítez was attacked for not playing more senior players, and yet a collection of senior players on the night were guilty of under-performing alongside the young lads. Sometimes in modern football managers are damned if they do, damned if they don't.

Following the defeat, the FA Cup assumed a revered new status, more in keeping with its heyday back in the 1950s. Suddenly it was no longer the competition Manchester United didn't even bother to enter in 2000. Liverpool fans began to question if the club was more interested in making money by finishing 4th than winning trophies — which, after all, was what the club's great tradition was founded upon (it certainly wasn't founded on finishing 4th, that's for sure).

If winning the league was the club's 'bread and butter', as Shanks liked to claim, winning the European Cup became its champagne and caviar. The four (sorry, *five*) cornerstones of the club's reputation are those European Cup successes. It is a fact of current life, however sad, that finishing 4th in the Premiership allows access to the 'Champions' League. Not only does participation in the competition guarantee the money to finance deals for new players — and Benítez would obviously like all the funds he can get his hands on in the coming seasons — but entry into the competition also attracts the best players, from overseas as well as the Premiership. The Champions League is where all top players want to ply their trade. By prioritising the FA Cup lower than the league, the League Cup (given that a draw at Watford the following week would see Benítez reach a final six months into his first season) and, of course, the Champions League, the manager was trying to balance a heavy schedule of games with a threadbare squad.

While his selection at Burnley backfired, there was no evidence that a full strength squad would have fared better. Even when Liverpool were the greatest team in Europe, their strongest teams came unstuck in the FA Cup: at Second Division Chelsea in February 1982, and a year later when they were defeated at home to lowly Brighton & Hove Albion. A week after the Burnley defeat in 2005, Manchester United were praised for not taking the competition lightly away at non-league Exeter, when a scratch United side had earlier struggled to a 0-0 draw in the Old Trafford tie (surely in many ways a more embarrassing result than losing away to a 'decent' side?). Maybe because Benítez is Spanish, he suffered xenophobic and patronising accusations of not understanding the importance of the FA Cup, when compared to his country's less revered *Copa del Rey*. It would certainly explain why, in comparison, Alex Ferguson escaped similar accusations. At home to Birmingham in the 4th round, Chelsea rested eight senior players and (crucially) won a tightly-contested game, without criticism. How Benítez must have wished he had the depth of the Stamford Bridge squad, and that the majority of the squad he did possess were fit and healthy.

In order to win the *major* trophies in the coming years, doing well in the FA Cup will have little bearing. Winning 'lesser' competitions breeds confidence, as we saw under Houllier, but it didn't help the club attain its ultimate goals of winning the two biggest club trophies. The Champions League now dwarfs the FA Cup in terms of importance and prestige. Simply qualifying for the Champions League, while not in itself a guarantee of success, remains a vital part of the process. No world-class player will join Liverpool to play in the FA Cup; they will, however, join to play in Europe's premier competition. (Or do so as a result of Liverpool's amazing success in 2005, which proved the club retained a special pedigree.) Similarly, there is more chance of those red devils freezing over in hell than there is of Manchester United pulling out of the Champions League due to other commitments. (Unless, of course, it's to take part in the formation of a European 'Super League', but then that's another story entirely.)

Speaking at the start of February, Liverpool Chief Executive, Rick Parry, took time to praise the work of Benítez: "During the summer, everyone was talking about this being a season of transition and stressed how the new manager needed time. It seems to me this all went out of the window last week and suddenly we are in a 'crisis' again. The common sense had gone."

Unfortunately you don't always get common sense where Liverpool Football Club is concerned.

Criticism is never slow in arriving. Individuals like Alan Hansen, at one time regarded as the best of pundits, are only offering their opinion, of course. But given their status, approval (or more often inflammatory disapproval) carries a great deal of public impact. It's certainly hard to think how bitter criticism (often scathing, from some quarters) benefits the club, rather than simply the author's bank balance. All fans grow frustrated, but those in a position of power need to wield it wisely, and responsibly — it is not like a fan venting his spleen to his mates in the pub after a game, because it gets worldwide exposure.

Liverpool FC needs to elevate itself from its current domestic perch (somewhere above mediocrity but well short of greatness), but that takes time. The process is not aided and abetted by ex-stars putting the boot in when the club is already down and looking for a hand up. The club will never move successfully into the future with a ten-ton weight fettering forward movement. With every passing year, that weight of elevated expectation increases. A sad paradox of Liverpool Football Club is that its glorious past is both its greatest asset and its most dangerous enemy.

Any new player the club signs has to live up not only to the realities of the past, but to the subsequent inflation of player reputations, with mere mortals deified by rose-tinted memory. You could be forgiven for thinking Liverpool never lost a game between 1965 and 1990, never produced a lacklustre showing, never failed to create chances in a game, never conceded a sloppy goal, and that no player ever misplaced a pass or mishit a shot. (I recently saw some rare 1970s television footage of Liverpool in Europe, and watched Kenny Dalglish hit the most appalling shot which sailed high towards the back of the Kop. Surely there must have been some kind of mistake? Was it video trickery? The Dalglish I remembered was perfection personified.)

Players such as Dalglish, Hansen, Souness and Rush were truly great indeed; their abilities were never in question. (Especially the key men of those sides — although mere squad players are also somehow referred to as *legends*. 'Super-sub' David Fairclough scored a legendary goal, but does that make *him* a legend?) The true legends earned that status, they didn't merely inherit it on the back of a couple of great performances, or one good season (as can happen nowadays). The problem is that the lens of time distorts to the point where *nothing* can compare. Older fans guard the club's achievements with a burning passion that is quite amazing to behold, but some won't acknowledge how it simultaneously holds the club back. (While winning the 2005 Champions League was a great achievement, it is even now raising expectations — and those expectations are partly tied to the phenomenal domination of the past.)

Nothing can beat the initial rush of success, like the flush of first love. Time never fights fair. Memories are linked to the triumphant youth experience, an exciting time both in terms of supporting Liverpool but also in terms of *life*. These men and women were young, vital, and discovering the world through Liverpool Football Club. Nothing will ever mean as much to these people again, just as no Beatles fan from the 1960s will be as excited by music again. The perfect new experience can only mean so much once.

It took the most remarkable victory in the history of the European Cup in 2005 just to put the achievement *on a par* with those from the past. In 1985, in reaching the final, Liverpool played just four ties: Lech Poznan, Benfica, Austria Vienna and Panathinaikos. In the last three rounds of 2005 Liverpool disposed of the English champions, the outgoing Italian champions, and the newly-crowned winners of *Serie A*.

You have to wonder if some of the retired players (even if only subconsciously) resent the idea of the club scaling the heights again, as if it would in some way dilute their achievements. Any current mediocrity merely portrays them in an even better light. As a result, the more fans think fondly of achievements from previous decades, the further the club appears from repeating them. On the fans' part, there is no longer any 'taking for granted' of that success, as some felt to be the case while it was occurring. The club, for a very long time, made winning seem *so* easy.

To propose a metaphor, we may not wish our past lovers harm, but we rarely wish them to be as happy — or worse still, even *happier* — than when we were together. It would injure our pride and dent our ego. While ex-players still have a lot of affection for the club (witness the reactions of John Aldridge and Phil Thompson in Istanbul), perhaps some of them are secretly happy to see it fail. Not fail miserably, or disappear from the 'big time', but to fall *just a little bit short*. Then there remains the excuse to say "Ah, but they don't match up to our day". All supposition, of course. But credible nonetheless. While some ex-players were effusive in their praise of the team on that night in Istanbul — Terry McDermott describing it as a bigger achievement than those between 1977-1984, and Alan Hansen calling it the best comeback of all time — some of the recent critics were noticeable only by their silence. As amazing as the success of 2005 proved, there is still a long way to go before the club is back on the footing of the 70s and 80s. If the win over AC Milan gave many ex-players the chance to share in the glory, the league form also gave them a reason to gripe and hark back to the days when the Reds were a truly dominant force.

The club these players represented with such distinction isn't even there any more — the managers they played for have either died or moved on. It's a different place these days. The ex-players almost certainly retain great affection for those who supported the team so loyally, so vocally, so passionately, so *famously*. That will remain constant — a unique bond. But unless these ex-players were boyhood fans who stood on the Kop (or indeed, took their place elsewhere in Anfield — the other three stands rarely getting an acknowledgment), it is hard to see how it makes them *supporters* once they retire. It's a totally different concept. They may still go to the games, but mostly as VIP guests of honour, or in their roles as pundits. Players often say they check for their old team's result first; even the most half-hearted and casual of fans does that. These erstwhile stars may have a great affection for the club, and an affinity with its supporters — but that doesn't make them fans, in the way fan is an abbreviation of *fanatic*. Fans look to vicariously experience their aspirations through the club, while retired players have already done that first hand. More often than not, footballers spend too much time playing the game — as kids, and then later, as professionals — to be 'real' supporters. They retain a different viewpoint, an altered perspective. The exceptions merely prove the rule.

The strangest type of comment from those who now work in the media involves the desire for a return to the old ways — as if they are still wholly relevant in this millennium, and that it will somehow automatically conjure the glory of old. (Or maybe it's just another excuse to draw attention to their heady exploits?) In an impassioned speech towards the end of his reign, Gérard Houllier — his voice trembling with anger, his accent strangely distorted — claimed that if the club wanted a return to the culture of the 1960s and 1970s it wouldn't be under his guidance. It's easy to mock the notion that the successes of the 1960s and 1970s would prove equally beyond his reach, but he was correct in what he was saying: you can no longer approach the game the same way. It is now unthinkable that a club would spend the week before the European Cup final on holiday, getting drunk, as happened at Liverpool in 1984. The level of athleticism required twenty or thirty years ago was far inferior to current standards. There have to be other ways to foster that kind of team spirit and unity. It would be lovely to have a collection of players as good as the ones the club could call on in those days, but the methods and approaches have moved on.

In many ways football remains a simple game, and there are many 'constants', such as the desire to win, the ability to pass a ball (and the courage to go looking for it), the tenacity to win tackles, and the knack of finding the back of the net. But so much has changed, from formations and training routines, to tactics and psychology, to preparation and diet, and — mostly — fitness, and the ferocious speed of the game (now that it is played by highly-tuned athletes, and not beer-guzzling relics of Saturday night culture). The same battle plans that once won wars aren't used indiscriminately in conflicts for the next thousand years. Advances are made, and new ideas are necessary. Shankly and Paisley didn't blindly repeat the formulae that were successful when they were players: they invented new systems, and pioneered fresh methods. They were innovators.

While Shankly and Paisley were undoubtedly blessed with genius, they were equally *of their time*. They may well have proven just as successful were they managing in the modern game, as they would be backed by the knowledge of modern ideas; after all, these were football men to the core, and outstanding thinkers on the game. (It's also easy to imagine, conversely, that they'd have fallen out of love with the sport as it now exists. Many from the 'old school' have, and understandably so.) But the disciples of these two great men have all had pretty miserable managerial records, especially in the last decade — ever since the renaissance of English football, when it embraced continental players and continental methods. Kenny Dalglish's managerial record suffered serious setbacks after leading Blackburn to the title in 1995 — achieved with a good old-fashioned British style of two wingers delivering early crosses for two big target men, Shearer and Sutton. (Incidentally, far less stylish fare than that produced by his Liverpool sides, especially the golden class of 1987/88: a side Michel Platini described as 'continental' — a unique distinction in England at the time.)

Kevin Keegan looked a potentially great manager in the mid-90s, until his Newcastle side imploded in spectacular fashion in the run-in of the 1995/96 season. Since then it's been mostly disappointing for him at the very top level, with an admission after his failure as England manager that he just wasn't as tactically astute as he needed to be, and towards the end of 2004/05 found himself without a job. Roy Evans — the last of the Bootroom graduates — produced a fine attacking team, which reached its peak around the same time as Keegan's Newcastle. Unfortunately, Evans' side had a similar inability to defend for 90 minutes. Graeme Souness has yet to do anything of any great or lasting significance as a manager since leaving Scotland in 1991. All of these in some way cut the figures of *yesterday's* men, possibly clinging to principles and ideas that just don't work in the modern era. Perhaps much of their failure as managers has been down to the fact that Liverpool, in its pomp, never really bothered too much with tactics, and that it was in the *construction of the team*, on top of psychology, in which their mentors excelled.

Much of Shankly's success was attributed to his motivational skills. While there was clearly far more to it than that, as a skilled all-round manager, it does remain his defining characteristic. Tom Saunders (the youth team coach under Shankly) recalled a pre-match team talk. The subject? *Boxing*. When, after 15 minutes of pugilistic discussion, Shankly switched to the game in hand, it was only to dismiss the opposition in summary fashion: "Don't let's waste time. That bloody lot can't play at all!" He was an inspiring character, that much is inarguable; others could later regurgitate the words he used, but render them less meaningful (especially to the pampered stars of the modern game — these players are 'made' for life by the time they are 22). With Paisley there was an uncanny knack of knowing *precisely* which players to buy, and then — without any special instructions, other than to 'go out and play your natural game' — they were sent out to add their specific talents to the blend of the unit. The players Paisley signed could think for themselves. They didn't need telling what to do — their hand being metaphorically held — in the way lesser players did. Mark Lawrenson's appraisal of the club under Paisley was, "Everything seemed to go like clockwork at Liverpool, as though nobody was in charge". That was no accident.

Once the team — constructed by Shankly and then improved-upon by Paisley — was up and running, it was like a well-oiled Rolls Royce, in need of a minor piece of tinkering each summer, by way of a service; add a superior component every close-season and the maintenance was complete. The machine then largely took care of itself, and did so until the late 1980s. That was, until old age and rust had it creaking, and the replacement parts were, for once, far inferior to the originals.

It was a process that started at the end of Dalglish's tenure — if only he'd kept buying players of the calibre of Barnes, Aldridge, Houghton and Beardsley — and accelerated at alarming pace by Souness, under whose tenure — to take the metaphor to its natural conclusion — the wheels, spectacularly, fell off. It was interesting to see Alan Hansen criticise Houllier and Benítez for not buying what he believed to be "Liverpool" players (i.e., they were either average, or inferior), and yet the onset of that failing can be traced back to two of his best friends, and continued by "Mr Liverpool", Roy Evans (who, in fairness, inherited a pretty shocking squad). It is hard to explain what *kind* of players they were, but one thing is for sure — some of the signings made by Dalglish, Souness and Evans were *not* "Liverpool" players. Jimmy Carter, David Speedie, David Burrows, Nicky Tanner, Steve Harkness, Torben Piechnik, Julian Dicks, Istvan Kozma, Paul Stewart, Nigel Clough, Mark Walters, Dean Saunders, Phil Babb, Oyvind Leonhardsen, Mark Kennedy and Sean Dundee did not come even close to matching the quality of their predecessors. The litany of names reads as an embarrassment to all Liverpool fans. Some, such as Clough, were almost certainly better players than they ever proved while in the red of Liverpool, while others never had much of a run-out, but none cut the mustard, or even came close to removing the lid from the jar. (In Sean Dundee's case, it is rumoured he couldn't even *find* the mustard.)

Liverpool had become a Rolls Royce reconstructed from so many alien components it resembled a badly assembled Ford Escort, with the engine of a 49cc moped. Turning it back into a Rolls Royce would represent a near-impossible task for subsequent Liverpool managers, and it became more of a burden for each successive boss.

Those men who played under Shankly and Paisley rarely had to witness radical team rebuilding. They never had to play with colleagues whose ability was far inferior to their own. They merely saw how to keep a great team at the top of its game — or rather, to return to Lawrenson's comment — they didn't see *anything*, as it appeared "as though nobody was in charge."

The instruction manual was bare when it came to building a team from scratch with a collection of average players.

It is an explanation that doesn't cover all the reasons behind the overriding failure of ex-Liverpool players as managers in the modern game, but there must be something in it — it's hard to believe it is merely coincidental. Souness and Dalglish in particular were such great 'thinking' footballers, you would think they'd still be managing hugely successful sides. (Souness' first season at Newcastle — his biggest job since leaving Liverpool — proved disastrous, while Dalglish also failed at the same club, as well as in a spell at Celtic with John Barnes.) Other great ex-Liverpool players were rather spectacular failures as managers. Many now work in the media as pundits.

The cloying past

The past just won't go away. Every new player who signs for Liverpool, no matter what his position, has a legend from yesteryear looming large; a spectral presence following him around the pitch, breathing down his neck, looking to trip him up or get in his way. Most teams have a couple of past legends the fans revere; Liverpool have several for *each position*. Even a position like left-back — hardly noted for its eye-catching performers — delivers you Alan Kennedy, Alec Lindsay, Emlyn Hughes, Joey Jones and, as a stand-in, Steve Nicol.

Javier Luis Garcia Sanz (happily known more simply as Luis Garcia) is a case in point: a signing never designed to be the final piece of any jigsaw, and never proclaimed as some kind of awe-inspiring world-class talent in the Maradona mould; just an extremely good player signed from a top team, Barcelona (where he'd done well the previous season), for his effectiveness and idiosyncratic qualities. He started his Liverpool career in spectacular fashion (perhaps *too* well, if that is possible), excelling in early games when deployed in the 'hole' behind the main striker — a position, of course, synonymous with Kenny Dalglish. At first, Dalglish's name was mentioned in some quarters, merely as a positional reference point (in the way Ronnie Whelan is still associated with the deep-lying defensive midfield role), and suddenly Luis Garcia was — ludicrously — being compared *to* Kenny Dalglish. A hiding to nothing, if ever there was one. When it became clear he wasn't as good as the great Scot (and let's face it, who is?), disappointment set in. And when, as Christmas approached, his form dipped further, to the point where he was woefully out of touch and lacking confidence, he suddenly *wasn't even fit to wear the red shirt*. Fans (of the impatient variety) and media alike compared him to the biggest flops of the Houllier regime, despite having a far-superior start to his Liverpool career than either El Hadji Diouf or Bruno Cheyrou, in terms of goals scored and chances created. By April he had scored 13 goals for the club — more than any Liverpool midfielder had managed in well over a decade — and was exalted once more (albeit now, with common sense, to a more appropriate level).

A club like Liverpool needs players good enough — and with shoulders metaphorically broad enough — to be able to handle the pressure and the expectation, and to not let comparisons faze them. But they remain human beings, who need time to adapt and adjust. Not an indefinite amount of time ("trust me, he'll come good in his ninth season"), just a realistic amount, especially if the player is coming from abroad, and in need of adjusting to a new style of football and learning a new language — as well as all the other *human* problems the process entails. Too many good — even world-class — players have initially struggled to adapt to the Premiership. Thierry Henry and Robert Pires of Arsenal are the most-cited recent examples. Both were fairly appalling in their first few months, with Henry looking shell-shocked and scoring just twice in his first 17 games, and Pires only showing any kind of form by the Easter of his first season. Both went on to win cups, league titles, and Footballer of the Year awards. Because a player struggles at first does not mean he will be a success at a later point (for example, Bruno Cheyrou). But if even the best players — experienced internationals — can take time with cope with the transition, even merely 'very good' players can do likewise. Some, like Xabi Alonso, hit the ground running; others don't. Just look at the inauspicious first few months of Peter Beardsley's Anfield career, and how he eventually cast aside the initial burden to become one of the club's great attacking talents. Beardsley was English, and used to the English league. Any change — whatever it entails — means a period of adaptation. When players join a club like Liverpool — even if they are moving from another Premiership club — there is a whole new level of pressure. It is not simply a case of turning up and fitting seamlessly into the side.

(Having said that, Bob Paisley had a knack of instantly aligning round pegs with round holes. But he could also send players to the reserves for their first season or two, to acclimatise to the 'Liverpool way'. You cannot easily do that in the modern age, as the player would call his agent in a sulk and all hell would break loose. Also, as the modern game sees a full squad utilised, players often need to be integrated into the first team from day one.)

It also has much to do with temperament. After his dismissal, Gérard Houllier never openly questioned the ability of his 2002 signings, El Hadji Diouf, Salif Diao and Bruno Cheyrou. He did, however, admit that hindsight proved they didn't have the special character needed to play for a club such as Liverpool. Some players are only capable of flourishing in less pressurised environments, as big fish in smaller ponds. Fans call for the signing of X or Y player on the back of great form for a fair-to-middling club, but we've seen plenty of those types of player fail to cope with life at a bigger club, where expectations are far greater, and their place in the team is in jeopardy (in fact, they might not even *get* a place). Diouf had a fine season on loan at Bolton, but expectations were far lower, and he was guaranteed a place in the side. Nine goals may constitute a success the Reebok Stadium, but it doesn't at Anfield.

Liverpool is unlike all but a very select collection of clubs in the world; it is virtually unique. It has a past so immense, so auspicious, that it casts a shadow into the present, and even on into the future.

Eventful, to say the least

There have been numerous key periods in the illustrious and highly-decorated history of Liverpool Football Club, but perhaps the lead-up to 2004/05 — and the early months of the season — will prove to be as monumental a time as any in its 113-year existence.

The arrival at Anfield in 1959 of Bill Shankly remains the one single factor — the one undeniable turning point — that did more to alter the fortunes of the club. However, that was one event, one lone managerial change. The events of the summer of 2004 comprised a combination of far-reaching decisions, the result of which came close to being beyond remarkable, and entering into the realms of the previously unthinkable. Where the future leads English football's most successful club — and the most successful it still very much is — remains to be seen. What is not in question is that a new direction is being sought, both on and off the pitch.

In June 2004 the club sacked its manager — something that had not occurred in the lifetime of many of its fans (and indeed, the lifetime of the new manager). In fact, the previous dismissal even pre-dated the advent of the Beatles, who seem to have been part of Liverpudlian history since the dawn of time. It had been fully 45 years since Don Welsh cleared his desk and made way for the great Bill Shankly.

Gérard Houllier bade the club farewell (with a handsome pay-off causing controversy later in the season) and in came Spaniard Rafael Benítez, fresh from winning the *Primera Liga* title — for the second time in three seasons — and the Uefa Cup with Valencia. It was hard to think of a young European manager with a better pedigree. Jose Mourinho, who claimed to have rejected Liverpool before joining Chelsea, had an equally impressive CV — a better European trophy but an inferior league championship — but most Liverpool fans were more than happy with the appointment of Benítez. If looking overseas, either of those two would have placated the fans. (Of course, another debate arose: Why not appoint someone local, with a connection to the club?)

With Gérard Houllier went his entire backroom staff, with the exception of Alex Miller, who was promoted from Chief Scout to Head Coach, and the medical professionals. Of the departing local element it was no surprise to see Phil Thompson receive his P45, given he was so closely linked to the failure of recent seasons, and therefore guilty by association. (It was very refreshing to hear his honesty, and praise, when commenting on the new regime, when he returned to work for Sky Sports.)

More disappointing was the exit of the highly regarded Sammy Lee — a promising coach and a great motivator — who opted to take up a role with the England team. Lee's time as a player in Spain made him an ideal candidate to work with the new Iberian staff, and indeed, he had crossed paths briefly with Benítez in 1986 at Osasuna. His was a great loss to the club, and one which has been largely overlooked. Ian Rush was another highly-qualified coach and ex-Liverpool player to make way.

To help the club manage its plans to build a new stadium as well as a new side, financial advisers Hawkpoint Partners Limited were appointed. Investment in the club was subsequently discussed over the following months with consortia from the Thai government, Hollywood, Jersey (via Liverpool) and the Middle East. Newspapers were full of proclamations from interested parties, each announcing that their bid would be successful. Suddenly Liverpool fans were highly aware of, and concerned by, the human rights record of the Thai government. If Liverpool had to "sell its soul", then it should not be to the devil. (Which is not to suggest that the Thai PM, Thaksin Shinawatra, was the devil.) Despite brash statements from the Far East, no deal was forthcoming. The bid of Steve Morgan — exiled-scouser, shareholder at LFC, and building magnate — was an attempt to take control of the club, following long-running ill-feeling between himself and the Chairman, David Moores; clearly the pair could not share power. Acrimony rumbled on until, following Morgan's wife's impassioned plea at the AGM, the Morgans took their metaphorical ball and stormed off home. By the end of the season the issue was still not settled.

In June 2004, planning permission was finally granted for an £80m, 60,000-seater stadium in Stanley Park — four years after the plans were first announced, and nine months after the application was submitted. The club looked all set to vacate Anfield — as revered as almost any club stadium in the world, and with a terrace (once containing — *somehow* — 24,000 swaying fans, and now a 12,400-seater stand) without equal in terms of reputation. Moving such a short distance would essentially help retain the club's heritage, and indeed the name *Anfield*. (Unless the name of the stadium ends up being auctioned to the highest bidder — the route Arsenal took for their new ground.) It would also mean things never being quite the same again, making it a transition primed with both excitement and trepidation. (*Excitement* and *trepidation*: two words the modern Liverpool fan knows only too well).

Reports of rising building costs caused more concern for all involved, with the paramount need for the club to not over-stretch its finances; Leicester, Derby and Sunderland stand as examples of Premiership clubs who had built impressive new stadia, only to end up relegated due to a lack of quality in the team. (Sunderland have now returned to the top flight. However, their place in the division below has been taken by Southampton. After 30 years in the top flight, the Saints have been relegated just three seasons after moving to a new stadium.) Investing in both the stadium and the team will no doubt prove to be a fine balancing act. Done correctly it will leave the club with one of the best stadia in the world, filled to capacity every game, as people flock to see a great team winning trophies once more. Done incorrectly, it could result in a half-empty soulless bowl as a team comprised of also-rans and journeymen plod their way to mid-table obscurity.

So in July 2004, everything was set. Then, with a large oar to insert, the government, at both local and national levels, urged the club to share the new Anfield (or, indeed, an alternative venue) with its bitter rivals and next-door neighbours, Everton. An old adage was brought to mind: the course of true love or building a new stadium will *never* run smooth.

Naturally there was an outcry from supporters both Red and Blue, who saw this as a step too far with regards to change. In England, a football club's stadium is its castle — it's own fortress. Inviting the enemy in — however much sense it makes, on a purely financial level — is just unheard of, and the majority of fans voiced the opinion that football is more about identity than fiscal concerns. Everton's need to share was perhaps greater, given their financial impoverishment, and far inferior "revenue streams" (two words not heard during Shanks' time). The plans to share a new stadium were officially pronounced dead in the water in January, 2005 — but still the issue rumbles on.

In amongst all of this, Michael Owen — at the time the club's most famous player, and top scorer for each of the previous seven seasons (in other words, every season he spent in the first team, including those blighted by serious injury) — left for Real Madrid in a cut-price deal (reported at between £8-10m), forced about once he entered the final year of his contract. Rick Parry needed to avoid a repeat of the Steve McManaman fiasco, where a home-grown star with a high market value was permitted to run down his contract and leave the club on a free transfer under the Bosman ruling. (A ruling the club exploited in its favour, with great success, in the summer of 2000, when Gérard Houllier procured both Gary McAllister and Markus Babbel without paying a fee.)

July and August 2004 became the summer of the Spanish-English transfer. Rafael Benítez, who until the age of 21 was on the Real Madrid playing staff, without ever making the grade (and who later coached their youth and B teams), was the man who had produced a team to outshine the Estadio Santiago Bernabéu's collection of expensively-assembled 'galácticos' (surely the most tiresome term in football) in the previous three seasons. In that time, Valencia won the league twice, sandwiching Real Madrid's solitary success. Many in Spain felt Benítez was the man Real Madrid needed to help them return to the summit. He was widely regarded as his country's top coach, the no-nonsense kind of man who could tame those galáctico egos. As it transpired, Benítez moved to Liverpool, and it was Owen who went to Madrid. Where Madrid needed leadership, they instead procured a striker for whom they rarely had room in the team. Just as Benítez left Valencia on the grounds that whenever he asked for one player he was given another instead, someone he often didn't need ("I asked for a sofa and they bought me a table lamp"), then so too had Madrid given their manager an unnecessary lighting accessory — and for that matter, one which would would be given little chance to shine — when they didn't even have the best possible manager running the team. In reply to Owen leaving for Madrid, Benítez made a bid for Fernando Morientes, but the Spanish international had already given his word to Jose Camacho (the man Madrid appointed as coach) that he would stay and fight for a place. It would only be another six months before Benítez finally received the very sofa he requested, at a very reasonable price.

The scale of the shock of Owen departing (an unthinkable prospect back in 2002) would have been magnified a thousand-fold had Steven Gerrard — the club's local icon and its best player — followed him out of Anfield by agreeing to join Chelsea in a £30m deal, as seemed inevitable. Benítez, in his first task as Liverpool manager, dashed to Portugal to meet the player for crisis talks at the England Euro 2004 camp, and it later transpired that only friends and family talked Gerrard out of a move to London. At least Liverpool fans could reconcile the idea of Owen joining the most successful side in European history; just as they had come to terms with losing other greats to the continent when Kevin Keegan joined Hamburg in 1977, and when Ian Rush moved to Juventus a decade later. Losing Gerrard to English rivals who had never won the European Cup and whose last league title success was 50 years earlier would have stuck most gallingly in the craw, however close the west Londoners were to becoming a successful side. Also, Owen had spent two more seasons than Gerrard in the Liverpool first team (and in that sense, had 'given' more), and while not totally 'past it', as foolishly portrayed, there remained a widespread belief that Owen was not quite the player he once was. With Gerrard, the improvements to his game were happening apace — he was on a steep upward curve — and he very much represented the future of the club. Unlike Owen, he was a Liverpudlian born and bred, and a fan from childhood. He was in many ways the *heart and soul* of the club.

While the "Gerrard To Chelsea" saga rumbled on, Milan Baros was becoming the first-ever Liverpool player to finish top scorer at a major international tournament, winning the Golden Boot for his five fine goals for the Czech Republic in Euro 2004. No sooner had the competition ended than his departure for Barcelona was being mooted, and more uncertainty surrounded a major star. For several months Liverpool fans did not know whether they were coming or going; just as they didn't know which players were coming or going. The club was in transition in every conceivable area. Was it in meltdown, or the incipient stages of yet another rebirth?

The summer months were actually bookended — in that crazy way the sport has a habit of doing — by a few games of football. (I know — whatever next?) The 2003/04 season ended with the frantic chase for a Champions League spot in May (achieved, but insufficient to save Houllier from the axe), and 2004/05 kicked off early with the two-leg play-off qualifier against AK Graz in August. Qualification would mean that the club was back in the Big Time, even if hopes of progressing beyond the groups stages were slim to a nascent Benítez side. Although hope, as ever, sprang eternal.

(As a sidenote, it is worth noting the shift in the yardstick which the intervening years had set for Liverpool Football Club. The aforementioned Don Welsh was sacked because the club was relegated from the old First Division — coincidentally, and gallingly, on the very day Everton were promoted. It is a measure of how the game has developed, and Liverpool's reputation grown, that finishing in 4th place — and thereby earning the right to once again challenge on the top European stage — was ultimately insufficient to save Gérard Houllier from dismissal.)

Truth be told, the return to the Champions League was more than anything about gaining experience (and in the process repairing a damaged reputation) after a two-year absence, and, of course, securing the financial rewards necessary to fund the essential squad-rebuilding programme. The first leg in Austria was won 2-0 at a canter, with Gerrard winning the match with two superb goals (and with a brilliant third chalked off), but Owen grabbed the headlines after he was left on the bench, so as to not cup-tie him ahead of any potential transfer. It was one of those games where the television director decides to spend more time covering the dugout than the match itself. Every expression on Owen's face (and there weren't many, as he looked on stonily) was analysed to see if it confirmed his Liverpool career was over.

A shock 1-0 reverse at Anfield almost undid all the good work on the continent, but it remained only a scare (with the bizarre sight of an opposition player being booked twice and remaining on the field). The club was drawn in Group A, along with Olympiakos (hailing from Greece, a footballing nation so recently relocated to Cloud Nine, and still celebrating its remarkable victory at the European Championships), and two of the previous season's top sides: semi-finalists Deportivo La Coruna, and beaten finalists Monaco. It was a group with a lot of Champions League pedigree.

Wasting no time in opening the chequebook, Benítez' first signing was Josemi from Malaga, for £2m. His second, third and fourth signings were rubber-stamped in the knowledge that progress in the Champions League was as good as in the bag as deadline day loomed. With money in the bank from the sale of several assets, Benítez went out and purchased three more compatriots: Antonio Núñez, from Real Madrid, valued at £2m as part of the Owen deal; Luis Garcia, a valued squad member, if not a regular starter at Barcelona, for £6m; and the manager's *coup de grace* — young Spanish international playmaker Xabi Alonso, who had been the subject of interest from Real

Madrid that summer, and Manchester United the preceding year. (Alex Ferguson was widely reported as saying 'Alonso is definitely one I'd take', though he was concerned at a reported buy-out clause of more than £20 million.) Liverpool paid just £10.5m to Real Sociedad to secure his sevices, and from the very first moment it looked an absolute bargain.

The season was only just beginning, and nothing that followed was as straightforward as any Liverpool fan would have hoped for — there were surprises good and bad aplenty. While success at Anfield has been sporadic in recent years, there has rarely — with the exception of some limp displays — been a dull moment.

Rafael Benítez' first year proved no different.

Chapter two

Gérard Houllier:
haunted by the ghosts of champions past

It is a maxim that remains true: football managers rarely gain employment at clubs devoid of problems. Something has nearly always gone wrong for P45s to be dispensed. Sometimes it's a long losing streak, at other times a creeping, insidious malaise and a failure to meet objectives — a 'slipping back' from previous standards. It may be that the players are behind the manager, but incapable of helping him out of a tight spot; or that he's 'lost' the dressing room. (Or, as in the case of Southampton's Paul Sturrock who departed two games into the 2004/05 season, never having *gained* the dressing room in the first place).

Liverpool simply do not sack managers; until the summer of 2004, it had been 45 years since the previous dismissal. In football — where, like politics, a week can be a long time — that's an eternity. So Rick Parry and David Moores will have taken no pleasure at all from releasing Gérard Houllier — a man they liked and respected — from his contract. (Nor will they have enjoyed making the payments to Houllier and his staff, which were substantial.)

In some ways, you can say that Houllier hardly deserved that ignominy (after all, two less successful managers had preceded him). It was made all the more difficult by the Frenchman (and I don't use that term dismissively, as Ian St John tended to) having *almost* made a strong enough case to be kept on: the minimum objective of a Champions League spot had been achieved. It was touch and go. Had the team finished mid-table, Houllier would perhaps have fallen on his own sword, instead of maintaining, until the bitter end, that he would remain at Liverpool and, after his sacking, claiming he would have liked to have seen out his allotted time. As in previous seasons, a late spurt (which hadn't been enough to ensure finishing above 5th in 2002/03) almost disguised the myriad failings of the winter months — but ultimately, the run-in of a football season commences mid-August.

The defining factor was that Liverpool appeared to be getting not closer but, gallingly, far further away from the summit. While that is true, the club hadn't fallen so far off the pace it was stranded mid-table, or worse, suffering relegation worries.

The club still owes Houllier a debt of gratitude of sorts for keeping the club fairly stable (although the £10.7m payoff he and his staff received tempered any sympathy). Treading water might not seem anywhere near good enough for a club like Liverpool (and in the grand scheme of things, it isn't), but it is better than sinking; better than drowning. It was a small mercy that Liverpool, despite being 30 points off the pace of Arsenal, still qualified for the Champions League. It would make Benítez' job that bit easier, given the money and prestige — not to mention experience — the competition could bring the club and its players. (And how!)

Any manager's main priority will be to make his team hard to beat — especially to steady a rocking boat in the early days. But at the top clubs, a manager's task is to make his team favourites *to win every game*. Houllier ended his reign — especially at home — not only losing too many games, but failing to win a whole host more: a draw being two points dropped and only one point gained.

History, however, will be fairly kind. Gérard Houllier will ultimately be remembered as a "good" manager — no other adjective seems acceptable for a man who brought some *good* times, just couldn't keep them. He was the Frankie Goes To Hollywood of football --huge, defining hits in the space of 12 months then very little of note. Liverpool had been used to being the footballing equivalent of The Beatles: the Fab Four of Bill, Bob, Joe and Kenny keeping the club at the top of the charts, year after year. (Still, on the bright side, at least Houllier wasn't Joe Dolce or Chesney Hawkes.)

If you were to list every Liverpool manager, Houllier would rank somewhere near the middle, courtesy of one remarkable season (which still fell short of the markings on the old yardstick); placing him safely ahead of his predecessor and one-time joint-manager, Roy Evans, the Bootle-born Boot Room boy (although Evans obviously deserves great credit for his part in the glory years), and well ahead of the man before him, Graeme Souness. Go any further back into the history of the club — in fact, all the way back to 1959, to when Bill Shankly took charge — and the comparisons do not make good reading. Every single manager delivered either the league championship or the European Cup. Bob Paisley and Joe Fagan won both. Kenny Dalglish, unable to field a team in European competition, settled for winning the league and FA Cup double in his first season. Expectations had dropped somewhat since those heady days, but the benchmarks remained; unbelievably high standards that ex-players were always quick to remind Houllier about. Unlike Paisley, Fagan, Dalglish and even Souness, Houllier did not inherit a side that had won the title in the previous twelve months.

At Liverpool it was often said that 'first is first, second is nowhere'. But now, even second place — achieved in 2001/02, when the club finished seven points behind the winners, Arsenal — remained the high-water mark for more than a decade of football. In the new millennium and the revamped world of the Premiership, first is first and fourth *actually is somewhere*, but at the end of 2003/04 the powers-that-be at Anfield had to decide if that was good enough. Ultimately they concluded it wasn't. The quality of the football — increasingly dull and uninspired — helped to hasten Houllier's departure. He had met his minimum objective, of 4th spot, but the gap between 1st and 4th was a colossal 30 points. In terms of points, Liverpool had finished closer to being relegated than winning the league. So while Houllier's side was treading water at best, it appeared ready to slip beneath the waves.

However you choose to look at it, it is hard to avoid concluding that Gérard Houllier's time at Anfield ended in ignominy. Like an ageing rock star he had — in many fans' eyes — outstayed his welcome in the spotlight. (He wasn't quite a bloated Elvis Presley in a white sequined-jumpsuit, seams straining, but you get my drift.) Houllier's allocation of benefit of the doubt had run dry, and like a player being substituted, his number was up.

Nearly all managers have a shelf-life. In the modern game, a hero one season — an undoubted *genius*, no less — is often a buffoon the next. Houllier's transition from former to latter took a little time, but he was rarely labelled anything too complimentary after the start of 2002/03. By the middle of the following season, he was on borrowed time; local newspaper polls suggesting the majority of fans wanted to see the back of him, following the club's second successive dark and disastrous winter. Death threats had been daubed — disgracefully — on the walls of Melwood, and while such vile actions cannot be condoned, it was the (somewhat twisted) product of the rise in local antipathy (voiced also on the ever-popular radio phone-ins and, of course, the many websites). Fortunately most fans wanted only that he resign his post, and not that he befall a more sinister fate. They got their wish in June 2004, when — purely metaphorically, of course — the axe fell.

The beginning of the end

While the good years under Gérard Houllier have already been fairly well documented in other books on the subject, it is still worth asking: where did it start to go wrong for the Frenchman? Was there a point in time when his fortunes reversed — when the man who at one time could do no wrong lost his bullet proof status, and misplaced his ability to pull rabbits out of a hat? Or did it instead give him a God Complex, where he felt he was untouchable, no longer a mere mortal? Was it a series of unfortunate incidents, or can his demise be traced back to one single event?

Was it a consequence of his dissected aorta in September 2001? Or the sale of Robbie Fowler to Leeds a month later, with no adequate replacement found? Was it the moment he withdrew Didi Hamann in the Champions League quarter-final in Leverkusen, minutes away from a monumental semi-final clash with Manchester United (at the time, a team Liverpool had the Indian sign over), only for Lucio's goal six minutes from time to destroy that prospect? Or was it at the end of that summer, when Houllier spent the best part of £20m on three players to take Liverpool to the next level — in so doing rejecting the talents of Nicolas Anelka — and all three failed to deliver?

History tells us that the steady progress of the club under the Frenchman's guidance came to an abrupt halt in his fourth season as sole manager. For three successive years the team had finished one place higher in the league than the season before: 4th, 3rd and then — tantalisingly — 2nd. The sequence was crying out to be completed, and Houllier was often quick to mention the fact. However, where first should have followed, to complete the rise, the club's fans were left despairing at 5th place, and not even the consolation of a Champions League spot. Perhaps the players and management thought it was merely a matter of completing 2002/03 and finishing as Champions, riding the building momentum to its apex; fated to yet again improve their position by one league place. It is doubtful that anyone connected to the club was *that* blasé, but there's no doubting it seemed a very 'neat' pattern destined for completion. Victory over Manchester United in the Worthington Cup final in February 2003 was not enough to rescue credibility for the season, but it did buy Houllier one more stab at things — and given his previous record, deservedly so.

So — would 2002/03 prove to be a mere blip, or the start of a serious regression? Unfortunately, it proved to be the latter. The next season was equally dismal. There was to be no cup final victory against Manchester United to gloss over shortcomings, and only a last-ditch qualification for the preliminary rounds of the Champions League with a fourth-place finish. While some fans supported Houllier to the bitter end, their number began to dwindle, and the nature of their support was not particularly vociferous. It remains the 'Liverpool way' that while fans may show signs of disenchantment at Anfield with a (very rare) smattering of boos at full-time — and even then, booing is frowned upon — and inadvertent groans during frustrating periods of a match (also articulated with the war cry of of "Attack attack attack"), they will never chant for a manager to be sacked. One or two "Houllier Out" banners appeared, but were quickly hauled down by stewards, or other fans who knew this is not the way things are done at Anfield. The club's fans retain a sense of pride in their actions. Perhaps it is arrogance, but they see themselves as the most knowledgeable around. There are unwritten rules that go with a seat on the Kop, a code of conduct that many new or 'day tripping' fans fail to realise. Disillusionment and disenchantment with Houllier was widespread, but there is a time and a place — and a way — to voice these frustrations.

It had been a little over two years since the Kop had held up a mosaic comprised of 12,400 cards, combining to form the letters 'G' and 'H', when Houllier returned to the dug out against Manchester United, following his heart operation. (Banners at Anfield remain for declarations of support only. If a manager's time is up, the board, the Chairman and the Chief Executive will get the message themselves, and act accordingly: and give the manager a 'gentle push'.)

There was no getting away from the fact that going to Anfield had become a chore for most fans. The fun had evaporated. Even the games Liverpool won were rarely done so with conviction, and while Liverpool is not one of those clubs where entertainment or 'pretty football' is more important than success, it is fair to say that glory and good football tend to go hand-in-hand. Very few dull or uninspiring teams reap the heady rewards of league titles; you can be miserly at the back, but will also need imagination in attack. Style *with* substance is the key. Had Liverpool been playing great football and narrowly — or unfortunately — losing, at least the fans could take some encouragement from the skill and commitment on display, and see improvement on the horizon. (After all, isn't being a football fan so intrinsically linked to *hope*: the belief in a better tomorrow?) The situation at Anfield became a vicious circle, with the pressure on players and management leading to increasingly rare expressions of quality and control; the fans, in turn, arriving with a negative mindset, and waiting for the team to inspire them rather than vice versa.

A clutch of performances shone out like beacons in the run-in to 2003/04, with Portsmouth and Blackburn dispatched three- and four-nil at Anfield, and a thrilling 3-0 destruction of Birmingham at St Andrews. There was also the superb first sixty minutes at home to Middlesborough — but even on that occasion, as soon as Liverpool took a 2-0 lead, many of the failings of the team became painfully apparent. The players seemed to lose composure, and instead of keeping possession and seeing out the final thirty minutes (while looking to score a third with a sensible counter-attacking approach), the entire side began clearing their lines as far as possible, and conceding possession of the ball as if it were the proverbial hot potato. The outcome was a nervous conclusion to the match, when Boro (who had nothing to play for, having barely been interested in the match at all) were the only side who looked capable of scoring. If this match highlighted how good the team was capable of being under Houllier, it also displayed the major flaws in the mentality of the side, which people took as coming from the manager's inveterate caution.

With two games to go the club secured qualification to the Champions League — but Houllier wouldn't be around to lead the assault on Europe's premier competition.

Successes behind the scenes

It is perhaps Houllier's off-the-field achievements which people will remember most in years to come, as his tenure is retrospectively assessed and re-assessed. Ultimately proven to be a flawed tactician and arguably an inconsistent judge of a footballer in the transfer market, he was a meticulous planner of the details that go into preparing footballers for a match. In 1998 there was a culture of complacency and unprofessionalism that needed overturning, and he was the right man for the task of reversing those trends.

Attitudes were changed. A player's body was suddenly something to be treated as a temple, not as the rubbish bins of a fast food outlet. Mobile phones were famously banned from Melwood. (Although in what sense they were being used remains an amusing image: Roy Evans, for all his lack of discipline, surely didn't oversee five-a-sides where the players stood around nattering to their girlfriends, mates and bookmakers, as well as booking their next modelling assignment.)

Houllier deserves a lot of credit for helping Owen and Gerrard to blossom as players and reach their true potential. Neither player was in danger of ever being merely average in their careers, given their natural talent (both were taken on tour with the U19s when just 14-years-old), but Gerrard undoubtedly benefited from Houllier's wisdom with regards to his off-the-field activities.

Where they perhaps owe Houllier their greatest debt is in getting them fit to play any football at all. Gerrard was beset by a series of growing pains, manifesting themselves in various muscle tweaks and pulls. Owen's hamstrings became an on-going news saga in themselves, with every report on the player referring to concerns about the ability of these muscles to stay intact for 90 minutes of football.

Houllier also helped Owen work on his weaknesses. If hamstring-strengthening exercises robbed the player of a yard of pace (and he had a few yards going spare), this was compensated for with improvement in both his heading and the use of his left foot. (The perfect example being the surgical precision of the winning goal in the 2001 FA Cup final. Tony Adams, using all his experience, 'showed' his erstwhile England teammate onto his weaker side. Little did he realise that Owen had been working at improving his left foot, and the rest, as they say, is history.)

Houllier's philosophy could be summed up by the four short phrases he had printed onto banners to display around Melwood and the Academy, and which were also exhibited on his office wall:

Respect.
Be a winner.
Always think team first.
Be a top pro.

He also had a myriad of pithy sayings, including "Sometimes the will to win is more important than the skill to win"; "If you fail to prepare, then prepare to fail"; and "Only in the dictionary does success come before work". All make good sense, of course. But Liverpool ultimately needed something extra, especially once teams like Bolton and Middlesborough started using advanced dieticians and top sports psychologists. Once all the other teams had the will to win, Liverpool needed the *skill* to win.

Reputation

At the time of his arrival at Anfield, much of Houllier's reputation in world football came from youth team development. His one league title in club football came at Paris St Germain, back in 1986 — twelve years before taking the Anfield hotseat. In the interim Houllier had been part of the French national set-up. When he led France, from 1992 to 1993, it finished in the disaster of failing to qualify for the 1994 World Cup, having been in the box seat with two games remaining. Before that, between 1988 and 1992, he worked as assistant to Michel Platini. Houllier was teased by both the legendary ex-French maestro and his midfield teammate, Jean Tigana; Houllier was dubbed 'the Professor' — a man who had never played professional football (being a mere semi-professional centre-forward), and whose ideas they mocked as merely theoretical. Although mostly jocular, perhaps this was the start of Houllier's self-consciousness around players whose stature and experience meant they could challenge and threaten him.

The failure of senior players against Bulgaria and Israel, in 1993, as the wheels flew from Houllier's World Cup qualifying campaign, may have confirmed such doubts. David Ginola's actions in trying a cross-field pass late in the final game — leading to the goal that eliminated France — were compared by Houllier to those of a criminal. At the time of his greatest failure as a manager, Houllier had already been heavily involved with setting up the now-legendary French academy in Clairefontaine, and it was this that played a massive part in his country becoming the dominant force in world football at the end of the millennium, winning both the World Cup (1998) and the European Championship (2000). In 1998 he received his own winners' medal from Aime Jacquet, the leader of that team, in acknowledgment of all the work Houllier had done in laying the groundwork.

It can be argued that it was behind the scenes, away from the pitch on matchday, that Houllier's philosophies — based mostly on attitude, professionalism and respect — were at their most effective; and that his tactical acumen — or at the very least, tactical *flexibility* — remained short of what's required to manage at the very top level. You don't have a career as richly-decorated as Houllier's without being a very good manager. League titles and European Cups, however, are what distinguish the great from the good. Securing the less-valued cups and promotions from the lower leagues (as had Houllier in France) are not what top leaders are measured by — only their achievements at the pinnacle.

Youth development will be remembered as Houllier's forte. It was with the boys at Clairefontaine he could make the most marked difference; young men who, if they adopted the right approach, could quickly excel. They were malleable, ready to be formed and moulded in the manner he desired. Those rookies had yet to play under a wide variety of managers and coaches, and were open and susceptible to his ideas. They knew no different, and — in terms of advice on lifestyle and attitude — it's hard to believe they could have been told any better. They didn't have to adhere to Houllier's tactics, merely his philosophies.

Where Houllier was on less firm ground was with older pros, who had been around the block a time or two; men who may have played under some of the best managers around, and as a result of which would now have their own ideas. Of course a manager's word is final, and it's not acceptable for the players to question or undermine the boss' authority. But the more trust you put in your players in terms of letting them express themselves, the more able will they be to make decisions on the pitch to influence proceedings, and take control of matches. Younger players cannot be expected to play with a maturity and wisdom beyond their years. They are fallible by virtue of being youthful.

Houllier was right to discard a character such as Paul Ince, whom Alex Ferguson (do I risk impeachment for treason because I omit the 'Sir'?) had previously dismissed with the tag 'big-time Charlie'. Ince was someone seen as a destabilising influence on the dressing room. That is not something to be tolerated. The manager has to assert his own authority. He needs players who can think for themselves, but he needs to be big enough and strong enough to rise above such players if he doesn't agree with their standpoint — the manager's decision is final, as the buck stops with him. He should engage the opinion of his players, but they cannot be allowed to have the final say.

There were rumours that Houllier fell out with Jari Litmanen, and that Litmanen was too opinionated. Litmanen's entire time on Merseyside was an oddity: a superb passer of the ball, he was rarely utilised by his manager. When the Finn said he was unhappy at being on the sidelines, Houllier remarked that the player was valuable and could expect 5-10 games the coming season — plainly insulting, and about the amount of games you might promise to a 19-year-old rookie (in fact, in 2003/04 Houllier said John Welsh could expect 15 games, although he eventually played just five minutes of league football). Litmanen seemed — in theory — the perfect kind of player to have around, with his experience of Champions League finals with Ajax, and time spent at Barcelona. He genuinely wanted to play for the club, as a boyhood Red. Whatever the reasons for his apparent distrust of the player's effectiveness, it is fair to say that throughout his entire reign Houllier didn't have enough experience in the ranks when it came to attacking talent. At the end of 2001/02 Phil Thompson acknowledged that the team needed more experience in the attacking third. None was forthcoming. Instead, in came Cheyrou, Diouf and Salif Diao, with a far lower combined average age than the departing McAllister, Fowler (earlier that season) and Anelka, whose loan period came to an end.

Houllier's side was built on defensive experience only. Dudek, Hyypia, Henchoz and Babbel were all at a good age when they arrived at the club (26-29). The same applies to Didi Hamann, who during Houllier's tenure was an entirely defensive player. For several years this was the only *consistently* successful part of the side.

The one problem these particular players presented was that, on the pitch at least, they were all quiet, introspective types. None apparently coaxed or advised those around them. They were all men who went about their own business with great honesty and dedication, but who were unlikely to act as a 'manager' out on the pitch, in the way Alex Ferguson trusted Roy Keane to rule the roost and call the shots during the 90 minutes of play. Keane was a massive presence in the United side, but he was never in doubt that Ferguson was the main man. Keane went head-to-head with Republic of Ireland manager Mick McCarthy during the 2002 World Cup, but you couldn't see him doing the same with the Old Trafford boss. You certainly couldn't see a player as headstrong as Keane playing for Houllier — neither man would enjoy the situation.

What made Houllier's reluctance to trust experienced players all the more frustrating was that on the rare occasions when he did employ a player with those credentials, it paid handsome dividends. Gary McAllister was a masterstroke signing — a 35-year-old fresh from a 13-goal season in the Coventry midfield. (It's one of those 'what if' debates — a shame he wasn't still in his late 20s, with all those extra years ahead of him in the red shirt.) Many were shocked at the time, but it made perfect sense — McAllister had looked after himself, ever since he had been the lynchpin in Leeds' title-winning side of 1992.

Houllier's best two years in charge were when the Scot was in the squad. First, the Treble season of 2000/01, then the 80-point league campaign and progress to the Champions League quarter-final the following year. In all that time, McAllister only actually excelled in terms of performances for a two month period from March to May 2001, when he scored six crucial goals: three high-pressure penalties, and three sublime free-kicks, and when his all-round game was superb. But what cannot be overlooked was his presence and calming influence on those around him. When he was on the pitch, even if he looked positively geriatric next to the seemingly super-human Steven Gerrard, he was still capable of setting the tempo and conducting the play. Gerrard was his 'legs', and in return, Macca was Gerrard's 'brain'. Was it a mere coincidence that Macca's two-year stay at Anfield was the club's best spell in the 13 seasons between 1991 and 2004? When McAllister left, he was never adequately replaced. Once again Houllier opted for young players, and in Bruno Cheyrou, a talented midfielder who, unfortunately, appeared afraid of his own shadow. Cheyrou had been told during his time in France that he needed to toughen up. Perhaps, despite his ability, he stood little chance of succeeding in England.

An example of Houllier's constant reduction in the average age of players is best illustrated in his perennial replacement of strikers: Robbie Fowler, aged 26 at the time of his sale in 2001, was sold to Leeds. In his place came Nicolas Anelka, aged just 22. By the time Anelka had turned 23 he was on his way to Manchester City, and in his stead arrived 21-year-old El-Hadji Diouf. Before long Diouf ended up on the right wing as, in 2003/04, 19-year-old Florent Sinama-Pongolle came in for a run of games. Had Houllier remained in charge for a further five years (and he wanted to) then we may have seen the Premiership's first eleven-year-old centre-forward plucked from the Academy's under-12s.

Tactical limitations

Despite what the naysayer's — and those with short memories — claim, things weren't always so bad under Gérard Houllier. From very early on in his reign he was castigated for the counter-attacking football his team produced, but all football teams use the counter-attack when the opportunity presents itself. There's yet to be a team who, when faced with a breakaway opportunity against outnumbered opponents, act with some kind of misplaced spirit of altruism and happily allow the opposition to get men back behind the ball — at least, probably not since the Corinthian Casuals. As with boxing, the best blows are often struck when the guard is down. There was the element of surprise: Liverpool were known in the past for their patient passing style of play, keeping possession until an opening presented itself. Suddenly, under Houllier, Liverpool were letting the opposition have the ball, and waiting to draw them on in order to catch them out as soon as they gave it back to the men in red. The first full season of this style of play was 2000/01, and Liverpool completed an historic treble — League Cup, FA Cup and Uefa Cup — that meant the ends justified the means. All was looking distinctly rosy in the Houllier *jardin*.

The problem was that teams, in seeing what was happening, simply stopped trying to play football against Liverpool, and packed their defence with as many bodies as possible — as was their right. They didn't have to come to Anfield with any ambition beyond drawing 0-0. The bigger problem was that the lesser teams set up their stall the same way *at their home*.

Gary McAllister, speaking after Houllier's sacking, summed it up to perfection: "Having been fortunate enough to win the league before with Leeds, I've always believed that there is a certain way to win it and it is not a counter-attacking style. You have to go out to win it, believing that if the other side score two, you will score three.

"Gérard was criticised for being defensive but the season after I left he tried to open up the style a wee bit and it seemed to upset the team. When I was there, the back four were excellent but that was because they were well protected by the midfield and even the front men. There were a lot of disciplined players in front of the defence."

Speaking in April, 2005, Jamie Carragher hinted at another weakness. "Maybe under Gérard Houllier we were encouraged to defend a little too deep at times, but now [under Benítez] we are asked to push out more."

While nearly all title-winning sides are constructed around a miserly defence, it is not their only asset. As McAllister attested to, in recent seasons, if Arsenal or Manchester United conceded two goals in a match, they proved able to score three or more in reply. Under Houllier it was too often the case that if Liverpool conceded first, the game was up; there was no Plan B to revert to, let alone Plan C or Plan D. If Houllier's side didn't take the lead to start with, there was no chance of getting all three points.

Predictability was the regime's greatest failing. Get men behind the ball, keep it tight, and hit the long ball to Heskey, to flick-on to Owen. Done well, it could still get results, especially if Heskey was having a good day, and given that Owen was as reliable as anyone around. It tended to get results away at places like Old Trafford, where Liverpool were happy to come away with a draw but, usually, thanks to Danny Murphy, stole the victory, much to everyone's delight. Snatch-and-grabs took place at Stamford Bridge, and in the FA Cup final against Arsenal, but it was only at its most effective when the opposition poured forward.

Generals who repeat — on an eternal basis — the successful tactics of previous victories lose subsequent battles. Gone is the element of surprise; and if your tactics were based mostly on that very thing — surprise, ambush — you've lost your main weapon. After a while, you need to be the cleverest, the bravest, the strongest, the fastest, the fittest, and the most united. Put simply, you need to be the *best*. Catching teams out with a fast counter-attack no longer worked as well, given that teams were now *expecting* it.

What does £129 million buy you?

It is often said in football circles that a manager succeeds and fails by his dealings in the transfer market. Clearly this doesn't tell the whole story. For starters, there is the squad he inherits — which could contain world-class talent, unpolished gems, or a collection of ageing over-paid journeymen with little sell-on value. Also important are his behind the scenes handling of players, his tactical acumen, and a million and one other factors.

But it remains true that how he spends whatever budget he is endowed with will ultimately have a massive say in the level of success. Buy only duds and you will almost certainly fail; mostly successes, and you will have a strong team with which to compete for the top honours.

Gérard Houllier spent £129m in six years. In most people's eyes that's a lot of money. Of course, he recouped a further £60m; in fairer assessments, that will always be taken into account. That leaves a net expenditure of £70m, just over £10m a season. Not cheap, but far from excessive. Compared to Chelsea's £213m in the last two seasons, at an average of £100m+ each summer, that's peanuts.

No manager gets it 100% right in the transfer market. In fact, 50% seems to be a more accurate figure to pluck (semi-randomly) out of the air — if half of your signings are roaring successes, it's fair to say you'll do pretty damn well, given you should have inherited some top players as well. On balance, Houllier had a rating less than 50% in terms of outright successes. The split was probably closer to a third each on outright successes, adequate or average players, and flops.

It is perhaps damning to Houllier that the best two players during his tenure remained graduates of the Academy he inherited. No one he purchased matched the enduring success and influence of Michael Owen and Steven Gerrard; Sami Hyypia and Didi Hamann perhaps come closest, and Gary McAllister — during his Indian Summer on Merseyside — sparkled for a handful of months before the light dimmed on his career.

On the whole, Houllier bought well defensively, but poorly when it came to attacking talent. Perhaps it could be argued that it was actually his tactics that led to defensive players impressing most: the team was geared towards two 'banks of four', with the defence sitting deep and enlisting the protection of four conservatively-minded midfielders (if not in natural tendency, then from instruction), while the strikers were often isolated 50 yards upfield, chasing lost causes and looking like lost sheep. Attacking midfielders had a lot of ground to cover to supplement the attack, and, on bad days, long balls were launched from the back with over-regularity.

Goalscoring midfielders were always Houllier's Holy Grail. The most successful during his tenure were Patrik Berger, Steven Gerrard and Danny Muprhy — all inherited. To his credit, Houllier managed to coax the best (previously seen only in his first months at the club) from Berger on a consistent basis. He also instantly promoted Gerrard from the youth ranks to the first team squad, and blooded him a week later. And, after a lot of psychology (and a loan spell back at Crewe, his old club) found a role for Danny Murphy, that would eventually lead the young man to international honours and the award of Liverpool Player of the Season in 2002/03 — unthinkable back in 1999, when he looked destined to leave the club. Of Houllier's signings, only John Arne Riise — with 14 goals spread over three seasons under Houllier — was a regular goal threat, although the third of those seasons was totally goalless (in fairness, he did spend the majority of it at left-back, before rediscovering his scoring touch under Benítez).

Gary McAllister had one purple patch, scoring six set piece goals in the run-in to 2000/01, but only managed two further goals for the Reds. Diouf was an unmitigated disaster in front of goal, and Bruno Cheyrou, fresh from a prolific season in the Lille midfield, never looked like scoring regularly with the exception of one four-game spell in January 2004. Vladimir Smicer, so prolific for his country — 25 goals for the Czech Republic from 72 games — never found the net anywhere near as regularly for Liverpool: instead of a ratio of one goal every three games, it was one goal every ten. (His assist rate was pretty impressive though, when he was fit.) Nick Barmby had a prolific start to his Liverpool career but trailed off in the second half of his debut season, much like Harry Kewell, while Bernard Dioméde managed just four goal-free games for the club.

Christian Ziege, who scored goals for his previous clubs, never found his true form at Liverpool.

It was much the same story for the strikers: Heskey doing okay, but not getting as many goals as his talent and physique demanded, while Erik Meijer and Jari Litmanen rarely troubled goalkeepers during their brief sojourns on Merseyside. Nicolas Anelka was not fully fit when he arrived, and never received an extended run in the side, but still never managed the amount of goals he had for Arsenal, or later would for Manchester City. Titi Camara had one good season before being sold, and Milan Baros had one fairly prolific season (based on the games he started). Despite scoring only three goals between them in their debut seasons, Anthony Le Tallec and Florent Sinama-Pongolle were both clearly astute signings for the future, and it's unfair to be too harsh on men who were mere teenagers at the time Houllier was sacked.

It is true to say that Houllier did not sign one single player who proved to be prolific; perhaps he didn't *desperately need* to, with Owen so reliable, but it would have helped lift the burden from the No.10's shoulders.

Every signing a gamble

There are so many vagaries, intangibles and imponderables that go into whether a purchased player is a success or not, including luck, fate and timing, on top of footballing reasons. You only have to look at the club's record signing, initiated by Houllier and completed by Benítez: Djibril Cissé. Not only was the French international trying to settle into the frenetic pace of the English game (whilst learning the language and transferring his entire life north of the English Channel), he suddenly found himself unable to prove himself in the Premiership when both his left tibia and fibula snapped in a game at Ewood Park in October. It is impossible to adjust to the English game sat in a wheelchair. Cissé, while far from impressing to the degree most fans had hoped for, had scored more goals during his first fifteen games in this country than had Thierry Henry in his debut season. Now much of any future success will be down to the level of recovery he makes from a potentially career-threatening injury. The early signs are very promising, with an early return to first team action, and at least he will have had time to learn the language and get to know his teammates (and watch how they play) while recuperating. His second season should see him finally deliver.

The chemistry between a new player and his teammates cannot be tested in advance. A manager is never afforded the luxury of giving the player a trial (unless a rookie or a player without a club) to see how he blends. They spend their money — often obscene amounts — and hope for the best. (If the player is talented enough, there should be no problem — all being well.) A good manager should be able to tell what style of player is needed to fit any given system, and from research get to know any potential signing's character inside-out. But how that player adapts to a move (especially if leaving a smaller British club, or an overseas side) is virtually impossible to predict. Plenty of 'sure things' in the transfer market — players whose arrival would help attain the previously out-of-reach — have turned out to be false gods.

You only need look at the dealings of Houllier's closest rivals: the men who ultimately stopped Liverpool winning the league. They weren't foolproof.

Alex Ferguson *lost* £14m (equal to Liverpool's record outlay) on Juan Sebastian Veron, selling him after just two years for half of the incredible (then-record) £28m he paid. Veron was supposed to be the final piece of the puzzle for their assault on the Champions League, but instead looked like a piece from someone else's puzzle shoe-horned into the wrong position. Karel Poborsky never lived up to expectations, and yet continued to shine for the Czech Republic. Several embarrassing goalkeeping mistakes came and went, most notably Mark Bosnich and Massimo Taibi. Diego Forlan was a complete joke figure in England, and yet as soon as he was transfered to Spain he scored 20 league goals in his first season. It's easy (not to mention fun, if it involves Liverpool's rivals) to label players as 'rubbish', but often they just don't fit in, for one reason or another, and will find good form elsewhere.

In the successful half of north London the mistakes are just as evident. Arsene Wenger lost Sylvain Wiltord on a free transfer, following an outlay of £13m just a few years earlier; while never setting the Premiership alight, Wiltord still scored 50 goals in his time at Highbury, many from an unfamiliar role on the right of midfield — goals that would help Arsenal win two championships, and two FA Cups — but was that enough of a return on the outlay? (I'm sure Wenger, with titles in the bag, would say 'yes'.) In fact, Wenger — good friend of Gérard Houllier — is an interesting comparison, having bought players who failed at Highbury such as Christopher Wreh, Gilles Grimandi, Luis Boa Morte, Igors Stepanovs, Kaba Diawara and Pascal Cygan. There are plenty of black marks against Wenger in the transfer market. It's the ones he got right that will be remembered longest, however.

Just a handful of months before Houllier paid £10.5m for Emile Heskey, Arsene Wenger had rescued Thierry Henry from his poor time out on the wing at Juventus, and converted him back to a centre-forward — the role in which he excelled as a young man in the French system at Clarefontaine, and in which Wenger had previously coached him at AS Monaco. It is not necessarily fair to compare the two signings in terms of one being the work of genius, the other of negligible miscalculation, as the two clubs had different needs during 1999/2000. Even had Gérard Houllier wanted Henry, he had spent heavily that summer on players in other areas of the team — where the need, it was universally agreed, was most urgent, with Fowler and Owen already leading the attack. It was only towards the end of that season that funds were made available to Houllier to procure Heskey, with an extra premium paid to Leicester for an early release, to help with the push for the Champions League spot (which ultimately backfired — the team failing to score in its final five games). Heskey was bought to do a job alongside Michael Owen — to take the physical brunt of defenders' ire — whereas different things were expected of Henry at Arsenal.

The point of the comparison is that Wenger ended up with arguably the best footballer on the planet in the early years of the new millennium, while Houllier was still trying to coax some self-belief into his talented — but flawed — striker, who had only shown his best colours during his first full season. In the final analysis, the signing of Thierry Henry led to league titles and a value of £50m being placed on him by his club; the signing of Emile Heskey led to him leaving Anfield for a fee that was approximately half what Leicester received four years earlier. Houllier would go on to spend £10m on El Hadji Diouf — ahead of Nicolas Anelka — which would ultimately lead to the manager's downfall. Had that £10m been spent on a radical success, it could all have been so different. At least it would have been *better*.

The arguments about whether Emile Heskey was good enough will rage on, even following his transfer to Birmingham. The only way it could have been *proven* was if he had key contributions, goals or no goals, in a side that won the league title. Any player in a successful side, whatever role they are performing, can rightly feel that they have contributed. As it was, Heskey helped the club win six trophies, so on that count he can feel satisfied.

But let's be clear: Houllier's task in his first summer in sole charge was to sort out a defence labelled 'comical' on too frequent a basis. Phil Babb, Neil Ruddock, Steve Harkness and co. could not be relied upon to keep clean sheets, and behind them David James was too erratic for comfort. Houllier plumped for Stephane Henchoz, who would prove an astute capture from Blackburn, given the deep-defending style the side would adopt. Next to Henchoz was Sami Hyypia, the best money, pound for pound, that Houllier spent. Just £2.6m was enough to secure the services of a man who would go on to be regarded as one of the best in Europe — a true colossus in the Ron Yeats mould. It was a hugely becalming sight to see the tall Finn rise into the air and head the ball 50 yards upfield; suddenly the team's soft core was as hard as nails, and as tall as towers. James was replaced by the Dutch national No.2 Sander Westerweld — a fine shot-stopper who contributed to the club's revival in winning five trophies, but whose inability to command his area saw him head for the exit (in no little ignominy) just two years later. His replacement, Jerzy Dudek, had one truly sensational season, and despite several high profile mistakes, remained a very fine goalkeeper.

Out went Paul Ince in a blaze of publicity — the former club captain regretting that he hadn't punched Houllier on the nose when the urge arose. In his place Houllier signed £8m Dietmar Hamann, who would patrol just in front of the back four in a role made famous at Anfield by Ronnie Whelan. Hamann's name became synonymous in English football with that advanced-sweeper role — he was the apotheosis of the art of being in the right place at the right time, to thwart an opposition thrust before giving the simple pass that sets the team on attacks of its own. Hamann was the final piece in Houllier's defensive diamond.

Another inspired signing was the experienced German international, Markus Babbel, snaffled on a free from Bayern Munich. Had illness not struck, the player could have gone on to become one of the club's greatest full-backs. As it was, his one full season resulted in the treble, and as well as defending stoutly, he scored six important goals.

Mixed legacy

Much was made by Gérard Houllier upon his departure — later echoed by Phil Thompson — about what they saw as the fine legacy they bequeathed Rafa Benítez and his staff. So precisely how good a shape was the club in during the summer of 2004? Would it be fair to say 'not that great' considering the massive gap between Liverpool and Arsenal (not to mention Chelsea and Manchester United) in the league? Or were there — as with the planting of bulbs in spring — many shoots of promise ready to blossom?

There are two distinct parts to this legacy: the playing staff, and the bricks and mortar (and hydrotherapy tanks) that made up the training facilities. Melwood was much altered by Houllier.

On the playing side, one of the cornerstones of Houllier's legacy was Michael Owen — a player Houllier had himself inherited upon Roy Evans' departure. Here the club had a guaranteed 25-goals-a-season (in all competitions) man, and a true world-class talent (whatever your definition of 'world-class' is, Owen is surely included). And yet Owen never got to play a competitive game for Benítez: sitting on the bench during the Grazer AK Champions League qualifier, and then promptly departing for Madrid.

It is fair to say that Houllier's disappointing final two seasons played a large part in Owen leaving: the player's future would have been settled sooner had the club been more successful on the pitch, or at the very least shown signs of progressing — and not, as appeared the case, regressing at an alarming pace. As it was, Owen procrastinated on signing a new deal, and however much his heart may have told him to stay, his head surely saw his future elsewhere; he had many new beginnings during his time at Anfield, and all had proved — ultimately — to be false dawns. In short, Benítez's arrival came too late. Perhaps had any other club come in for Owen, the player would have said no; Real Madrid, on the other hand, are notoriously difficult to turn down.

Owen's value had depreciated rapidly during Houllier's time in charge; had the player been on a four year deal during the summer of 2004, he'd have been worth in excess of £20m. As it stood, his value was less than half of that, and in just five months Owen could begin negotiating a Bosman transfer ahead of 2005/06. When he left, with him went a large part of Houllier's legacy to his successor.

Initially Anfield didn't have so much as a revolving door as a lengthy queue for the exit: arrivals were slow in materialising, departures were swift. Emile Heskey had already been sold to Birmingham with Djibril Cissé's impending arrival in mind. Also heading out of Anfield, following pre-season assessments by the new manager, was Danny Murphy, making it three England internationals to leave that summer (although only Owen was still a regular part of Sven Goran Eriksson's plans). There could be little doubt that Heskey and Murphy were good players, but compared to the very best — the players at the top three clubs — they appeared too inconsistent when judged over a number of seasons. Both could be brilliant on their day, but neither had their day quite often enough. The best players excel eight games out of every ten, whereas these two players (and others at Anfield) could manage just three or four good games out of every ten, and maybe only one or two great ones. Both Murphy and Heskey had managed one great season at Anfield, but fans were growing increasingly impatient with the players they saw as underachieving. Benítez, of course, could only guarantee Murphy a squad place, so the player chose to move to Charlton.

A bevy of Houllier's signings departed on loan, meaning that whatever the quality of Houllier's legacy, the quantity wasn't anywhere near as abundant.

Anthony Le Tallec, told by Rafa that he wasn't yet ready to feature in his first-team plans, went on loan to St Etienne — but with the clear instruction that there would be no chance of a permanent deal at the end of it, given the 19-year-old had far too much promise to discard, despite the petulance that led to the loan in the first place. Alou Diarra, after two seasons on loan in France, returned to his homeland for a further year, this time at Lens (amazing many Reds by making his debut for the French national team before he'd played a competitive game in a Liverpool shirt). Young French reserve Carl Medjani would spend a year at Lorient in the French second division, and Gregory Vignal, whose bright start at Liverpool in the Treble season seemed a distant memory, exchanged Anfield for Ibrox. John Otsemobor went to Crewe to gain experience, and Neil Mellor turned down a similar move to Gresty Road. Bruno Cheyrou and El Hadji Diouf, given that no team wished to pay the asking price in order to buy them, were sent away in order to get them off the wage bill — Cheyrou to Marseille, Diouf to Bolton. Salif Diao would later make a similar move to Birmingham. All in all, this accounts for over £22m of investment in players being farmed out on loan.

So that left a fairly threadbare squad for Benítez to begin working with. (While many of the decisions to let those players go were the Spaniard's, some had been taken before he arrived.) He was in the tricky position of having to quickly assess his squad before pruning the deadwood and seeking replacements. In years gone by, an Anfield manager would have been able to add players all season long, up until late March. Under the new transfer window regulations, Benítez had only until the end of August, and another four week period in January. He had a pretty good knowledge of the Liverpool squad upon arrival (Rick Parry was impressed that Benítez knew many of the reserve players), but he would obviously need to work with these players at close quarters to form a first-hand opinion. It was one thing encountering Houllier's Liverpool team — playing Houllier's way — in the Champions League and a pre-season friendly, but it was another to see if these players could adapt to new ideas and different tactics.

Houllier bequeathed a very young squad, given that he became increasingly loath — give or take the odd exception to prove the rule — to signing experienced players. Those he did sign, such as Jari Litmanen, were treated with strange contempt, or at best, apparent distrust. Houllier was planning for tomorrow the entire time. *Tomorrow never arrived* — at least not during his tenure. There was never quite enough quality and experience for *today*. Houllier would never have time to see canny purchases, such as Florent Sinama-Pongolle, come to fruition. By 2004 he had used up all five years of his self-confessed 'five-year plan'. His successor — at the start of his own five-year plan — would surely be given a season or two's grace, to bed in new players as he rebuilt the side, before being expected to challenge for the ultimate prizes.

In 1999, the average age of Houllier's side was 23/24. The idea was that the team would grow up together in the coming years, and gel as a unit as they matured. But towards the end of Houllier's reign, the average age was still 23/24. Certain individuals had matured, but others had been replaced by less-experienced players, and it was almost a case of 'back to square one'. (It was interesting to note that Houllier, after many of his players had been involved in the Champions League semi-final victory over Chelsea, expressed pride at having signed mainly 20-24 year-olds. While a sensible buying policy to a degree, it left a shortfall in experience, especially in attacking terms, which Benítez was left to address: signing Luis Garcia, 26, and Fernando Morientes, 29.)

Just as players reach their peak between 27-31, you will find nearly every successful team has an average age between those two figures. Success tends to be based around a clutch of young starlets, a smattering of players either in, or approaching, their peak years, and a small number of older players whose legs may be waning but who offer unique experience from all their years in the game — the kind of players who can act as coaches in training, offer guidance from the sidelines, and be a 'manager on the pitch'. It is worth noting that Houllier's most successful season, when he won the Treble in 2001, came when he was fielding his 'oldest' side. Westerveld, Hyypia, Henchoz, Babbel, Barmby, Ziege, Hamann, Berger, Smicer, Litmanen, McAllister and Fowler were all over 25. It was only after this season that his gradual reduction of the average age started to gain pace.

Gérard Houllier deserves some credit for Benítez' success in the Champions League, although precisely how much remains open to debate. Given two of Benítez' signings (Morientes, Pellegrino) were ineligible for the Champions League, another (Carson) was a back-up goalkeeper who featured only once, and two more (Alonso and Josemi) missed several months — and a series of key games — with injury, it was mostly Houllier's players who got the team to the final. It just needed a better tactician to guide them, with the Spaniard having added a little more quality in the areas the Frenchman left underdeveloped. Just as José Mourinho could not have won the league without the players he inherited, and the level Chelsea had reached the season before, then nor could Benítez have taken Liverpool to the final without the European experience the players gained under his predecessor. (It was funny to hear ex-Evertonian Kevin Ratcliffe suggest Everton could reach the Champions League final — on the basis that if Liverpool could, so could they. Finishing three points above Liverpool appears to have gone to the Toffees' heads. Was he forgetting the extensive European experience Liverpool had picked up in the previous four years, while Everton were busy in relegation battles?)

Unless Benítez rebuilds the entire squad — which will be highly unlikely, unless he is in charge for five years or more, or given an astronomical budget — he will be working heavily with inherited components. While the manager who actually achieves the success deserves the lion's share of the praise, some credit must also go to the man who had done some of the groundwork.

Chapter three

Michael Owen – saint or sinner?

Footballers differ from many other athletes and sportsmen, in that, exhibitionist ball-jugglers aside, they exist exclusively in the realms of a *team sport*. Golfers may join together for the Ryder Cup, tennis players may unite for the mixed doubles, and the fastest men and women on the planet may exchange (or in Britain's case, drop) batons in the 4 x 100 relay, but otherwise they exist in isolation, loners in their chosen sport, pitting their wits one-against-one, or one-against-all comers, to be crowned *the best*. It is highly instructive to watch how golfers, for example, visibly wilt under the pressure of a team game in the Ryder Cup, when they are playing for themselves and a collection of other golfers, not to mention their country/continent. But that's only once every two years, and for the rest of the time they just have to concentrate on their own game.

Consider the lot of a top footballer who trains his heart out from a tender age, leads an abstemious life away from the pitch, and generally attempts to do all he can to get the most from his God-given talent. Whatever his destiny in the sport, he is beholden to his teammates. Still judged as an individual, but part of a collective. Diego Maradona aside, a footballer cannot win games single-handedly; he can make winning contributions, as did Michael Owen so memorably on so many occasions, not least the 2001 FA Cup final, but the little Argentine is the closest the game has come to a one-man team (in an attacking sense, at least — Maradona wasn't much of one for tracking back).

Modern-day footballers are trained, with almost nauseating predictability, to thank their teammates at every opportunity — after all, they cannot do it alone. Even Maradona would have struggled in a match of one versus eleven. (He may have looked like he was doing everything in a game, but of course in reality he wasn't.) A united team of journeymen can overcome a collection of over-confident superstars — we've all seen that happen enough times, with Real Madrid being the perfect example: the more superstars they sign, the less successful they become. It is a team sport, and as the annoying phrase confirms, there's no 'I' in 'team'. But if the best players need the assistance of their teammates, it's equally true to say that their teammates can also hold them back. There's no point being the best striker in the world if your goalkeeper cannot catch a football and concedes five in every game; similarly, there's no point being the best keeper in the world if your strikers can't hit a barn door, and never score a goal. No one should be in any doubt that whatever the power of the team, *football revolves around individuals*. They are the ones who make the telling contributions. However great a team move, it needs one person alone to finish it off.

A team is always a collection of disparate, autonomous human beings who come together for the cause; it is not eleven conjoined people, like a freak of nature. A team will always need someone to move above and beyond teamwork, and to take responsibility to be the *individual* who makes a difference. Not in a display of irresponsible showboating, or the reckless abandon of trying to shine while not caring about the fact that it might be counterproductive winning the game. Someone — a single player — has to *make it count*. These are the 'match winners'.

For example, take Arsenal's 'invincibles' of 2003/04. Whatever their team spirit, and however great their collective unison — where the total exceeds the sum of the parts — that team relied on the individual abilities of key players, not least Thierry Henry's ability to 'go it alone' when the occasion demanded it. Had he spent the course of that season turning back and laying off 'easy' passes, and been only a 'team player', they'd never have won the title, let alone have gone the entire season undefeated. At times Henry had to assume the responsibility to be the one who made the difference. (As did

John Barnes in the late 80s, in Liverpool's *near*-invincibles.) Henry was still playing for the team, of course. But not in the bland sense of the word.

At Liverpool, Michael Owen was often that man. Never as flamboyant as Henry, of course. But often as deadly and clinical.

Aspirations

All players have different ideas of how to attain their own personal objectives. Any player has the right, if out of contract, or nearing the end of his deal, to opt for a different environment if he feels undervalued, under-deployed, under-stimulated, or underpaid at his current club. It's not always a clear-cut case of loyalty or disloyalty. He may even intend to stay at his current club, and say as much — but a better offer comes along, and the challenge is too great to refuse.

It's fair to say that this was the case with Michael Owen. His aspirations — to win the major honours — were not being assisted at Liverpool, due largely to the limitations of his teammates, and the growing concerns at the inadequacy of the team's manager. No, Owen wasn't always perfect. Yes, he missed sitters. But his consistency is backed up by his record — stats like that don't tell lies. It's fair to say that in Michael Owen's position, any fan would have felt that his or her enduring high-class contribution was worthy of something more significant than sporadic cup success. Before casting the first stones, fans should put themselves in the player's position. Would they have acted any differently?

While at the club, Owen was viewed with some suspicion by a section of the support, and his departure was no different. Many wished him the best, and his first goal for Real Madrid was roundly cheered at half-time at Anfield when George Sephton announced the news over the tannoy. But plenty felt cheated by his departure, having believed he'd promised to sign a new deal, while others used it as a chance to say "I was right — he was always looking to leave". There was a fair level of enmity, of a kind unthinkable towards Robbie Fowler.

The summer of 2004 saw another English 'superstar' exit a Merseyside club. But there were radical differences in the two situations. Wayne *once a blue, always a blue* Rooney, at just 19, was leaving his beloved hometown club for the lure of the bright Champions League lights of Manchester United. He had a lengthy contract remaining, and his sum contribution to Everton — the team he supported in a 'diehard' manner — was a small collection of goals and a far larger collection of disciplinary points. Everton may not have matched his personal ambitions, but he hardly gave them much of a chance.

What Rooney allowed — or arguably, *forced* Everton to do, in contrast to Owen, was receive a transfer fee in line with the going market rate. In agitating for a move, Rooney gave Everton little option but to cash in. Once a player asks to leave, it's counter-productive to try and keep him against his wishes. Was Rooney worth £27m? To Manchester United, clearly so. Was Owen worth as little as £8-10m by comparison? Of course not. But Owen had just one year left on his contract, and had he seen that out, he'd have been worth nothing to the club — so that's a depreciation of £10m in less than a year. He always maintained he would never leave on a Bosman transfer, and in many respects he was as good as his word. (It would have been interesting, had Madrid not made their last-minute move, to see what Owen would have done once the transfer window closed. If he meant what he said about never leaving on a 'free' — and he may well have done — the obvious solution would have been to sign a short-term deal with a reduced buy-out clause.) One thing Owen had done (in contrast to Rooney) was give his club full value for money — and more — during his time in Liverpool. He gave the club the first half of his career, not two inconsistent and temperamental teenage years.

Losing players for less than their 'usual' market value is never an easy pill for fans to swallow, but did Owen cost Liverpool anything other than seven years' worth of wages? (Which, in themselves, were high but not exorbitant when compared to players of similar standing in the game, and who, like Owen, also generated sizable incomes for their clubs with their worldwide commercial pulling power.) In his seven full seasons, he was the club's top scorer on each occasion.

So had he paid his debt to the club, whatever that 'debt' was? (Presumably, the act of its scouts discovering and nurturing him, although he was coveted by a clutch of clubs throughout his youth — in truth, *he chose Liverpool*. Liverpool did not choose him. His talent was not created by alchemists who knew how to turn normal boys into superstars. He was an outstanding prospect long before he reached his teens — the club helped him develop, but it did not 'create' him.)

Seven years, 158 goals, four major trophies later, and having just helped to ensure the third Champions League qualification of the new millennium, he eventually exited for a £10m transfer fee. It's hard to argue that Owen did anything but benefit Liverpool Football Club during his time there.

Any fan who wants to harbour a grudge should ask whether they would do the same in similar circumstances; or indeed, *in their own circumstances.* If they have refused all opportunities to better themselves, all offers for promotion or a pay rise, and never felt professionally unfulfilled — bored, unchallenged, stale — or undervalued, then they can adopt the high moral ground. I doubt many would pass such stringent hypocrisy tests.

The issue of 'greed' also raises its ugly head. How many Ferraris and mock Tudor mansions does any single footballer need, after all? But money for a footballer is not *solely* about greed (although there are plenty of money-thirsty mercenaries out there) — it's a symbol of his value to the club, and a reward for his achievements on the pitch. Players know how valuable they are to their employers, and how they rank in the pecking order of importance among their peers. Very few are altruistic enough to think "well, this new Bosnian Bosman left-back is on £80,000 a week, due to his strong bargaining position, and he's not even making the bench. But I am happy to keep scoring 50 goals a season and busting a gut for £5,000 a week".

We, as fans, worship the players, but the relationship is different for them. Their trade may not be a 'job' in the most mundane sense of the word, but it is, all the same, their *profession*. It's their livelihood, and it's also how they define themselves. Not all are into the *bling bling* culture, or take part in seedy hotel 'spit-roasts'. Despite the stupidity of a number of footballers, they were still the ones who made sacrifices as teenagers while 'we' either weren't good enough, or couldn't be bothered going out in the cold or the wet, maybe snug inside some pub getting drunk with our mates. They are the ones who trained in a way that would have made Roy Castle proud, and, while brittle bones were still growing and setting, played an obscene amount of matches every week that a Victorian chimney sweep would have baulked at. (The kind of schedule that led Rob Jones to have all sorts of crippling injuries, and surely contributed to his premature retirement.) They are the ones who will doubtless have suffered injuries intent on shattering their dreams, and had to battle back through excruciating (and lonely) gym work. Largely unconcerned with schoolwork, they put all their eggs into the 'professional footballer' basket, and from that point on have to do all they can to make it. It's a dog-eat-dog world. A Darwinian system is in place, where it's survival of the fittest; the weak fall by the wayside.

Deluded (and possibly arrogant) fans are liable to say 'I'd play for free', in response to those who need to earn fortunes for the 'privilege'. It's an easy thing to say *when you are not actually good enough to do so*, or *haven't been bothered in doing so*. Those uttering such statements haven't invested the time and energy to earn the right, and nor have they ever had to play under anything resembling the kind of pressure the professionals have to deal with. (It's easy slating a player, but try doing better with 40,000 people groaning and wincing at your every touch.)

There is nothing stopping a fan of any club, who possesses the necessary ability, progressing to the point where he can play for his beloved club, and to then offer do so for free. As far as I'm aware, it hasn't happened yet, despite all those representing the club of their boyhood dreams. Many say they'd walk over hot coals, but none ask for YTS wages. And if a talented fan offered his services for free, got a few games and did extremely well — ended up doing better than players on £50,000 a week — they'd soon think 'balls to this, where's my share of the pie?'

It may seem like an easy life, but even the laziest of players have worked hard at some stage to get where they are. Owen was one who never stopped working hard, and never stopped caring, once he got there.

The ones at the top of their profession are handsomely remunerated (although it's the journeymen who are laughing hardest, getting millions for being average). To stay there they need to produce the goods. They have also earned the right to decide what to do with their careers, when their contracts are nearing conclusion. (It's hard to have much sympathy for footballers who sign lucrative five-year deals, with all the long-term benefits that it represents, and then cry foul or want away within a matter of months; they want the security of that contract, and then want to be able to ignore the binding nature of it — the very thing that protects them.)

Twelve months from the end of a contract is the one time when both club and player hold an equal amount of cards. It is when a player is still tied to a club and therefore doesn't yet possess freedom of movement, but when the club knows it has to make a decision: offer a new contract or risk losing the player in a year's time. Put bluntly, it's make-or-break time, although two years before the end of any deal is the true key time from a club's point of view. After that point, the value of their 'investment' quickly depreciates.

Clubs do not *own* players, as they are human beings, free to do with their careers what they please, so long as it's legal. Fans can be too possessive, and understandably so: a lot of emotion gets invested in watching, and worshipping, these stars, and it can take next-to-nothing to have us crying foul, or questioning their loyalty or commitment. Sometimes fairly, other times unjustly.

If Owen, by letting his contract run down to its final year, was keeping his options open, who can blame him? Was that not his right? Why should he narrow his options, when he clearly doesn't have to? The club could, of course, have offered him enough money to make it virtually impossible to refuse to sign a new deal. Perhaps they did. What he was clearly waiting for — given he had enough money for several lifetimes — was unequivocal proof that the club was moving in the right direction. While his contract was running out, that clearly wasn't the case; it was regressing. When the club was improving, he never hesitated to sign a new deal — and this includes the time between 18 and 21, when his star was burning so brightly he could have easily declined to put pen to paper and opted for a more lucrative move abroad, or agitated for the kind of move Wayne Rooney pulled off.

Had Houllier won the Premiership, or taken the club to a Champions League final, between 2002 and 2004, I think it's fair to say that Owen would have felt suitably impressed to commit his future to the club beyond his final deal. And even when it came to the summer of 2004, a less impressive offer than that of joining Real Madrid (the footballing equivalent, it seems, of being invited by Hugh Hefner to the *Playboy* mansions) may not have tempted him. However much he rated Benítez (and Owen, along with other senior pros, was consulted by Rick Parry on the appointment), it was clear that the Spaniard had his work cut out and the striker, who'd seen his fair share of false dawns at Anfield, was entitled to think it could take a number of years for the team to get where he wanted it to be. Real Madrid offered a ready-made team of quality, and even though the side were lacking certain attributes, it's fair to say that the Madrid of Ronaldo, Raúl, Beckham, Zidane, Figo and Roberto Carlos were closer to the finished article than Liverpool. (How ironic that Liverpool should progress far further in the Champions League. Owen must have been disbelieving at what took place in his absence, and no little jealous — anyone who walks away immediately before something special occurs would feel the same. It must be akin to dropping out of the work lottery syndicate the week before it wins the 'rollover'.)

It's hard to argue that Owen didn't outshine the vast majority of his teammates during his time at Liverpool. Some were fit to play alongside him; others clearly weren't. Had Owen and Ian Rush swapped eras, then it's not inconceivable that the former would have matched the latter's goalscoring feats and won as many league titles and European Cups. Both were supreme strikers, but whereas Rush had ten top-class teammates, including Dalglish with his sublime vision (any goalscorer's dream partner), Owen was often left to feed on scraps, or make his own good fortune.

Owen craved to be surrounded by peers on a par with himself. While Houllier helped Owen overcome his hamstring nightmares, and turned him into a more complete striker — not least with regard to his left foot and heading — it's also the case that the manager failed Owen with regard to building a team to match his talents. The good times under the Frenchman were a thing of the past. Owen had won four cups under Houllier, and his efforts were rewarded with the European Footballer of the Year in 2001; the *Ballon D'or* the ultimate recognition of his individual talent in a way that being part of that Liverpool team — unable to procure the biggest prizes — could not deliver. Owen's remaining ambitions were no closer to being met. In fact, by the time Houllier was sacked, they were disappearing further into the distance.

Accusations abounded about Owen being past his best (which some say was when he was 18), but in his final year at Liverpool he actually scored more goals — in terms of the percentage of the team's final tally — than ever before, at an ever-impressive ratio, while his goalscoring record at international level has been better under Sven Goran Eriksson than prior to his appointment in 2001. He remains one of those players who has to go to great lengths to re-prove himself, and still be considered a failure in some respects. But it was also clear he wasn't totally enjoying his football — the smile was gone, and the body language often dejected. The time was as good as any for a change.

From Liverpool to Madrid — and back to Liverpool?

Michael Owen will look upon his first and, if rumours are to be believed, only season in Madrid as a success, and as a great learning experience. It doesn't mean he will be happy with being third choice, or 'super sub', but his goals-per-minutes ratio was the best in *La Liga* — whenever he got a game, he often scored. It is abundantly clear that Owen is not a quitter, but clearly something has to change. He may not have Ronaldo's amazing skills, but the sight of the bloated Brazilian lumbering around mid-season with his gut hanging over the elastic of his shorts left much to be desired, while Raúl appeared to be living off the reputation of yore. Ronaldo remains a great footballer, but the lack of professionalism — or dedication — was summed up by turning up late to training twice in the week in which he'd organised an engagement party in Paris — which was also the week of an important game. Owen had the right attitude, but the wrong image — a kind of semi-galáctico, unable to oust or usurp the fully-fledged variety. Glamorous, just not glamorous enough.

Liverpool retain the first option on Owen if Real opt to sell and in early April Benítez said: "He is a Liverpool supporter and it's always an option for him and us. He has the spirit you need, he loves Liverpool and it's always an option." All the same, outsiders believed Benítez was less than keen on re-signing the player, and the inevitable rumours about a rift leading to his leaving resurfaced — and it is a given Real will demand closer to double the fee they originally paid. The arrival of Morientes and rehabilitation of Cissé give Liverpool two extremely strong attacking options, and Florent Sinama-Pongolle was developing well before injury struck; while Milan Baros remains a fine player, albeit one not as clinical as Owen (few are), and one whose season was very hit-and-miss. Baros' contract has just two years left to run, and he has made no secret of his desire to play in Spain. Of the strikers still on the books, Baros looks the likeliest to leave the club. And while Morientes is still adjusting to life in the Premiership, on the rare occasions he and Owen took to the field together in the white of Real Madrid they appeared to gel very well.

Benítez was responding to reports in the media suggesting Owen favoured a move home. Owen had only just told *Shoot* magazine, "I left Liverpool on good terms, they are still the first result I look out for and I have a lot of friends there. I have no bitterness at all towards Liverpool and they are still a club very close to my heart." The interesting thing about his experience in Madrid was his teammates' opinion that he was so introverted — like Ian Rush, he perhaps wasn't a natural for life overseas. The parallel led to much of the speculation that Owen, like Rush, would return to Liverpool, who have first option on his signature, after just 12 months. Owen admitted to missing certain things about England: "Being around your family, your friends, being in your house. I had just had my house reshaped and virtually the minute it was finished I was leaving. It is my dream house [with] two dogs, my horse and all the land that I want. I got it perfect for living in and then I had to uproot."

Rumour-mongers this season have persisted in linking Owen with a move to Arsenal, who may be able to offer Madrid the talented and unsettled young Spaniard, Jose Antonio Reyes, and who could certainly use a penalty-box poacher of Owen's ilk, given Henry does most of his work out wide. Owen re-igniting the near-telepathic understanding with Steven Gerrard is, of course, a mouth watering prospect, given the added style and substance of the Liverpool side under Benítez, but it seems as likely that both could be at Liverpool next season as *neither*. They could be reuniting in Madrid, or even at Chelsea, if you believe all you read. (And, as with this book, *I* wouldn't.)

It was a grand irony that in leaving Liverpool in search of the major trophies, he ended up missing out on the biggest of them all. At least he proved to himself, and to his doubters, that he could cut it in *La Liga*; though he won no medals in his first season in Spain, he did win plenty of acclaim. He was also humble enough to admit that had he stayed at Liverpool, he would have done things differently to Milan Baros, and the team may not have had such a remarkable season in Europe. Where Liverpool missed him most, however, was in the Premiership.

Chapter four

Replacing an idol

The signing of Djibril Cissé proved to be Gérard Houllier's final piece of business as Liverpool manager before clearing his desk and bidding his colleagues farewell. The young French striker was also the last in a lengthy line of replacements Houllier tried to find following his most controversial transaction: selling 'God' (otherwise more modestly known as Robbie Fowler) in October 2001. Houllier was sacked before Cissé — the club's record signing at £14.2m — had even arrived for his first training session: after three years pursuing France's hottest young prospect, the deal came to fruition too late to save the manager his job. The striker chose Liverpool ahead of other tempting offers, on account of the club's long-standing interest, and also the involvement of Houllier, who Cissé felt had great trust in his ability.

Following the dismissal of his compatriot, Cissé quickly claimed that he was equally happy to play for Benítez (while he may have been nervous at how the new man regarded him, he would also have approved of Benítez' pedigree), and Benítez soon made it perfectly clear how pleased he was to be inheriting a player he'd coveted while in charge at Valencia: he was quick to relate that his technical director and chief scout always talked about Cissé, saying 'If you'd had him you would win the league for another three years'.

It could be argued, with hindsight, that Cissé's chances of settling quickly were hindered by the exit of the club's French manager, its Gallic coaching staff, and a whole raft of French-speaking players. As it was, settling into the English game and learning the language proved to be the least of the player's problems, as tragedy — in footballing terms — struck, and he ended up in hospital undergoing surgery to repair his shattered leg.

The curse of the Liverpool no.9 shirt — which dates back to the late 1990s — lived on for yet another season. Such a potent symbol for so many years — the bold white numeral '9' on a blood-red shirt shorthand for the word 'goal'. Now a symbol of hex, as goals scored by the players wearing the famous shirt dried up.

First Fowler succumbed to a succession of serious injuries, to the point where, when he was fit enough to play, it was blindingly obvious that while still gifted, he was no longer the player once so venerated by the Kop. Struggling for peak fitness, he was low on the one thing he once seemed replete with: confidence. Weighed down with the worries of the world, and a few extra pounds, he was no longer playing with the carefree enthusiasm that had been one of his greatest strengths. (What a sad sight in subsequent seasons, seeing Fowler as a pale — and sometimes overly-large — shadow of the player so fondly remembered by the Anfield faithful.) Eight years in the Liverpool team, and it was a career of two halves: the first four years producing a sackful of goals, the second four resulting in a far less impressive return. If Manchester United fans still mourn the exit of George Best at the age of 26, and all the unfulfilled potential (despite achieving much, and being brilliant for most of his time at the club), then Fowler — while clearly not Liverpool's greatest-ever player — must go down as its greatest under-achiever. Or rather, to put it more accurately, the player who lit up the pitch for a number of seasons, only to leave in his mid-20s, denying the fans the later years of a career that seemed destined to be played out in red, and in so doing, leaving a sense of incompletion and unfulfilled promise. If it seems daft to suggest someone who scored 171 goals for the club in 330 games failed to deliver on his potential, then such were the standards he set from 1993 to 1997, as he edged towards 40 goals a season.

Next, Nicolas Anelka had a short spell in the shirt, but was overlooked by Houllier when it came to a permanent deal; a situation which led to recriminations in the press, and bafflement from many fans. If the sale of Fowler, for £11m, looks better business with each passing season, the nagging reminder is that £10m of that fee went on El Hadji Diouf: a player who would hardly cover himself in glory at Liverpool, either on or off the pitch. Even in Fowler's last full season he scored 17 (mostly crucial) goals for the club. Diouf became the first ever no.9 in Liverpool history to go a goalless league season at the club, and scored only one further league goal after his bright home debut. (Diouf, while on loan at Bolton, scored nine goals, and was hailed as a great success. And yet nine is hardly very many by Liverpool standards.)

Milan Baros arrived at Liverpool on the same day as Anelka, in December 2001. He actually signed for Liverpool in the summer of 2001 but had to wait until he was granted a work permit in the winter, after he had played a couple more games for the Czech Republic. Initial impressions weren't good — many of the coaching staff questioned why the club had paid £3.2m for a player who was slightly overweight and who didn't appear especially happy to be at the club. In the pre-season of 2002/03 Baros knuckled down, and suddenly Houllier's reasoning became clear. The Czech scored 12 goals in his first full season, from 25 starts, and a bright future appeared ahead of him.

Finally, Cissé arrived with a massive reputation and rampant expectation, but before he'd even had a chance to adjust to the English game he suffered a comminuted fracture of the tibia and fracture of the fibula. A truly gruesome injury, from an innocuous-looking challenge at Blackburn Rovers in October. (How on earth can one league fixture throw up — and that is an apposite phrase following the slow-motion replays of Cissé's leg snapping — broken bones to three Liverpool players in just 180 minutes of football over a 15 months period?) A little over two months into the season, and his campaign was over. Reports later confirmed that a complication with damaged nerves in his leg meant it came close to being amputated, but a full, and speedy, recovery appears to have taken place. Cissé taking to the pitch as a late substitute at the Stadio Delle Alpi on April 13th, with Liverpool leading Juventus 2-1 on aggregate, was one of the sights of the season. It was also slightly surreal, in that not only was he back four months earlier than anticipated, but Liverpool were just minutes from the semi-final of the Champions League. It capped a perfect night.

The first couple of months of Cissé's Liverpool career were, on balance, little more than average — displaying some promise without hitting the heights expected. While comparisons between Cissé and Thierry Henry were inevitable, given both are tall, black, turbo-charged players of French descent, their styles are actually rather different: Cissé preferring to work centrally on the shoulder of the last man (like a taller, faster Michael Owen), while Henry's unique talent sees him drifting all over the pitch looking for space to influence the game, especially favouring the left wing. For those who wrote off Cissé's career after an inauspicious start it is worth noting that Thierry Henry started his Highbury career even less impressively. It took the Arsenal man 17 games to reach the three goal mark, while Cissé had three in fifteen when injury struck (plus three more on the pre-season tour of America, including two fine finishes against Celtic). As Cissé worked his way back to full fitness via a number of brief cameos, his stats only looked less and less impressive, but 2005/06 is when the club can expect to see the player at his best. As it was, the final league game of the season, at home to Aston Villa, provided the first true glimpse of the Frenchman approaching such levels, when he won and scored a penalty, and then soon after tucked away another fine finish. There were other shots of note, and some sublime touches, while the old pace was starting to return in earnest. However, he made it clear after the game that he was still only 70-80% fit. If he wasn't at his best physically, he certainly was mentally — replete with confidence, he also appeared fully at home in English football for the first time. Although he'd previously shown glimpses of his class, this was his first match-winning performance. He was electric.

In the early part of the season Cissé had played as a striker, in rotation with Baros, but as the autumn approached, he either started or ended matches on the right wing, where he proved surprisingly effective. There were no fancy tricks, just the simple tactic of knocking the ball past the full-back, safe in the knowledge that he could give anyone a five-yard head-start and still beat them over twenty. While centre-forward remains his true position, with Benítez, like so many of his peers, employing the 4-5-1 formation in many games, it could be that Cissé spends more time on the right once he regains his fitness — especially as Fernando Morientes is ideal for the lone striker role. If that proves to be the case, then there is still much Cissé can offer, as well as the prospect of dovetailing with the Spaniard when the manager opts for a 4-4-2 formation.

Anyone who saw the goals Cissé regularly plundered in France will tell you what a special talent he is. Instant judgments in England have tarnished his reputation somewhat, but he looked a 'proper' finisher in his homeland, scoring all kinds of goals: volleys, chips, headers, poacher's goals, as well as the obvious examples where his blistering pace left defenders not so much for dead as readily embalmed and entombed. Make no mistake — he is not some quick 'headless chicken' type, but a player with capabilities on the ball (as his reverse nutmeg on his home debut against Man City evinced), even if he will obviously never have the guile and craft of a Dalglish or a Beardsley. Cissé's record of 72 league goals in 123 starts (and a further 14 substitute appearances) for Auxerre is absolutely top-rate by anyone's standards. Anyone who claims, in the hope of demeaning Cissé's achievements, that the French league is easy for strikers, should note that the top scorers in that country rarely match the amount of goals plundered by the Premiership's top scorers. Goals are more difficult to come by in *Ligue Une*. French football is one of the five major leagues in Europe, along with Spain, Italy, Germany and England. The pedigree is there.

For example, Didier Drogba managed 18 *Ligue Une* goals in 2003/04 at Marseilles, and as second-top league scorer in France that season earned a £24m move to Chelsea (based also on his fine European record during that campaign). At Monaco, Fernando Morientes managed just nine league goals, but of course also scored that many again in a dazzling run to the Champions League final. So when put into context, Cissé's 26 league goals during that campaign are not to be sneezed at, especially as he wasn't playing in one of the truly outstanding French sides. In fact, during his time at Auxerre, the club had spent most of its time just outside the top three: a good side, but never a great one.

There was one moment, in the home fixture with Charlton, when Cissé appeared to break the speed of sound — or possibly even the speed of *light*, as he caught up with a ball he knocked 30-yards into space *before it had even left his foot*; he was near the halfway line, and in the blink of an eye down by the corner flag. It is harder to recall a quicker burst of pace in the history of Anfield. (Paul Stewart certainly never came close.) As the quickest striker in the country — all being 100% well in his rehabilitation, as appears to be the case — Cissé will force defences to drop a lot deeper than they need to against the sprightly (but not super-quick) Baros. Teams know their quickest defender can catch Baros — that won't be true of Cissé. Of course, the deeper a defence sits, the further forward Fernando Morientes (if Benítez opts for two strikers) can position himself, and therefore the threat of him scoring from crosses into the box greatly increases. If teams push out to negate Morientes' aerial prowess, to keep him 40 yards from goal — and even he doesn't score 40-yard headers — then that provides the space for Cissé to run into. Only time will tell how effective the partnership proves, or indeed, if Benítez opts for something, or someone different. That Cissé got himself back into contention so quickly owes a lot to the fine medical staff, but also speaks volumes of the player himself.

He was told he'd have to work hard, and work hard he did. Many reports from inside the club emphasised his diligent approach and positive attitude. The hairstyles may suggest a flash young man preferring style over substance, but the way he reacted to adversity, and the dedication shown in his rehabilitation, clearly proves otherwise.

The best thing, from Liverpool's point of view, was the perspective it gave the player. His comments, as his return to first team action beckoned, were extremely refreshing: "I want to say that to all the football players in the world, all the professionals who think they are hard done to or have things to complain about. They all complain, you know, about things like having to run for 30 minutes or do something they don't fancy, and they moan. But that is ridiculous — we are so lucky and I really appreciate that now. I just wish all footballers could realise that. It is a job, sure, but it is a passion. Can you believe we get paid to do that? You see so many stupid things happening in football, and I just want to tell those guys how lucky they are. I'm not exaggerating to say that it is close to a miracle that I am playing again at this stage. It is miraculous and I count my blessings that I can be playing now in this game."

Amen to that.

El Hadji Diouf

Djibril Cissé arrived at the club to find negative parallels instantly drawn with a previous expensive signing of Houllier's from France, El Hadji Diouf. Such a judgment was pronounced, by the *Daily Mirror*, after just one game — in which Cissé also happened to score a great striker's goal. Others took a little longer to reach that conclusion, but it was still a premature assessment. The 'logic' ran, that *even Diouf* scored two goals on his debut. (A statement in itself incorrect: it was his *home* debut, and his second league start — the first being at Villa Park.) The implication was that Cissé would prove equally useless.

That paper's opinion that Cissé didn't even *look* like a footballer would remain one of the most bizarre pronouncements of the season. The hairstyle and bleached-blonde goatee may have differed from the 'norm' (and certainly wasn't something stylistically akin to World Cup-winning footballers like Jackie and Bobby Charlton, while it is equally implausible to imagine Ron Yeats or Tommy Smith sporting a peroxide-blanched style), but aside from his tonsorial extravagance it's hard to think how much more you could want in terms of physique — surely the only way to judge whether or not someone *looks* like a footballer. If Cissé was fractionally less muscular than Emile Heskey, the man he was replacing, then that was more to do with Heskey having a heavyweight boxer's musclebound build (despite an all-too-frequent failure to punch his weight).

That Cissé later found himself utilised on the right wing seemed to compound such bizarre and hasty parallels drawn with Diouf. The two players couldn't be more different; they just happen to come from French football, be black, and cost £10m or more. Beyond that, the similarities are scarce.

Both arrived in England at roughly the same age and an identical stage of their careers, but whereas Cissé had 72 league goals to his name, Diouf had only managed fractionally over a quarter of that amount — a very modest 20. To be blunt, Diouf had never been a goalscorer, so it remains a matter of some puzzlement that he arrived with the nickname 'Serial Killer'. Cissé, by contrast, always appeared a thoroughbred. In fact, despite a decent scoring run during his loan period at Bolton, the Senegalese is still nowhere close to matching his career league goals tally to the amount of league bookings he has accrued. (As of June 2005, Diouf's league career statistics show 56 yellow cards, 3 red, and just 35 goals in 194 games.) While he has undoubted skill on the ball, such statistics over the course of a series of seasons don't lie — they merely confirm that the player doesn't score enough goals, and gets himself into far too much trouble. Houllier's thinking in signing Diouf seems to have been along the lines of deploying him just behind Owen, in the 'hole', to link the midfield with the attack — a long-standing problem for his side. (Something Nicolas Anelka had shown promise with during his brief stay at Liverpool, and a role Jari Litmanen had earlier been earmarked for, without ever getting the chance to fully prove it.)

Diouf's international record for Senegal was fairly impressive, but due mostly to plundering hatfuls against minnows in qualifying campaigns. In the finals of three major tournaments — two African Nations Cups and a World Cup — when up against superior opposition, his record stands at just one goal in close on 20 games. While the World Cup of 2002 brought him to the world's attention (and to the attention of Liverpool fans), it was more for his work outside the box, not least turning an ageing Marcel Desailly inside-out on the left flank in the build up to the winning goal in Senegal's shock 1-0 victory over holders France, in the showpiece tournament-opening game.

Things could have been very different for Diouf, Houllier and Benítez. Before the World Cup, Diouf had been close to signing for Valencia. It is unclear how much involvement Benítez had in the decision to pursue the player, given that transfers were handled by the club's Director of Football. Liverpool then made their move, and secured the player's services, after which Houllier claimed the deal was agreed before the France game. It's fair to say the Liverpool fans would have been far from impressed by the club paying £10m for a player few had previously heard of. The game in June 2002 changed that overnight, so fans were understandably excited by the arrival of a player who had played a large part in destroying the reigning world champions. Hindsight tells of the distortion of that game: France went on to have a truly atrocious tournament, and Diouf had just played the game of his life. If Liverpool fans were to conclude that this — on their first glimpse of him — was the level the player reached on a weekly basis, they would be very much mistaken — and not a little disappointed. While many fans had hoped to see the Robbie Fowler fee spent on Anelka, given that the player's abilities were well known and tested, they were also happy to accept the possibility that a relative unknown could present a pleasant surprise. The fact that the Italian press contained mournful editorials about how another gem had eschewed their league and instead opted for England, seemed to merely confirm that Liverpool had captured a real prospect. The Liverpool strike-force would be led by the reigning European Footballer of the Year, and his African counterpart. The side which finished 2nd in 2002 would now have the attacking quality to make the push for the title 2003. In theory, at least. How different it proved.

Emile Heskey

A perennial under-achiever at Anfield, Emile Heskey promised so much but ultimately delivered far less than was wished for. Aside from his first full season, when at times he looked a world-beater (despite the familiar periods of ineffectiveness), his contributions — still often telling — were just too few and far between. It's hard to think of a player any central defender would less like to face, assuming Heskey was fired up and on top of his game; alas, that wasn't always the case. There were no physical frailties, just mental ones.

Heskey wasn't purchased to replace Fowler *per se*, but Houllier long had the burly Leicester player in mind as a more suitable partner for Michael Owen (dating back to an England U21 match he watched), and the Heskey-Owen axis duly became Houllier's no.1 pairing.

That great debut season was as good as it got. There was a two-month spell when he could do no wrong, and was simply sensational. He tried things, and they came off — such as the subtle lob with the outside of his foot, arcing over Coventry City's Chris Kirkland and into the Kop net. Heskey played his part in the run in on the way to securing the treble, but the goals had dried up — and such barren spells became the norm, not the exception. Like Diouf he has since scored a reasonable amount at a club with less pressure and expectation, but both have been considered successes without reaching double figures. Liverpudlians *expect* twenty goals.

There can be little doubting Heskey's ability — witness his demolition of the Argentine defence on his England debut at Wembley, or when he ran Maldini, Canniavaro, Nesta and co ragged in Italy — but the self-belief was never what it should have been, and his positive contributions, hard work aside, became increasingly fitful. Houllier fought an ultimately futile battle to try to rouse the big man, repeatedly stating that the player just needed to believe in himself. The sale of Heskey to Birmingham, for £6m, was rubber-stamped by Houllier, and Cissé — a less introverted player on the pitch — was signed as his replacement.

Nicolas Anelka

The loan signing of Nicolas Anelka in December 2001 signalled one of the more surprising transfers in Liverpool's history, but an intriguing one nonetheless. Houllier remembered how jaw-droppingly impressive Anelka was in the French youth system, and the Liverpool manager had seen some wonderful talent emerge during his time at Clairefontaine, the French national coaching centre, in the mid-1990s. Thierry Henry was an outstanding player, as was David Trezeguet, and were partners in the side that won a European Youth Championship trophy. But on the bench for the final was Anelka, 18 months their junior, and seen as having even more natural talent. Subsequently it became clear that the main difference between Anelka and those two high achievers was purely down to attitude. Anelka's was possibly not as bad as the press made out, but it was far from perfect — he trained hard, and got on reasonably well with his colleagues, but he remains one of those strange personalities who never quite fits in wherever he goes, and who says the wrong things at the wrong time. Perhaps he just refuses to say what people want him to, and transgresses the diplomatic etiquette of football.

In 2000 Houllier had stated that Anelka was a future European Footballer of the Year. (Perhaps without realising that he had the next European Footballer of the Year on the staff already: one Michael Owen, who would win the award in 2001). And yet at the time of his arrival at Anfield, Anelka's career was in decline. After his stunning breakthrough into the Arsenal side as a 18-year-old — supplanting Ian Wright alongside Dennis Bergkamp and scoring the goals that led the side to the double in 1998 — he went on to complete just one further season at Highbury, before the £500,000 signing was leaving for Real Madrid at a 4600 percent mark-up. The youngster's knack of procuring major medals was as strong as ever, as Madrid won the 2000 Champions League. But his time at the Bernabéu was not a happy one, and he was soon moving back to his first club, Paris St Germain, for another £20m fee. Before too long he was on the bench, and not getting a look-in. When Houllier rescued him from the team he himself had guided to the title in 1986, Anelka was out of condition, and low on confidence. It seemed like he needed someone to show faith in him, and to get him enjoying his football again.

The Frenchman, nicknamed 'Le Sulk', slotted back into English football with relative ease, and scored a fine goal in the 3-0 FA Cup win over Birmingham City, where he linked impressively with Michael Owen. Surely a sign of things to come? As it transpired, Anelka never really managed a regular run in the side, and found himself behind goal-shy Emile Heskey in the pecking order. Anelka's arrival perhaps helped provide Heskey with the kick-up-the-backside he'd been in need of — it won't have helped his fragile confidence, but it did appear to make him more proactive for a while — but it was no accident that the fine end to the season coincided with valuable contributions from Anelka. His link-up play was at times exceptional, and his positive approach with the ball at his feet when drifting wide put Heskey's 'safety first' attitude to shame. (Funnily enough, Heskey had impressed in his early days at Anfield by running at defenders, but perhaps his sizeable self-doubt stopped him taking these 'risks' more often, and had him opting to play it safe.) There were several memorable moments of brilliance from Anelka, not least in the 3-0 defeat of Newcastle — whose defenders simply could not get to grips with the way he dropped deep to collect the ball, before sprinting at pace at their back line. It was an electric display, and with his increased fitness came greater sharpness, and the old confidence — or arrogance — came flooding back. One single drop of the shoulder at Middlesborough sent no fewer than *three* defenders the wrong way, before his pinpoint cross set up Didi Hamann for a shooting chance, the rebound of which Heskey tucked away from close range.

If Anelka had promised much, it was also true that he didn't make it impossible for Houllier to refuse a permanent signing, when the time came to make the loan deal permanent with a £13m transfer from PSG. It was fair to say that a consistent run in the side — which all strikers need in order to find their form and rhythm — would have helped him make his case more emphatically. If managers are ultimately judged by the players they sign — and what those players achieve — then overlooking Anelka was arguably the one mistake Houllier made in terms of players he opted *against*. There can be no guarantee that Anelka would have been an outright success at Liverpool, and you can never accurately predict an alternative version of future realities, but his full seasons at Arsenal and Manchester City — who pounced when Houllier said *non* — suggest a consistent goalscorer and, judging by his Opta stats, a player who created goals for others, and who was involved in all of his team's best attacking moments. That Diouf was instead chosen led to direct comparisons between the two, and while Diouf struggled to procure anything other than yellow cards and trouble during his two years at Liverpool, Anelka was banging in the goals for City, and scored more in the league *against* Liverpool in four games than Diouf managed *for* Liverpool in 66.

Whereas Anelka had a reputation for being difficult, no-one had a bad word to say about him during his time at Anfield (nor did anyone at Arsenal — Wenger always spoke highly of him, despite the nature of his exit), while Diouf brought shame on the club. He was late back from the African Nations Cup, and broke late-night drinking curfews. Diouf's greatest crime at Liverpool was spitting at a Celtic fan during a Uefa Cup tie, and he continued to cultivate this habit while on loan at Bolton. Not so much Serial Killer, more Phantom Phlegm-Flinger.

Anelka had many advantages over Diouf that, looking back, Houllier may have paid more heed to. The Frenchman had played in three top leagues, as opposed to the Senegalese's one. Anelka had played for major clubs — Arsenal, Real Madrid, and Paris St Germain (twice), so knew what it was like to handle the pressure and expectation; Diouf had only experienced life at less-fashionable French clubs. Not only that, but Anelka had helped two of these clubs to major honours — proof that he could handle the big occasion. Most crucially, Anelka had played — and been an undoubted success — in the Premiership. He knew how to beat English defences. When plenty of overseas players fail to settle or adjust, the chance to sign something so close to a 'sure thing' has to be seriously considered. As he had on many occasions, Houllier went for youth and inexperience ahead of proven quality — although the reasons behind the change of heart remain something of a mystery. The official reason was difficulty negotiating with Anelka's brothers, but they were always part of the player's posse. Anelka had claimed he was happy to take a wage cut, and even be third choice (although that was surely a calculated gamble, trusting he could displace Heskey, given time).

Whatever went wrong with the signing of Anelka, the failure of Diouf played a large part in Houllier's downfall. After his dismissal, Houllier openly admitted that signing

Diouf was a mistake — and that the player, while talented, just didn't have the specific mentality required to play at a club like Liverpool. Even in the winter of 2004, Anelka was still being linked with a return to the club, to finally make the move permanent. Benítez went as far as to publicly praise the player, but his first choice was always Fernando Morientes, and Anelka ended up in Turkish football, with Fenerbahçe.

Morientes, upon his arrival, would suffer a fate similar to Anelka in 2002, in that he joined Liverpool when decidedly ring-rusty after half a season of inactivity, and was then in and out of the side (in the case of the Spaniard, down to a thigh injury, and being ineligible for Champions League games). But once El Moro is fully into his stride, Benítez knows the fans will see the qualities of a world-class striker, to supplement the other attacking he options he now possesses.

Whether Morientes, or Cissé, or both, it is clear that Liverpool need a regular 20-goal-a-season striker. Benítez has seen goals from Luis Garcia, Gerrard and Riise in midfield — now he just needs the centre-forwards to weigh in with their fair share.

Golden Past, **Red** Future

48

Part Two

Chapter five

Enter *El Jefe*

At the time Gérard Houllier's aorta split in October 2001, Rafael Benítez was still settling into the manager's role at Valencia, a club that hadn't won the Spanish title for 31 years. Remarkably, they would only have to wait a further seven months. Benítez' star was on the rise as, across Europe, Houllier's waned. Their fortunes almost crossed in the firmament: one heading upward — a shooting star; the other — then coruscating with a blinding light — entering the end of its life-cycle, before burning out and disappearing from the constellation.

Maybe Houllier's luck was passed to Benítez, like a contagious condition, when the two shook hands before the meeting between Liverpool and Valencia in Amsterdam, in a pre-season tournament in July 2001. Houllier certainly experienced little luck from that point onwards, and Benítez could apparently do no wrong. It was Benítez' first game in charge of his new club, and Jari Litmanen's goal consigned him to a losing start. Within three months Houllier was not so much fighting for his job as fighting for his *life*, and while he would recover to lead his side to within six minutes of a Champions League semi-final and within eight points of winning the Premiership, it was Benítez who would be crowned in glory at the end of the season. The two men would meet again the following season, this time in more meaningful circumstances, and so — as far back as the autumn and winter of 2002 — the wheels were set in motion for the process of Benítez replacing Houllier.

Two years later, Rick Parry would sit down with senior Liverpool players to discuss which had been the best team they had faced in recent years. To a man they said Valencia. It is an interesting symmetry, and proof that football really can be a 'funny old game'. Benítez and Houllier crossed swords in the first group stage of the 2002/03 Champions League, and the Spaniard won their first competitive dual with staggering ease. At the Estadio Mestalla, Valencia dismantled Liverpool's defence with alarming regularity — the phrase 'hot knife through butter' was coined for such events — on their way to a 2-0 victory. It was a scoreline that rather flattered Houllier's side. While Liverpool would later self-destruct against a decent (but far from spectacular) Basle side, and beat a poor Spartak Moscow outfit, it was Valencia who exposed the shortcomings of Houllier's side. The ease with which they found their way through to goal was embarrassing. The Reds simply could not live with their Spanish opponents.

Any ideas Liverpool fans harboured that their team was capable of topping the progress of the previous season was seriously dented that night. Houllier's side were torn to ribbons at the Mestalla, but if anything it was the Spanish side's 1-0 victory at Anfield that was to prove more eye-catching and instructive; it confirmed the fears about a gulf in class. Losing away in Europe and being outclassed in the process is one of those things that can happen from time to time, but to be so outplayed at home was a different matter entirely. Everyone there that night knew they'd witnessed a special side. The 3-1 home defeat to Barcelona the previous season had been cited as some kind of high watermark in terms of attacking football, with the Catalans being hailed as some 'miracle' team, but the truth of that particular occasion was that Liverpool had been the better side for the first 60 minutes, and missed a number of chances to go 2-0 up and effectively kill the game. It was only once Barça took control in the latter stages that they displayed the kind of breathtaking passing usually reserved for exhibition matches.

Valencia, on the other hand, controlled the game from first to last. They were fast and skillful, displaying wonderful passing interplay, but it was the way they attacked and defended 'as one' that made the deepest impression. It was like a swarm of white bees buzzing all around Liverpool players — not ten outfield players following the ball like a collection of eight-year-olds, but a team with a set shape working for each other, chasing and harrying with a commitment you would never usually associate with continental football. They suffocated the life out of the team in Red, and when in possession the reigning *La Liga* champions were not about to give it away cheaply — they weren't particularly 'flashy' in what they did, in that they didn't resort to tricks and showboating, but it was wonderfully free-flowing 'pass and move', and devastatingly professional and efficient. Whilst they didn't tear through the Reds' rearguard with quite the frequency and ease of their Spanish assault, the lesson they imparted was one in how hard it is to beat a team when they don't give you a kick of the ball.

Anfield was once home to such traits on a regular basis. Suddenly Houllier's more prosaic and pragmatic brand of football looked horribly limited.

In many ways it delivered the first real sign that Liverpool had hit a brick wall in terms of progression, although of course it was possible at that stage to try and write it off as a blip, given the amazing strides the club had taken in the previous two seasons. Only time would prove that the problem was endemic, and that the high point of the Houllier reign had passed. The team was no longer in rude health, and a kind of sickness had set in. From that point, the world would see an ailing patient who showed occasional signs of a miraculous recovery, but ultimately continued to struggle and decline.

Rafa the gaffer

Many ex-Liverpool players were instantly cynical at the appointment of Benítez. They stated, without really researching their facts beforehand, that Liverpool's new manager was more defensive than his predecessor in the Anfield hotseat. (The inference being that Liverpool fans were in for a testing time — it was, in truth, the last thing they wanted to hear.) Noted Spanish football correspondent and Sky Sports' *La Liga* pundit Guillem Balague revealed that it had taken a chance meeting with Mark Lawrenson on a flight during Euro 2004 to point out that Benítez, while he would never be famed for Keeganesque gung-ho attcking, was not a negative tactician. Perhaps the antipathy from ex-players stemmed from seeing another overseas coach — another outsider — handed the responsibility of running *their* club.

Benítez himself claimed he was interested in the balance between defence and attack — not explicitly one or the other, to answer accusations that he felt the two were mutually exclusive. (Perhaps because, compared to Real Madrid's top-heavy line-up, *any* Spanish team can seem a little cautious.)

The appointment of Rafael Benítez was generally very well received by Liverpool fans. Many of the other names in the frame weren't exactly awe-inspiring, including Alan Curbishley, who had done a wonderful job at Charlton, but whose brief at Liverpool, if offered the job, would have been considerably different. (Maybe he has the talent to succeed at a big club, and no one will know until he gets the chance, but it's a different task handling world-class talents and the egos that are often attached, not to mention the added pressure and expectation, than it is to over-achieve at a small club — but ultimately achieving nothing truly remarkable.) Liverpool wanted a proven *winner* and, Benítez aside, a further two names were in the hat, the first of which was the shy and retiring Portuguese, Jose Mourinho, who had just led Porto to Champions League glory, but who, at the time, was believed to be heading for Chelsea.

The other name was Celtic's Martin O'Neill, who had achieved notable 'success' at every club he'd managed: promotion to the Football League with non-league

Wycombe; promotion to the Premiership with Leicester City, followed by two League Cup successes at Wembley; and at Celtic a number of league titles and cups, and some impressive results in Europe, not least in knocking out Liverpool on the way to the Uefa Cup final of 2003 (in which they succumbed to Mourinho's Porto).

Some fans had wanted a British appointment, following the problems in the latter stages of Gérard Houllier's reign — and there were calls for a return to the past, by appointing Kenny Dalglish. It seemed an odd call given he was now out of the game and that his recent CV was far from impressive, following failures at Newcastle and Celtic. It was hard to see how he could do anything other than damage his reputation in the eyes of Liverpool fans, having served the club so remarkably for fourteen years, between 1977 and 1991. The ultimate idol, he appeared a god who could only tarnish his standing. Everton offered the perfect example of why it's never a good idea to return: Howard Kendall having a further two spells at the club after a successful stint in the mid-80s, but both subsequent spells were unmitigated disasters. The expectation is always far higher the second time around, and as such, the pressure increases, and the acceptable timescale decreases.

When a manager is sacked you often see it followed by the appointment of his diametric opposite. Newcastle United have a habit of doing this very thing, dating back a number of years: the dour and deadpan Scot, Dalglish, seen as too boring in all senses, was replaced the younger, more overtly charismatic, continental aesthete, Ruud Gullit, with the Dutch legend arriving on Tyneside promising 'sexy football'. A 4-1 defeat at St James' Park by Houllier and Evans' Liverpool had the away fans singing with mirth and delight: "you can stick your sexy football up yer arse". When Gullit's tenure ended in failure — after he had the temerity to omit local hero Alan Shearer — the response was to appoint someone as contrasting as possible: Bobby Robson. Where Gullit was young, Robson was wizened and experienced. Where Gullit was modern, Robson was old-fashioned. Where Gullit was stylish and intelligent (speaking five languages), Robson was simple and straightforward (speaking only English with any advanced proficiency, although even then he sometimes appeared to be speaking a language no one fully understood). And where Gullit was a 'Johnny Foreigner' who commuted from Amsterdam, and had no connection to Newcastle (which he appeared to be snubbing by living in his homeland), Robson was not only English but a dyed in the (black and white) wool Geordie. For a couple of years it all looked hopeful for the Toon Army. And then finally, when Robson was accused of failing to impose sufficient discipline on his mega-rich stars, with their love of *bling* and nightclubs, the club appointed the hardline disciplinarian, Graeme Souness. (Typical, then, that the club would later find two of its players — Lee Bowyer and Kieron Dyer — fighting *each other* during a league game.) Every time a major problem was perceived, the club acted to rectify it, and the result was an absence of attention to the bigger picture. The Newcastle Chairman appeared to be firefighting the entire time, rather than constructing watertight long-term plans.

Where Newcastle lurched from one extreme to another, Liverpool had a clear strategy: a five-year plan, to find someone who could challenge for the Premiership crown (in theory at least), but who also knew how to win in Europe. It didn't always work, of course, but while Liverpool were at least consistently in the top five, the Geordies — who had pretensions on matching the Reds — lurched between the Champions League spots and the relegation zone.

Respect

Upon his appointment, Benítez was able to walk into Anfield and command respect for his achievements from afar — in the planet's most acclaimed league, no less — but also because of first-hand evidence of what a Benítez side was like to play against.

Unlike Houllier at the time of the Frenchman's appointment, Benítez had been directly responsible for enormous success months before arriving at Anfield; Houllier having only *indirectly* contributed to France's World Cup success of 1998.

Of course, the comparisons must be drawn between the Valencia side Benítez inherited — Champions League finalists in the previous two seasons — and the one acquired at Anfield. He was clearly bequeathed a more complete squad at Valencia — if, ultimately, one that continued to fall a little short. A group of *nearly men*, as opposed to a group of *not-so-nearly men*.

In his first season at the Mestalla, Benítez won the league on the basis of a miserly defence. The rearguard is often the starting point for a new manager: the first task is to stop losing games, and then concentrate on winning them. Skip the first stage and you concede too many goals; shore up the defence but at the cost of attacking verve, and you end up with too many 0-0 draws. Get the balance right, and you are in business.

It's easy to say that Benítez's work was already done for him before he arrived in Valencia, given the comparative success of the side under the previous manager, but the truth remains that 1971 was the last time the club won a league title. Hector Cuper left for Inter Milan at the end of 2000/01, star players were heading for the exit as the team began to break up, and the side was expected to falter under the surprise stewardship of Benítez, a man who, despite significant successes at two previous clubs, had yet to achieve anything truly remarkable in the game. His first task — as it would be at Liverpool — would be to sell the club's most famous asset: in that case, Gaizka Mendieta, who was looking to try his luck in Italy.

Up until that point, Benítez was famed for taking two small, unfashionable clubs — Extremadura and Tenerife — to promotion into the *Primera Liga*, but his CV was not without its blemishes. He started his coaching career soon after retiring as a player, at the tender age of 26, following a serious injury. Having been on Real Madrid's books between the ages of 14 and 21, he returned to the Santiago Bernabéu to work with the club's youth teams. He progressed to coaching their B Team, which he led to an impressive 7th-place finish in the Second Division in 1994 — as bizarre as that seems to English fans, used to reserve teams competing in the less glamorous environs of the Pontins League. He was soon assistant manager, working for Vicente Del Bosque — the man who would later lead the club to two European Cups, and still get sacked. (Del Bosque was also in the Madrid side beaten by Liverpool in the Paris final of 1981 — the exact same time Benítez was released by the club as a 21-year-old. Again the symmetry.)

Benítez left to take over at Real Valladolid but was sacked after just 23 games. He dropped down a division to Osasuna, but after one win in nine games was shown the door. To put it bluntly, a bright career didn't appear to be on the horizon. It goes to show that young coaches can struggle in their initial appointments; however, it does not necessarily mean they lack talent. Of course they still have many lessons to learn, but failure can also be down to the circumstances surrounding the club, or even a lack of time to put changes into place (nine games hardly seems a fair crack of the whip).

He bounced back, but his career remained up and down — quite literally. After leading Extremadura to promotion in 1997, the team were relegated by the narrowest of margins two seasons later. It was at this point he took a year-long sabbatical and travelled to both Italy and England, to study alternative coaching methods. In England he spent time with Steve McLaren at Manchester United's Carrington training complex. McLaren was known within the game as a very forward-thinking coach, and perhaps it was no coincidence that United's Treble (which, of course, was *almost* as remarkable as Liverpool's in 1984) was achieved with McLaren onboard; since his departure, United have seen their standards slip. It showed that Benítez was prepared to take his time to get things right.

That sabbatical also took Rafa to Italy, to study the methods of legendary AC Milan coach, Fabio Capello, and now manager of Juventus. "My idol was Arrigo Sacchi," Benítez said on the eve of the Juventus tie at Anfield, "but Capello did a fantastic job after Sacchi had left Milan. I spoke and ate with Capello, and watched how he conducted physical training. It must have been very difficult for him at Milan to win trophies after Sacchi's team but Fabio is a winner. You can see that in him." (How Capello must have been ruing that tutorial when, six years later, Benítez dumped his mentor out of the Champions League.)

Whatever he learned in those twelve months paid instant dividends. Tenerife, Benítez' next port of call, were led to promotion, as a certain young player called Luis Garcia scored 16 goals from the wing. It was then that Valencia came knocking. Any suggestion that he was merely an expert at getting small teams from lower divisions promoted (which, incidentally, was a speciality of Houllier during his time in France) were cast aside ten months later, when he led Valencia, one of Spain's biggest clubs, to the title. Benítez had arrived.

If Benítez couldn't replicate Cuper's feat of taking the club to Champions League finals, he did prove that it was sustained success he was achieving, and not high-profile valiant failure. Things looked to have gone awry when the title defence ended with a fifth place finish (mirroring Houllier's penultimate season with Liverpool), which didn't even result in a Champions League place. Undeterred, Benítez stirred his troups, and completed a remarkable double: the *Primera Liga* title, and Uefa Cup. The nature of this second league success was now more rounded: while still possessing the most miserly defence in Spain's top league, they were now scoring freely at the other end. Only Real Madrid, with their plethora of world-class attacking talent — Ronaldo, Raúl, Zidane, Figo, Beckham and left-back-cum-left-winger Roberto Carlos — managed to score more over the course of the league season: by all of one solitary goal.

What's more remarkable is that Benítez, while losing quality players, was given next to no money to spend on their replacements. The blonde-maned Gaizka Mendieta was the Steven Gerrard of that club. Claudio Lopez had been its star striker — its Michael Owen — and had been sold to Lazio the previous summer — the destination for Mendieta weeks after Benítez took over. Purchases were few and far between, with transfers decided by the club's Sporting Director, Jesus Garcia Pitarch. Benítez famously quoted, when discussing how he found it impossible to get the type of player he requested, that he "asked for a sofa and they bought me a table lamp."

Maybe the greatest testimony to Benítez' value to Valencia was how the club imploded in such spectacular fashion in the months following his departure. Claudio Ranieri returned to manage the side for a second time, on the back of his relative success with Chelsea, where he achieved his first-ever top-three finish in a league, and took the Stamford Bridge side to the semi-finals of the Champions League (where a certain Fernando Morientes put paid to his dreams, with a goal in each leg). Of course, Ranieiri had the privilege of almost £200m over five years to help him reach the lofty heights of *close but no cigar*. He'd have no such luxury at the Mestalla. He was, however, mysteriously given the kind of budget to buy new players that the club had denied Benítez. Ranieri's stock had risen considerably during his final season at Chelsea, and was on the receiving end of a massive surge of sympathy due to the way his employers appeared to be negotiating with every top manager in the game in an attempt to replace him, at a time when he appeared to be taking the club forward. Affable and often inadvertently humourous, at times he also appeared to be as mad as a bag of rabid rodents.

Under the Italian's guidance the Spanish side became inconsistent, until finally they became *consistently poor*. The club was sliding down towards mid-table, and the stylish football of Benítez had been replaced by a more direct 'long ball' style by Ranieri, with diminutive Argentine playmaker, Pablo Aimar (the player most Liverpool fans hoped would follow Benítez to Anfield), left on the bench. Elimination from the Uefa Cup by Steaua Bucharest was the final straw, having already fallen at the Champions League group stages, and on February 25th he was sacked. "We understand, and he understands, that the results in the last few weeks have not been the most appropriate," said club president Juan Bautista. Although Valencia may be lucky enough to find success again, it remains clear that Benítez's achievements will take some equalling — having led Valencia to, and through, the most successful period in its history.

A different kind of challenge entirely

In Spain, Benítez had to overpower the superpowers. In England, he was joining a jaded superpower, and needed to elevate it by not one but by two or three levels. Arsenal were in the rudest possible health, Manchester United were still a force to be reckoned with, and Chelsea, the *nouveau riche*, were breaking up the Wenger/Ferguson duopoly.

The main problem for Benítez was always going to be the way in which his new rivals were being run and managed, when compared to his Spanish rivals. Wenger, Ferguson and Mourinho were all proponents of a similar philosophy, and able to implement it with the patience and understanding of their employers. When in Spain, Benítez — while not backed in anything remotely resembling the way Wenger was at Arsenal, for example — still set about doing things differently to the hegemony of Real Madrid and Barcelona.

Barça only started to find direction under Frank Rijkaard in the second half of Benítez's final season at Valencia, and while they put up a fair challenge, it was too little too late.

(As an interesting side note, the vagaries of football — and the power of 'image' over achievements — were epitomised by the fact that Rijkaard was voted above Rafael Benítez in a Uefa poll for European Manager of the Year for 2004. Rijkaard's Barça won nothing, and finished second to Benítez's Valencia in *La Liga*. Not only had Valencia won the Spanish league, but also captured the Uefa Cup, while Barça again failed on the European stage. There was only one manager in Europe on a par with Rafael Benítez in 2003/04, and that was Jose Mourinho.)

Real Madrid, meanwhile, opted against the young, dynamic, goofy and godly Ronaldinho on the grounds that he was *too ugly*, instead opting for the marketing men's dream, David Beckham — whose main skill was sending searing crosses arcing like heat-seeking missiles into the box. Not only did they omit their best attacker of crosses — Fernando Morientes — they also allowed Beckham to play infield, where he could be the 'centre of attention', so to speak. Beckham was yet another player approaching his 30s, with most of the other 'galácticos' already past their peak. It was as though the president, Florentine Pérez, was trying to put together the footballing equivalent of the Harlem Globetrotters (relating to the basketball team's later media-friendly incarnation). Perfect for exhibition matches against stooges, but anyone putting up *real* competition would present an entirely different proposition. The big names *had* to play every game — the coach was apparently given no choice in the matter. Many of them appeared to have too many interests outside the game, and lacked focus. To make matters worse, coach Vincent Del Bosque was sacked — having won the Champions League twice — and it at times appeared like the lunatics were running the asylum. Pérez sold Claude Makelele — the man who held the midfield together, like a weight-bearing girder in the Golden Gate Bridge, and who would go on to do the same at the 'Stamford' variety — and, for too many seasons, Madrid refused to buy defenders as they weren't glamourous enough. In spite of the entertainment Madrid promised, the club still somehow managed to represent everything that was wrong with the game at the highest level: greed, superstardom, egotism, and a sense of utter superiority. At least, unlike 'upstarts'

Chelsea, it had an incredibly rich tradition both domestically and in Europe.

Pampered superstars were not indulged at the top end of English football. Compare and contrast the athleticism, hunger and professionalism of Thierry Henry to the bloated figure of the once-mercurial Ronaldo, whose commitment seemed questionable at the very least. Wenger, Ferguson and Mourinho all preferred the majority of their players to be young and with a burning desire to achieve everything in the game; at Madrid, there was very little left for most of the superstars to win.

Where Benítez made workrate and professionalism the cornerstones of his Valencia side, Wenger, Ferguson and Mourinho all believed in the same ethos. At least Liverpool now had someone cut from the same cloth as those three men, and, like them, knew how to get his side to play progressive, attacking football. The problem was that Benítez was starting his race already a lap or two behind the leaders, and without the boost of expensive isotonic power drinks whenever he needed them. Arsenal, Chelsea and Manchester United had stolen a march in the preceding years, and it would take a miracle worker to overturn such a deficit overnight. It takes time, simply because there is no short cut. Simply keeping some kind of pace with them, initially, would be an achievement in itself.

If Benítez couldn't compete with Arsenal's eight-year development (Wenger taking charge in 1996, with Benítez having to start from scratch in 2004), the Spaniard was also unable to get anywhere close to matching the astronomical budgets handed over to Mourinho, and those Ferguson regularly had to work with.

Benítez must also hope that the leaders trip, stumble and fall, at the time when his side starts to gel. While unlikely to happen in the next 12 months, he can but pray that Roman Abramovich finds a new plaything to distract his attention. Rafa will also hope that Alex Ferguson finally retires and is replaced by someone who is either incompetent, or who takes time to get his own ideas across; not to mention the complications surrounding Malcolm Glazer's purchase of the club, and how divisive it could prove. Finally, Benítez will hope that Arsenal cripple themselves financially with their ultra-expensive new stadium at Ashburton Grove, while their hugely promising array of young overseas players all get a serious bout of homesickness (not to mention Thierry Henry deciding to spend five years studying the rare wildlife on the Galapagos Islands).

It was no surprise to see Benítez' name linked to Real Madrid in March, 2005, once he had taken Liverpool further than the Spanish aristocrats in the Champions League. Perhaps one day Benítez will return to manage the club where he started his playing career. But it's hard to see the current regime at Madrid — one which employed *three* managers during 2004/05 alone — as one Benítez would want to work for. It is the antithesis of everything he stands for — individuals over the 'team', superstars over the cohesive unit — and provides none of the stability he craves, nor the control over team matters that all the most successful managers need.

In Spain, the manager is more of a 'coach', who works with the team, but doesn't necessarily choose what players to bring in, and in some cases, it is believed he doesn't even get to pick the team. Sporting Directors (such as Jesus Garcia Pitarch at Valencia) and Presidents all want their input; they are more concerned with their annual re-election than any long-term view. It is the autonomy of a role like managing Liverpool that is so appealing to a man like Benítez, who knows that his job is much easier if trusted to actually get on and *do it*.

The stuff of legends

Liverpool fans are very trusting — they tend to get wholeheartedly behind the manager from the outset. They start out expecting greatness — that he should be good enough is a *given* — and treat their leader like a king until he proves to be an imposter. Innocent (of being incompetent) until proven guilty; not needing to win the fans over, merely having to avoid losing their faith. He will be vocally supported. The manager *must* have a song, if not two or three. Maybe the 'cult' of leadership goes back to Shankly: a pied piper all Reds would have followed into the Irish Sea, had he beckoned them, such was his power. He inspired such faith and trust that the contract between fans and their manager — whatever his identity — seems to have endured. It is easy to forget that Gérard Houllier was hero-worshipped at the start of the 21st Century, before it all turned sour. Once he had departed, the next manager would receive their full backing.

To highlight the point, Benítez — still only six months into his debut season — had not yet done an *awful lot* to merit the scene at Cardiff, where fans paraded a large, ornately-gilded framed photograph of him around the streets directly outside the Millennium Stadium, calling to mind some kind of religious ceremony. It was a bizarre sight, but also a highly amusing one, as fans fought to touch his visage. But it was the events in Cologne, the night before the game against Bayer Leverkusen, that sealed Rafa's place in the fans' hearts, and have gone down in the club's folklore. With the team's hotel showing a German game on TV, Rafa made his way to a nearby bar in the hope of watching Manchester United play AC Milan. He walked into Jameson's Irish Bar to be greeted by wall-to-wall Reds, and his desire for a quiet evening out was shattered once his presence was discovered: serenaded by disbelieving fans, he would also spend the next 50 minutes posing for photos, discussing footballing issues. Rafa would get to see precious little of the game. At that point he called it quits and made his way back to the hotel, by which time photos were zipping from a clutch of camera phones and onto various internet fora. Suddenly he was 'a man of the people', and the fans could identify with him. While he clearly didn't *intend* to spend his evening in such circumstances (and in his low-key manner, perhaps he'd still rather he hadn't), it still took a man lacking airs and graces to stand around and talk to the fans. Instead of making his excuses after five minutes, it took him ten times as long. It helped lift the fans' spirits ahead of a potentially tricky tie, and the club as a whole received a boost. A bond was tightened; one that will hopefully remain strong for years to come.

Masterpiece

Leonardo da Vinci (the Renaissance painter, sculptor and inventor, not the *Serie B* wing-back) knew that the *Mona Lisa* looked pretty pathetic when, at the start of the 16th Century, it resided in an incomplete state on his easel. It was painted in layers, over a number of years, and he knew it would take time to perfect. The thing was, he didn't have to exhibit it to the general public until *after* the last brush stroke was applied. X-rays of nearly all of history's greatest paintings show altered limbs, people or objects painted-out in a change of heart, alterations to perspective, re-drawn features, even the first attempt — totally abandoned — still residing on the reverse of the canvas, in the way a child turns over the piece of paper to use the other side. Masterpieces start out as a few sketched details, an overlaying of colours and textures, as the artist gets the basic elements into some vaguely coherent form, and then an addition here, an alteration there, until it resembles something close to its finished state. Managers can cobble something together, in a rush to impress, but the creation of something significant and lasting takes much longer.

Benítez is creating his masterpiece in public: it remains to be seen whether the four years da Vinci took to create his, may or may not be coincidental.

Chapter six

The Benítez approach

Challenging and criticising a manager's tactics is one of the accepted liberties of supporting a team, along with debating the merits of his team selection, and indeed, the wisdom or folly of buying those players in the first place — let alone persevering with them.

But tactics is a grey area. It can be akin to those brought up on draughts questioning Garry Kasparov's decision to use the rook for a counterplay on the queenside. Paying our £30 makes us experts. Even those of us with a fairly decent background in the game, and knowledge of a variety of experiences on the pitch, cannot hope to always understand what a professional manager is trying to do, as their knowledge far exceeds our own (which makes sense, seeing as a manager's knowledge exceeds that of his own players). All we can do is draw judgment from what unfolds before our eyes, and guess at what the manager thought he was playing at. In truth, we don't have an insight into *everything* he is ever trying to do. We rely on the testimony of expert witnesses, but even they may not *fully* understand new thinking (if they've been out of the game for a long period) or be able to articulate what they mean. (Ex-players, in general, hardly being the most articulate of people — anyone who can understand Tony Cottee's assessments is a better man than I am. Some ex-players spend a lot of time *saying nothing*.)

Football is a simple game that can be complicated by fools, in that the basics remain unchanged: score goals at one end, keep them out at the other.

Simple.

But if it really was *that* simple, *anyone* could be a manager. Clearly they can't. (Although you do get those who, having done well with a 'management simulator' computer game, apply for vacant Premiership positions. Their delusion knows no bounds. You can but imagine them trying to handle a half-time teamtalk with a collection of angry and emotional men, some of whom cut fearsome figures.) Even great players can be spectacularly useless when in charge of a team. To return to the earlier metaphor of chess: once you know the rules, is a simple game — in that set things happen when you move certain pieces into specific areas of the board. It's easy to learn the movements allowed to a Knight or a Bishop, but the higher the level you go, and the better the opponents you pit your wits against, the more the strategy comes into play, and the more subtle the thinking.

To use myself as an example, I can just about beat my three-year-old son at chess, even though I know nothing about how to play the game, other than the *rules*. (His decision to wipe out my well-placed pieces with his plastic Tyrannosaurus Rex tends to thwart my attempts at a more thoughtful approach; experience teaches me that T-rex to F5 tends to result in checkmate, before the board ends up on the dog and the pieces behind the sofa.) I can "play" chess, but I cannot *think* like a chess-player. Anyone with half an instinct for the game could wipe the floor with me; lord-knows what a grandmaster would do, as I couldn't even begin to comprehend what would go through his or her mind. (My betting is that he or she wouldn't use the *Plastic Toy Dinosaur Attack*, but then, as I've explained, I'm no expert.)

We football fans are incredibly arrogant, in that — *somehow!* — we think we know best. We don't, clearly. But we are, of course, entitled to our opinions — especially at the price we pay for tickets, or subscription packages to watch a game on TV. Sometimes you just feel that if an Inuit, plucked from northern Alaska, and never before exposed to a game of football, were to sit at Anfield for the first time he'd be asking those around him why the manager is persisting with the flat back four, why he doesn't look to more width from his midfield, and why doesn't that young lad from the reserves get a game more often?

We look to experts — ex-players — to tell us what the manager is thinking, but often their comments do not tally with what we are seeing with our own eyes. Ex-players have a tendency to view the current scenario through the distorting lens of *their* day. The approach and methodology has changed, from the back-pass law, the outlawing of the tackle from behind (and indeed, the tackle from in front, and the tackle from the side), to offside now (supposedly) favouring the attacker. These are football men, who understand the game inherently, but perhaps sometimes they let how it was 'back in the day' cloud their judgment, if they are not prepared to allow for developments.

Perhaps it is more prevalent with ex-Reds, as they are everywhere in the media. Most former Liverpool players give honest, open and insightful opinions into the game, and nearly all clearly care deeply for the club, but occasionally there appears to be a hidden agenda, or a refusal to view the game in its correct context. We know when something is unjust, or just plain nonsense.

One of the most startling examples of the season was when plenty of Reds were left disgruntled by Steve McMahon's negative appraisal of Liverpool's sparkling 2-0 victory against Monaco. McMahon, a boyhood Red, could not acknowledge the good fare on offer, and persisted with his own personal rant. Liverpool were outclassing, and beating, a quality European outfit, and somehow it still wasn't good enough. What he was widely reported to have said on *Sky Sports* — that Liverpool were playing the same as the previous season, only with Spanish replacing French players, and a negative approach with just one up front — did not tally with what those at the game witnessed. Was he being controversial for the sake of ratings?

Benítez was fiercely criticised by the ex-captain for deploying Luis Garcia just behind Cissé. His words were spoken not as if Liverpool were facing the previous season's beaten finalists, but some Finnish part-timers. And his words were spoken without a hint of irony at the fact that Liverpool's greatest success came with Kenny Dalglish stationed just behind Ian Rush, and that McMahon himself played in the wonderful attacking side of 1987/88 where Dalglish, managing the side, used Beardsley in the hole, to supply the ammunition for John Aldridge. That side was so flexible that players ended up all over the field, and was the antithesis of rigid formations. But it still employed only one out-and-out striker.

When excelling in the second-striker role himself, Dalglish may have played further upfield at Anfield than in away games, but he still dropped into midfield to find space, knowing that doing so would pull opposing defences — packed tightly like sardines in a tin — out of line. The classic dilemma it poses for the man marking this kind of player is whether to follow him, and put his team's shape at risk, or whether to let the holding midfielder detail him. If clever enough, the striker can flit between the two positions — midfield and attack — so that, in the split second where uncertainty exists between the two opposing players (who cannot read each other's mind), he can end up in space, and in possession. If the centre-back leaves his position, and follows the striker all over the pitch — tight man-to-man marking — the striker knows he can create space for a teammate to run into; if the striker is being marked by the holding midfielder, he can take that player back so far that he gets in the way of his own centre-backs — somewhere he will not want to be — and may end up affecting the offside line they hold, as well as leaving their midfield underpopulated. Whatever a player like Dalglish, Beardsley or Luis Garcia does in that role, when the game is at Anfield, it is aimed at hurting the opposition, not *stopping* the opposition. How can that be even remotely negative?

There's also the confusion based on the unclear demarcation of the player who plays 'in the hole', just behind the out-and-out striker/leader of the line: it doesn't seem to have much to do with how the man plays, but more about the arbitrary nature of how someone draws his position on a piece of paper. Is someone like Raúl, or Paul Scholes, an attacking midfielder, or a deep-lying striker?

Does it matter? What's in a name?

In certain countries this player is seen as the "No.10" (whatever his actual shirt number), or even, as in France, the "No.9.5". (This number has yet to appear on any jersey, although decimal points could become the next fashion for the back of shirts.)

As a further example, Arsenal, for all their attacking verve, appear to at times play with *no* strikers. Henry drifts wide to a left wing position, and Dennis Bergkamp drops deep into midfield. That leaves the space for Pires, Ljungberg, Reyes or Vieira to go sprinting into, before Henry and Bergkamp join the fray when the time is right. It's not the starting positions of a player as detailed on a pre-match teamsheet, but where they find themselves over the course of the 90 minutes. The Dutch 'total football' of the 1970s, pioneered by Rinus Michels, still involved a pre-match teamsheet that detailed a collection of static players on a page — it was only once the whistle blew, and the full-back found himself in the centre-forward position, or the centre-back on the left wing (or both simultaneously), that 4-4-2 went out the window, and became largely and irrelevance.

It is so obvious, it shouldn't need pointing out. Football is fluid. The formation 4-5-1 (or 4-2-3-1 as Benítez' tends to be described) is roundly criticised for being negative, while 4-4-2 is seen as an attacking formation. Yet two goal-shy attackers backed by four defensive midfielders is not attacking by any definition of the word. Meanwhile, Real Madrid have the capacity to field a five-man midfield of Figo, Zidane, Beckham, Solari and Raúl, with the latter tucked in behind Ronaldo — and that's about as far from defensive as you could get. (Especially when you add Roberto Carlos, only nominally a full-back, given he spends almost the entire game stationed on the left wing.)

Attention to detail

The picture painted of Benítez is of an obsessive man hunched over his high-powered laptop like a Grandmaster over his chessboard (this metaphor will run and run), plotting every last detail of his team's performance. It ties in with the 12-year-old boy who would later become the man we know. Bested by a friend in a military board game, *Stratego*, (a clue to the nature of the game clear in its name), young Rafael stayed up all night pondering why he had lost, and how he could prevent it happening again. "Once I'd learned the rules and understood the strategies," he said ahead of the Anfield derby in March, "I didn't lose again. I worked out a way to win no matter who I played."

Defeat is not something that comes easy to Benítez. "I go home and mutter into my pillow all night wondering how I can change things," he said. "We've lost games and I've found it unbelievable. I've left a game thinking, 'We're better than them. How did we lose?' I have been trying to understand why, working 14 hours every day with my staff. At Valencia we'd change our game plan to combat a particular opponent. That's something we still need to learn how to do here. We're still far away from achieving what I want us to be but, in football, you can change things by working harder."

Fernando Morientes is clearly impressed. "Benítez is completely different to any manager I've worked with," he said, a couple of months into his stay on Anfield. "He lives for football. Every moment of every day, it's football, football, football with him. If you speak to him after training or you talk on the telephone, there is only one subject. I've never worked with anyone else like this and I've played under many managers. They would all concentrate on the game and the training, but after that their work was done." When someone with the experience of Morientes says this you have to take note. (Anyone who has been at Santiago Bernabéu for any length of time is more than qualified to speak on playing 'under many managers'.)

A familiar sight during 2004/05 was Benítez, following the final whistle of a match and while his team were still applauding the Kop, pulling a player aside and pointing to an area of the pitch and gesticulating. Not concerned with milking the acclaim from the crowd, the manager was still working as hard as he had during the 90 minutes of football, correcting — in his own mind, and in the mind of the player in question — an error that had taken place.

A level of planning takes place in a top manager's mind to which we are not privy. They don't celebrate goals, as they know their team is vulnerable to a loss of concentration — their first instinct is to get the team focused once again. Benítez — an undistinguished player, much like José Mourinho and Gérard Houllier — perhaps knows that, unlike those with a more famous grounding in the game, he must be extra special in what he does — and not what he *had done* as a player — to win the respect of the players. Alex Ferguson and Arsene Wenger were better players, playing in their country's top division, but they were not 'great' players. Fortunately the game has seen sense after the fad of handing distinguished players the reins to their club. It worked with Kenny Dalglish, but with no little help from 'Sir' Bob Paisley in the background, and the wonderful team he inherited. But now — and this applies to big clubs especially — it's the management record that secures an appointment, not a decorated playing career. Having said that, some clubs just don't learn. Newcastle are already openly lining up Alan Shearer to succeed Graeme Souness, which hardly bodes well for Souness' future: his successor already in the ranks, hovering in hope of his opportunity. While Shearer may prove to be a great manager, he has no prior experience, and has yet to learn from his mistakes in a footballing backwater, in the way Ferguson, Wenger, Mourinho and Benítez did.

As well as the necessary tactical nous a manager needs, there is his ability to motivate; his ability to understand the different psychological approaches different players need — the arm round the shoulder or the kick up the backside; his man-management skills; his communication skills — with both the players, and the fans; his understanding of science, and how the latest training and fitness methods can give his troops the edge; and so on.

Paul Gascoigne was a genius with the ball at his feet — the best English player of his generation — but you (surely?) wouldn't dream of making him manager of your club, whatever the level, unless as a desperate publicity stunt.

Questioning Benítez

Following the 1-0 victory against Bolton at Anfield in April, a broadsheet journalist openly questioned Benítez's tactical knowledge — in terms of the game in question, but also in the wider sense. He wasn't saying Frank Sinatra was having a bad night on a stage in Las Vegas — he was saying *Sinatra was no singer*.

As far as I'm aware, the journalist — not an ex-player or manager — had not won two *La Liga* titles in the previous three seasons, taken two different sides (Valencia and Liverpool, for those slow on the uptake) to cup finals in successive seasons, nor made it through to the quarter-finals of the Champions League with those same two sides.

You do all that, and *still* have your tactical ability as a manager questioned? How on earth did he achieve all of that, then? It seems bizarre that one of the game's recognised master tacticians can be so easily dismissed, by someone who hasn't had to prove that he knows any better. All managers are fair game for criticism, of course, and that is the job of football writers, but surely a CV like Benítez' — with major success so recent, and not a dim, distant memory — earns a little more respect, a little more leeway? The tactical "error" in question was in playing Gerrard behind the lone striker, Luis Garcia — not a situation Benítez himself would have preferred, given every recognised striker was either injured or suspended — but Gerrard had excelled in that role on numerous occasions earlier in the season, most notably in the 2-1 defeat of Arsenal in November, and was the top goalscorer in the ranks, with ten goals at the time (given Baros, with 13, was suspended). Benítez, seeing Liverpool outplayed (or out*bombarded*) in the first half, shuffled his pack in the second half, introduced all three subs, and saw a big improvement in his team's performance, capped by two once-mocked players, Djimi Traoré and Igor Biscan, combining to score the winning goal. More positively, the *Daily Express* report of the same game praised Rafa's tactical acumen, and his success in improving the performance levels of both players.

It is the broader picture that needs analysis. The circumstances of the match were as follows: Liverpool were just three days away from a monumental clash with Juventus, a fixture that was overshadowing everything, given the events of 1985; Benítez had only half a squad to select from, due to all the injuries and Milan Baros' suspension; and while many of the fit members of the Liverpool squad had been away on international duty, where two World Cup qualifiers had just been played, and with players only returning to the fold on the Thursday, Bolton's First XI contained mostly retired internationals, like Gary Speed and Fernando Hierro, or those not selected by their country.

Whereas Sam Allardyce had the full two weeks to work with key members of his team — nearly all of whom were fit and available to play — Benítez only had *one full day* to prepare his players; no wonder, as the journalist in question suggested, his preparation was found wanting. He is not a miracle worker. How can he prepare a side when he doesn't see the majority of his players — and none of his *best* players — in the fortnight leading up to the match? In trying to combat the inevitable fatigue, Benítez opted to employ a handful of players who hadn't played as much football over the course of the season, or who hadn't been away on international duty, and gave full home debuts to Scott Carson and John Welsh. Allardyce is on record as saying that much of Bolton's success is from catching the big teams fresh — or rather, *fatigued* (or jaded, at the least) from midweek Champions League action. The same applies to international matches. Benítez refused to make excuses for the shortcomings of the display, saying that if you have good players they will end up representing their countries — the latest being Luis Garcia, who that week became a full-international for Spain. Bolton make a habit of ruffling feathers, and they are the most direct team in the Premiership, while having a smattering of quality players who can do something a little different with the ball. But Liverpool still prevailed. If Liverpool had totally outclassed Bolton, it would have been reported as 'just Bolton', despite the Lancashire side frequently getting wins or draws against Arsenal, Manchester United and Chelsea. Given Luis Garcia's legitimate equaliser was incorrectly ruled out at the Reebok Stadium in August, it can also be argued that Benítez was in dire need of a stroke of luck. Playing poorly and winning is apparently the sign of a great side, so long as the team also has the capacity to play well. Irrespective of the amazing Champions League exploits, no one can say that this Liverpool side is a tuly 'great' one (yet), but sometimes Benítez must have wondered what he had to do to earn some credit.

Tactics are a big part of a football manager's remit — he needs to be adaptable in his approach, both before and during a game — but often circumstance, and cause and effect, have more of a bearing on proceedings; and tactics go out the window. The best-laid plans are well-known to falter in unpredictable circumstances: the Liverpool-built *Titanic* would have been fine without that pesky iceberg. You can plan for some eventualities, not all eventualities. You are constantly at the mercy of human error, and 'acts of God'. Freak events occur during football matches, and alter the course of a game: a goal is conceded after a defender trips on a divot of turf, and there is nothing the manager could have done differently on his chalkboard. Going a goal behind can adversely affect confidence — which becomes a psychological problem, not a tactical one (although one a change of tactics could help resolve). There is also the problem that the players, for all the extensive planning of the manager, cannot correctly implement the tactics. In *Stratego*, Benítez could manually manipulate the pieces — lift them from the board, to directly place them where he so desired. As a football manager, he can only *instruct* the players, and then it is down to the eleven individuals on the pitch to follow his directions, and, more importantly perhaps, to take it that one stage further, and *think for themselves*. While tactics are clearly essential — you don't want your team taking to the field without clear instruction — it is equally true that possessing the most talented, professional and committed players (not to mention them being *fit*) is what makes the most difference.

Jamie Carragher was in no doubt about the manager's quality. "We work a lot on tactics as a team, how the team is going to play and the weaknesses of our opponents," he said, his Scouse accent, already squeaky in its pitch, now sounding helium-fuelled in his excitement. "We probably do more tactical work now than I have done with any manager at any level in my career. That's how Benítez likes to do things. When he has the time to prepare the team properly you can see that it's reflected in the performances."

Criticising a manager's tactics is all well and good, but there can never be any certainty in the success of any of the proffered alternative approaches. Lose a game 1-0 and it can be said that the manager did *this* and *that* wrong; had he changed his approach, as suggested, his team could have lost 3-0. The naming of mistakes after the event is always unreliable, as you cannot replay the match in the exact same circumstances in order to prove the opposite would have happened, had something specific been altered. Even the most apparently obvious of mistakes — such as Houllier removing Hamann in Leverkusen in 2002 — cannot be proven to be the cause of a defeat. In that particular instance, Liverpool were being overrun, and the German, usually so reliable, hadn't done much to prevent Leverkusen's dominance. While it can be argued that replacing him with Smicer merely added to the problem, it is also true that *sometimes* an attacking player good in possession can help keep the ball at the other end of the pitch. A manager doesn't know if *this* — the here and now, the point at which he rolls the dice — will prove to be one of those times. Had Houllier not made that change, Liverpool might have prevented Lucio's devastating late winner. By the same token, they might have lost 5-3, instead of 4-2. No doubt Houllier wishes he could play that game all over again, and make a different decision; had he kept Hamann on and still seen his side eliminated, he would equally spend his life wondering 'what if' with regards to Smicer. 'If only' we'd held the ball up better, and 'taken it for a walk' towards the corner flag. Hindsight is something a manager cannot call upon *during the event*, only after. It would be nice if more of those who are severely critical of a manager after a game had to submit *their* game-plan before the kick off. It wouldn't mean much, of course, as it wouldn't relate to events that are yet to unfold, but it would at least remove some of the hypocrisy and smug *I know better*s that surround match reporting.

It is only long-term that tactics can be accurately assessed: the familiar mistakes, repeated time and time again — and thus not mere coincidence — are the only thing that prove a clear tactical flaw exists. A manager can fail in any given game because of bad luck (penalties denied, players wrongly dismissed, legitimate goals missed, injuries to key players), but over the course of a season — or a number of seasons — the effectiveness of his approach will be telling. Only then will a clear picture emerge. (Such as the way England and Liverpool played in almost identical fashion for four years, with Owen and Heskey spearheading a counter-attacking game — but proved effective only up to a certain point.) It is a manager's approach to the game in general — his philosophy — that matters most.

Get the balance right

Fortune favours the brave — but never the foolhardy. Aggressive, progressive and pro-active teams tend to end up champions, but rarely if allied to a weak underbelly.

Every side has its optimum point of attacking effectiveness. We've all seen games where a team has been losing but creating chances, and then the manager, in a pique of desperation, throws on three strikers from the bench, and as a result they don't get another shot on goal. Strikers need people to supply the ball from deep, and sometimes you end up with a striker, due to the necessities of the situation, finding himself doing the job of a midfielder, only *not as effectively*.

If it was as easy as saying 'the more attackers, the more we'll score — and win every game', then every team would start with five strikers. But then one forward-thinking manager would drop a striker in place of an extra defender — to negate the opposition — aware that while his own team would score less, they'd concede less too. The process would evolve to the point where teams settle on the approach that provides the optimum balance for what it is they are trying to achieve, be it to win games, or avoid losing them. In fact, that's how the game has indeed evolved, from the days of five forwards, to the present vogue for just one.

Benítez talks a lot about this need for balance, and over the course of his contract it is what he will set out to locate; it is not something you can hit upon in an instant, unless with the largest imaginable slice of luck. He is in possession of a large weighing scale, and every game, depending on what takes place, a grain of sand is added to the side marked Defence, or two moved to the side marked Attack. Every week the slightest alterations, until the team's equilibrium is achieved: the perfect balance between defence and attack, with every element of the team aligned, in synchronised harmony; able to keep things tight at the back, dominate in midfield, and create chances up front. This is what he achieved at Valencia: a unit so well created and so perfectly drilled it achieved a state of balance that it was almost 'as one'. Every time a new element is added to any side — such as Pellegrino and Morientes in the winter transfer window — the process needs refining, no matter how good the talent involved. It's why great teams, in the manager's desire to make them better still, sometimes end up being less effective after the addition of a top player. The perfect example is Manchester United and Juan Sebastian Veron: in trying to accommodate his £28m man, Ferguson lost the team's equilibrium. It's another reason why Real Madrid fail when, by all rights, they should win every trophy going; they insist on throwing in more and more world-class attacking talent, with no consideration to the problems it may cause, like a patient mixing a series of "feel good" medications with no heed to the hazardous side affects, or a chef throwing a series of sweet ingredients into the bowl, and ending with a sickly, inedible pudding. Madrid simply do not care about the balance.

While it irks to say it, Chelsea now provide the example of how to build a team whose main asset is *balance*. Arsene Wenger, in losing his Premiership crown to new-kid-on-the-block Mourinho, would still not swap his collection of attacking players for Chelsea's, but it was Mourinho's side who won the league, as they had a better all-round balance. Chelsea had a superb defence, of course, but it would have meant nothing without the quality of Robben, Duff and Lampard ahead of them; however, Chelsea didn't need the *phenomenal* talent of someone like Thierry Henry, nor the collective genius Wenger's side exhibited during their unbeaten season a year earlier, when the interplay and near-telepathic understanding took the breath away, and led many pundits to say it was the best domestic football ever seen.

Once the defence propping up a team with great attacking verve starts to wane, that great attacking verve gets negated as players are sucked back into the wrong positions, to plug gaps; or are under pressure to score four goals *just to rescue a point*. A great defence provides the platform for a less-amazing midfield and attack to attain — or exceed — its expected levels; exceed the sum of its parts. In many ways, it is better to have a good defence, a good midfield, and a good attack, than to have a potent attack and atrocious defence, or vice versa. The aim is to steadily improve each department, but not to the detriment of the others. And that was very much a Houllier failing: the lauded defence was suddenly alarmingly exposed once the midfield — so long its protector, its on-hand bodyguard — was asked to be a little more expansive and progressive. Just as a boxer who has his guard up for an entire fight won't get knocked out, he also cannot deliver his own knockout blow to win the fight. When Houllier's side let its guard down, it was seen to have a glass jaw; when it needed to throw its own combinations, its guard slipped too low (and the lack of pace at the heart of the defence was finally exposed). A great boxer is one who can get his devastating blows to land — to make them count — while not leaving himself exposed to frequent retaliatory bombardments and counter-punches.

The best teams, like the best boxers, can switch between defence and attack at will, reacting accordingly when the situation dictates. Houllier, for all the relative success he had, never quite mastered this aspect.

A game of two halves

The 4-2 victory at Craven Cottage in October 2004 completed a notable double for Rafael Benítez — albeit the kind of double that, while speaking volumes, still goes largely unnoticed. It summed up the new attitude.

The first part of this particular double came two months earlier, in August. What Gérard Houllier had failed to do for five years — turn a half-time deficit at Anfield into a full-time victory — Benítez achieved on his very first home game. The 3-2 victory against Spurs in May 1999 was the previous time it occurred; Houllier's home record in recent seasons was not such that his team never went in at half-time a goal behind.

To prove it was no accident, Benítez' Liverpool repeated the feat at home to Newcastle in December, following the Reds conceding the *most offside goal in the history of the game*. (I would say it was 111 yards offside, but Anfield is only 110 yards long.) Ideally Benítez would like to be taking his team in at half-time with a clean sheet, but it was refreshing to realise that going a goal down did not mean Game Over.

But it was the victory at Craven Cottage that caught the eye, and made the statisticians sit up and take note. It had been a long wait, encompassing three different managers: September 1991 against Notts County had been the last time Liverpool won an away league game in which they trailed at half-time. Souness never repeated the feat, and it totally eluded Evans and Houllier. Was it merely an accident that it took Benítez just a handful of games? Liverpool ended up winning more top tier games from a losing position than any other club: four.

It didn't end there. Although in a different competition, the 3-1 home defeat of Olympiakos in the Champions League was the apotheosis: the substitute Benítez introduced at half-time, Florent Sinama-Pongolle, taking just one minute to draw the Reds level, before he set up the second goal for fellow substitute, Neil Mellor.

If Benítez didn't know *everything* about the opposition before the game, he certainly did by half-time. His first season in English football was such a steep learning curve that there was not enough time to absorb what other teams were doing, or to bring himself totally up to speed with every element of the competing 19 clubs. He had to assess, and prepare, his own team; and while he admirably stated that he wasn't leaving his homeland to improve his very reasonable grasp of the English language, he of course needed to do so in order to get his points across. There are only so many hours. Even for a workaholic like Benítez, who doesn't switch off at the end of a working day but instead continues to ponder every last detail and nuance, there is only so much that can be done.

Some things a manager can affect in an instant, such as the act of selling a player: he doesn't rate Player A, and Player B is a disruptive influence, so he shows them the door. Problems solved. However, other aspects of management take a long time to blossom: seeds of ideas planted into players' minds, that won't bloom for several months. Education is a gradual process. If he sees the potential in Player C, it takes time to bring it out; he cannot suggest something and expect an instant transformation in the player. Butterflies only emerge from a cocoon when they are ready — try to skip that stage, and you are left with a corpulent caterpillar. If he sees a weakness in one area of the team, a quick fix is not always possible. If Player D is extremely good *but not quite good enough,* buying a better player might cost £15m. That's okay if you have the backing of an Abramovich. Otherwise — as in the case of Fernando Morientes — it can take six months to secure a top class player at a price the club can afford, where all the elements finally align: in this case, the player's disenchantment at Real Madrid; Madrid still owing money to Liverpool from the Owen deal; the player wanting to join Liverpool so badly that he turned down more lucrative offers, and ultimately, Madrid having to sell the player for the fee Liverpool wish to pay, and no more.

Chelsea manager José Mourinho — never backwards in coming forwards — suggested, as his team closed in on the Premiership title, that "the biggest myth in football is when a manager says he needs time". But when you inherit a team which finished the previous season with 80 points, and made the Champions League semi-final, and are then given an unlimited war-chest, you clearly do not *need* that much time. Being located in one of the world's major capitals — an incredibly cosmopolitan city — makes attracting top overseas talent that little bit easier still. It was also easy for him to say it with the title virtually in the bag — had his team stumbled, a different story would have arisen. His team suffered injuries, but he had the strongest squad in England (in terms of quality if not quantity), and also only lost Arjen Robben from those he would list as key players. Peter Cech, John Terry and Frank Lampard were ever-present. It was all part of Mourinho's self-styled image, as the 'special one'.

Would Mourinho have done any better at Liverpool than Benítez, had he been appointed instead? Perhaps, but I very much doubt it — unless he was the beneficiary of a lot more luck. Mourinho had some advantages, such as arriving into the Premiership when able to speak perfect English — having been a communicator, an interpreter, for his living — but Benítez will catch up on that score in time.

Regrets, I've had a few . . .

Of course, Benítez made his fair share of mistakes — inasmuch as all managers, as *human beings,* get things wrong. You cannot have a 100% record on judgment calls, especially as many are the 50-50 gamble of heads or tails. He himself feels he didn't react accordingly in certain situations, and admits he is on a learning curve. His frankness throughout the season was refreshing. "I have been self-critical," Benítez said. "I tried to change things when [in January] I saw Southampton playing better than us, but it didn't work. You can't always do the right thing as a manager." It takes a secure leader to admit his mistakes, to be able to hold up his hands without fear of losing the respect of his players. In fact, the players should only respect him more; they *know* he knows his stuff — he's proved that to them from his time in Spain, and from his early exploits at Liverpool — but at the same time they can see he is not trying to kid them that everything he does is without fault. Not only that, but it means that the players know they are not being blamed for every single failing of the side — the manager is prepared to take his fair share of the blame. They are 'as one'. Insecure managers will blame everyone but themselves, as they are scared of the spotlight falling their way, and being found out. Players are not stupid — and neither are the majority of fans — and I believe Houllier lost a lot of respect from both in his final year, when he clearly wasn't telling it as it was. Perhaps that was understandable — at that stage he was under tremendous pressure — but it didn't help him one single bit. The players had clearly lost faith in him, and the fans resented being told that the amount of corners their team had won represented proof of an attacking style of play.

Benítez had no such qualms. Straight-talking was his aim, although speaking in English sometimes took him on a circuitous route. "Sometimes I make bad decisions. But that's my responsibility. I pick the side, and if we win, as against Arsenal and Olympiakos, people talk well about me. If we don't, I can accept the criticism, though if I were always thinking about it I would lose my concentration."

Hopefully he will still be as honest in three years time (albeit as a record-breaking manager, picking fault in the one draw that blotted his 37-game winning copybook).

In the zone
For a while, in the autumn of 2004, 'zonal marking' was the buzz phrase. It was mentioned, almost exclusively, in attempts to ridicule Liverpool's new manager, and his *odd* continental ways. It was his grand folly, implementing a system that had proved hugely successful at Valencia, but which, many felt (myself included), may not hold up in the English game. At the time, many Reds were baffled by the system, and it was pinpointed as the reason for the team conceding a number of goals at set-pieces (zonal marking from open play is an entirely different concept), especially away at Olympiakos, Manchester United (twice) and Chelsea. The system — which entails placing defenders in set positions in and around the six-yard box — has only one main weakness, and that is how it allows the opposition to get a running-jump. Rather than run to attack the ball, zonal markers are already in the position they need to be. So what you gain by them being expertly positioned, you lose by the fact that they are already there, and therefore have no momentum. At times it worked against Sami Hyypia: while a giant, and clearly great in the air, he wasn't naturally 'springy', and suffered from a standing start.

Man-to-man marking from set pieces remains simple to understand: everyone 'picks up' an opposition player, and makes it his duty to stop him winning the ball. It is a universal system, but one which finds almost total favour in England. If a goal is conceded, it is easy to say who was at fault. Of course, it is therefore always an individual who is to blame, and never the system.

In January 2004, the game at Carrow Road between Norwich and Middlesborough ended 4-4. Both teams used man-to-man marking, and no less than *five* (five!) goals came as a result of players losing their marker from set pieces. Any time Liverpool looked uncomfortable from a corner — and let's face it, *all* teams look uncomfortable on at least two or three corners every game, if the delivery is sufficiently dangerous — the system was called into question. Yet the alternative, though patently flawed, remained free from scrutiny. That one game at Carrow Road yielded over twice as many goals as a result of negligent marking than Liverpool conceded due to the failings of the zonal system *between October and May*.

The logic behind zonal marking, as the nature of set-pieces evolves, is now clear to see. As players increasingly block the runs of others when marking man-to-man, and referees either turn a blind eye or simply don't see the offence in amongst the mêlée, then the incidence of goals increases. In the chaos it is impossible to guarantee sticking to a runner. It was noticeable that although Liverpool, in persevering with the zonal system, lost quite a few headers in their box to onrushing opponents, the fact that the Reds' defenders were all in good positions meant there was rarely, if ever, a *free* header conceded. There was a perfect example in the Champions League semi-final at Stamford Bridge. Didier Drogba — tall, athletic, and very powerful in the air — ran from the edge of the box to attack, with some force, a corner delivered towards the heart of Liverpool's six-yard box. He won the header above Sami Hyypia, but given the presence of Hyypia, and the challenge the Finn put in, Drogba couldn't direct his header on target. So while the system says *we may allow you to win the header,* it also makes it as difficult as possible to score with it.

Only time will tell if it's a complete success, but after a few teething problems, it proved hugely successful in Benítez' first season. It stands as an example of a radical change he has implemented that seemed a step backwards, initially, but which led to two steps forward.

Chapter seven

The twisted media

Liverpool are in a position unique to any English club, in that the most successful generation of footballers in the history of this country — all ex-Reds — are all long-since retired, with many now working in the media, given their enduring high standing within the game. Gérard Houllier was never slow to point this out. While Houllier's paranoia reached legendary proportions, it didn't help that from day one he had Ian St John referring to him — with what seemed a barely-suppressed sneer — as "the Frenchman". Liverpool are the most-criticised club in England. Most of the critics, as ex-players, have exceptionally (and unrealistically?) high expectations. As the club has the greatest history, it leaves more to fall short of matching. Of the five trophies English teams may get the chance to compete in, Liverpool hold the record for most amount of wins in *four*: league championships (18); European Cup/Champions League (five); Uefa Cup (three); and the League Cup (seven).

Manchester United are just about hanging on to their second golden period in the game (currently they are only the third-best team in England, for the second season running, and the third time in four years). Their empire might be getting fragile, but it is yet to conclusively crumble. Arsenal are as good and as successful as they've ever been. Chelsea simply have no *history* to weigh them down, just their weight in gold. Of the teams to *dominate* the English game over the last 30 years (therefore excluding Aston Villa, Leeds and Blackburn), only Nottingham Forest, twice winners of the European Cup, have fallen further than Liverpool. (Their recent relegation represents the first time any winner of the European Cup has sunk to the third tier of their domestic league, no less.) Any other summer and the same could be said of Everton — who, in most recent seasons, have slumbered in and around the relegation zone.

The critics

Alan Hansen remains a Liverpool legend, and given his experience and intelligence, an authority on football. He is not Liverpool's fiercest critic, and clearly retains a firm affection for the club he represented so majestically for 13 seasons. In the last decade he's been mostly 'hard but fair' in what he's had to say about the club. However, there appears to be some complacency and sloppiness in his appraisals of Benítez' first season. Hansen is used here as an example to prove how even the best get it horribly wrong, and, for whatever reason, are blind to the realities of certain situations. His standards certainly seem to have slipped, but along with Andy Gray he remains the most respected pundit in the game.

Many ex-Liverpool legends are working for the national media, and as such are expected to present an unbiased opinion. But in so doing, they can at times go too far the other way. Fans look to people like Hansen for sense, not sensationalism. There is a kind of moral responsibility on them, in their exalted position of 'experts', to get things right, especially about their old club, where their expertise should be at its strongest.

It started over the summer of 2004, with Hansen's ill-informed comments that Benítez was even more defensive-minded than Gérard Houllier. It didn't tally with what took place in Spain over the previous three years, and especially in Benítez' last season, when they scored freely while maintaining solidity at the back. Alas, it was not an opinion confined to Hansen. As noted earlier, the man who has either stood or sat alongside Hansen since 1981 — Mark Lawrenson — had to be put straight on the issue by Spanish pundit, Guillem Balague, on a flight to Portugal during Euro 2004. Before he even arrived, it appeared the knives were sharpening for Benítez. It may not have been malicious, but there was resistance all the same.

A third member of Liverpool's 1984 European Cup-winning squad (they also won the league and the League Cup, lest anyone forget) felt very differently. Michael Robinson, somewhat implausibly to those who remember the player (he didn't appear one of the game's great thinkers), has worked hard to become the main man — so well known he is simply referred to as 'Robin' — in Spanish football television. Speaking to Sid Lowe in the *Observer* newspaper on February 6, 2005, he launched a scathing broadside at his erstwhile teammates. "There is a screaming necessity for a journalist," he said. "Because they all speak now in a certain argot, they all sit down comfy, comfy — Lineker, Hansen, Lawrenson and the rest. And there's no journalist saying, 'Why?' Hansen thinks every goal that's ever been scored is a defensive error, because when you don't understand football, you can stop a tape anywhere running up to a goal and find a rick. But everybody makes an error. And when he says something Lineker goes, 'Oh, all right then'. Lawrenson simply underlines or puts inverted commas around what Hansen says. They need to be challenged. It's all happy families. I consider the BBC to be the mother and father of all television but they've become totally prostituted."

Perhaps Hansen has grown a little sloppy and complacent, like the defenders he bemoans — and is in danger of becoming a caricature of himself. As Robinson attests to, ex-players are allowed to speak their minds and have it taken as gospel, with no one challenging them. There was the strange suggestion about Benítez lacking the correct credentials; this, after his amazing exploits with Valencia. It makes you wonder who *would* have been good enough to take the job. (Under such harsh criteria, Bill Shankly definitely would not have warranted his appointment in 1959). Mourinho was Chelsea-bound, and Ferguson and Wenger were as attainable as gold from concrete. Sometimes you feel there can be no pleasing these ex-players.

All commentators on the game get things wrong. That's a given, and at times as unavoidable as guessing heads or tails on the flip of a coin. And of course, a pundit can be proved wrong one week, and then feel vindicated the next; seven days later, and it's back to being wrong again. What *is* inexcusable in the world of punditry is a certain hypocrisy, and the changing of opinion to suit the situation.

For instance, it was disappointing that many of the very people who had praised Benítez for trusting the youngsters throughout the season were then castigating him for playing some of those kids at Burnley in January. You can't have it both ways. Sometimes it will pay off; other times it will not. But you cannot fault the intention if it is an intention you have previously praised; you can just criticise the *performance*, which was poor. The kids had done the manager proud away at Millwall and Spurs, and Benítez obviously felt they could repeat the feat at Turf Moor. Surely a team that can win in the hostile environs of the former, and defeat a *full-strength* team replete with internationals in the latter, could overcome Coca-Cola Championship side Burnley? Managers have to make gambles every game, and sometimes they don't pay off — that's the nature of the sport. It's the same with television co-commentators — the ex-players — who say "the striker should have dinked it over the keeper" after watching him fail with a one-on-one. Had the striker tried the alternative, and the goalkeeper saved it, the co-commentator would have said "you have to take it around the keeper in that situation". So much football analysis revolves on being wise after the event.

Everyone is entitled to change his or her opinion when convinced by new evidence over a period of time; just not to suit the situation, and then change it back the next time the situation is reversed. Anyone can do that, as you are only 'proving' how clever you are with the aid of hindsight. At Burnley, either Benítez' players let him down, or his tactics let the team down; or a combination of both. There was enough quality in the side — full and youth internationals — to beat a mediocre lower league side. It didn't happen, and all teams have 'bad days at the office'. If it can happen to the best side in Europe (the Liverpool of Hansen and Lawrenson), it can happen to a team in the midst of a rebuilding programme. Benítez deserved some criticism — it goes with the territory — but not to be savaged by the press.

Benítez repeating Houllier's mistakes?

The greatest example of how Hansen got it grievously wrong was on January 24, 2005, when, in his *Daily Telegraph* column, he suggested that Benítez made a big mistake in signing players from *La Liga*, stating that the manager should have gone for "proven British quality". Hansen claimed that Houllier failed by going "totally French" in the transfer market, and that his successor was making the same mistake — only this time going totally Spanish. Hansen described it as a "conveyor belt of mediocrity". Many opinion pieces are just that — opinion. But the facts that back them up need to be correct, or at least in the ball park.

Now first of all, whatever the impression, Houllier didn't go totally French in the transfer market. Stephane Henchoz, Nick Barmby, Didi Hamann, Gary McAllister, Abel Xavier, Pegguy Arphexad, Emile Heskey, Christian Ziege, Steve Finnan, Chris Kirkland, Daniel Sjolund and Harry Kewell all came from the English league (and a mixed bunch that lot proved to be. It also accounted for almost half of the money Houllier spent, if you discount Djibril Cissé, who arrived after he was sacked.) Many more came from European countries other than England or France: Jari Litmanen, Igor Biscan, Markus Babbel, Sander Westerveld, Rigobert Song, Erik Meijer, Jerzy Dudek, Milan Baros, Sami Hyypia, and Frode Kippe. (Two Frenchman, Jean Michel Ferri and Alou Diarra, were also bought while plying their trade away from either England or France: Ferri from Turkish side Istanbulspor, Diarra from Bayern Munich.)

Even allowing for Hansen's "totally" being some kind of rough approximation, it's still horribly incorrect. In this case, "totally" equals one-third, and therefore well in the minority. If a journalist were to write "the population of the human race is totally over the of age 50", it would be labelled as the work of a madman. When you take into account that many of Houllier's French signings — such as Gregory Vignal, Djimi Traoré, Florent Sinama-Pongolle, Anthony Le Tallec, Patrice Luzi, Carl Medjani and Diarra — were youngsters snaffled on the cheap (at an average of less than £1m each), merely as hopes for the future, it leaves just eight of Houllier's 'major' signings as either French or coming from the French league.

You could label the same accusation of Francophilia at Arsene Wenger — a manager Hansen has (rightly) never been slow to praise. And yet Wenger has won three titles and achieved the double twice based on such a buying policy. Benítez could as easily be the Spanish version of Wenger, not the Spanish equivalent of Houllier. It is a sloppy, lazy conclusion that, given Houllier's French buys were generally his least successful, it follows suit that Benítez would suffer the same fate in Spain. Surely these are two very different men, with unique individual qualities? There is nothing to make the comparison in any way valid.

Houllier made some great signings — that is undeniable. But did he sign anyone from the French league who could match up to Xabi Alonso, Luis Garcia and Fernando Morientes? Alas, no. (Although hopefully Djibril Cissé will prove a late exception, and Sinama-Pongolle and Le Tallec still have massive potential and time on their side.) Riise, the Norwegian signed from Monaco, was perhaps Houllier's best buy from *Ligue Une*. As good as Riise is, he's not quite in the class of Alonso and Morientes (who will surely prove as much in his first *full* season at Liverpool), and certainly doesn't have Luis Garcia's silky skills. Josemi and Núñez look no worse than Cheyrou and Diao, but cost less than half the price, while Pellegrino was an inexpensive gamble which didn't really pay off — but given his pedigree, it was one worth attempting. At least two of these players were bought simply to bolster the squad. So already, based on the early evidence (and that's all there is to go on, at present), Benítez appears to have recruited far more astutely from his homeland.

Hansen went on to say that it was crucial that Benítez bought players good enough to go straight into his strongest possible starting XI — and clearly states that he did not believe this to have been the case.

It was abundantly clear that Alonso and Morientes (when fit) were good enough to be in the strongest starting XI, and in fact, will strengthen it considerably for seasons to come. Luis Garcia, meanwhile, added that little spark of creativity and the ability to bamboozle opponents, something which had previously been missing (even if, at times, he himself went missing). At the end of January 2005, when Hansen made his comments, Luis Garcia was admittedly struggling for form, but it was still too early to write off the little Spaniard as not being good enough for the Liverpool first team, given how brilliant he was at the start of the season, and the difficult personal problems he faced over the winter. Benítez clearly knew the player's quality. Luis Garcia's goals would soon knock out Bayer Leverkusen, Juventus and Chelsea in the Champions League, and he'd get his first cap for Spain. That's three players to improve the Liverpool first team, and almost one-third of the outfield starters. Not bad, considering that represented a £22m investment, and that the other players Benítez signed — Carson, Pellegrino, Núñez and Josemi — cost a mere £4.7m combined.

Or, to look at it another way, the exact fee for Salif Diao.

Procuring Carson was a fantastic bit of business: the best keeper around in his age-group, with a very bright future, and, as he proved on a handful of occasions, more than capable in the present (if, at 19, he still has much to learn, and much experience to gain). Players like Carson are hard to come by; had he been tied to a lengthy contract at Leeds, his value would have been closer to £5m (twice that if he had become a regular there), and therefore prohibitive. The very contract situation that wiped money from Owen's transfer value worked in Liverpool's favour this time.

It's far too early to write off two of the other three additions (Pellegrino having since been released), despite each having some tough games and coming in for severe criticism, but even if they only exist as reserves in the future, at an average of just over £1m each and unlikely to be on sky-high wages, they're still very cheap additions to a squad that — once the deadwood had been offloaded — needed bolstering. Inevitably, more deadwood would arrive, as no manager knows a player will flop until he's been tried and tested (and when it's therefore too late), and as such, the law of averages suggest at least one or two of Benítez' purchases will fall flat. They at least deserve the chance to adapt before being cast into the wilderness, or described as 'failures'. Núñez in particular came in for heavy criticism, from all and sundry, and yet he had a couple of outstanding games — against Everton and Middlesborough at Anfield — that at least prove he has talent. If it transpires that some deadwood has been replaced by more deadwood, well, that's just life — so long as it doesn't end up costing the club £50m.

Buy British?

The trouble Benítez faced in wanting to improve a first-team like the one he inherited from Gérard Houllier was that there were a whole raft of 'decent' players on the books — there were some flops and failures, but nearly every man offered *something*. These were not terrible players, they just weren't *quite* good enough, or consistent enough. The catch was that even *half-decent* players cost fortunes these days, especially from the Premiership. In recent decades, English players have seen their value soar — the best ones exponentially so. Even mediocre English players, or overseas players at English clubs, can eat dangerously into a manager's overall budget. A manager cannot just 'magic up' a series of quality signings who will all be guaranteed successes. There will be an element of trial and error about the whole process.

The accusation of 'going Spanish' is an example of a mindset that prevails in English football analysis: British is best, and to be trusted; foreigners are 'dodgy' and to be very wary of.

A great deal of football writing tends to be critical, but not offer a reasonable, *realistic* solution. The writers are often happy to suggest what's wrong, but make no detailed explanation on how to fix it. Perhaps they'd say: *well, that's what the manager is paid for!* While journalists and pundits cannot be expected to be able to solve a club's problems, their comments on what needs to be done often lack substance and depth; so 'broad' they actually say nothing.

In the instance of Hansen saying Benítez should have "bought British", where is the part where he takes into account the manager's circumstances, not least his budget?

Buy great British players? Sure! Of course!

But *who?*

Or rather, who is available and good enough, and who would cost under £20m? Benítez inherited a Liverpool side that had not only lost Owen, but arrived at a point when, for the first time in its history, the club had no power to resist the might of London's *nouveaux riche*, who were intent on unsettling and ultimately procuring Steven Gerrard, its best player, and who came perilously close to so doing. Although top Italian clubs managed to lure Graeme Souness and Ian Rush away from Anfield, Bob Paisley and co. never had to fight off *another English club* when it came to keeping Dalglish, Souness, Rush and, of course, Hansen himself.

Never mind signing the best English players, Benítez had his work cut out trying to *keep* them.

Liverpool couldn't even price this voracious predator — hovering, intent on the kill — out of the equation, as, in the modern age, a player (or rather, his agent) can make a move happen, if he so desires. Hansen seemed to be judging Liverpool by its old standards, in its old setting of the 1970s and '80s. While all Reds want to see Liverpool back at the pinnacle, the game has changed, and so have the club's competitors, resulting in an entirely new landscape. Manchester United and Arsenal were never this strong, and as for Chelsea — well, they were a joke for twenty years. There has never been a club like the 'new' Chelsea in the history of the game. Had Roman Abramovich not arrived in 2003, there is every likelihood that Chelsea would have continued to struggle for silverware.

If money was no object for Benítez, as is the case at Stamford Bridge, he would probably have spent some of his war-chest differently. As it was, he had to look for bargains, or players who, while not cheap, still represented fantastic value for money. Sometimes in life you get what you pay for. Other times you uncover an unpolished diamond.

Hansen spent most of the season in awe of Chelsea — and it was justified, given the way they swept all before them domestically, especially when Arjen Robben and Damien Duff were flying in tandem. Having spent £15m or more on a player *five times* during the summer of 2003, Chelsea, just one year later, added Peter Cech (£7m), Arjen Robben (£12m), Paulo Ferreira (£13.2m), Tiago (£8m), Didier Drogba (£24m), Mateja Kezman (£5m) and Ricardo Carvalho (£20m). Their average spend per-player was almost £13m — but if you count only the five men bought with the express intent of going straight into the starting XI, the average outlay rises to almost £16m per player: a fair way in excess of Liverpool's *record signing.*

That record signing, Djibril Cissé — signed by Houllier, but a player Benítez rated

— didn't even get a proper chance to prove he was worth £14.2m. Given his wonderful record in France, you could at least surmise that, once he had settled in the autumn months of his first season, he would have started banging in the goals and would have radically improved the first team (certainly in the absence of Owen). After all, at the time of his terrible injury Cissé had the exact same number of goals as Didier Drogba. Drogba would later go on to improve, finding his stride and scoring a fair amount of goals, though without really silencing his critics. The comparison is especially valid, as both came to England from France with the burden of being their new club's record signing. While in France, Cissé easily outscored Drogba every season (although Drogba was in a lower division until 2003), and managed fully eight more league goals during their final season in *Ligue Une*.

Hansen criticised Benítez for not going British, saying that he should have bought players from the home market as "you know what you are going to get". This is where such arguments get confusing. Hansen, remember, lavished extravagant praise on both Jose Mourinho and Chelsea, as well as lauding the newcomer's signings . . . *none of whom were British, or from the Premiership.*

Chelsea's reserve team and substitute bench, meanwhile, comprised players such as Scott Parker, Joe Cole and Glen Johnson — expensive signings from the Premiership. Chelsea's other British players were bought by Ranieri, with the exception of John Terry, who bucked the trend by coming through the club's youth ranks.

Why did Benítez have to have his hands tied by going British — which was almost certainly the best approach twenty years ago — when the club's current competitors, who were excelling, *were not?*

Signing players from England is just not cost effective, unless a player is nearing the end of his contract, or on a 'free'. It's hard to imagine the fees the club would have had to pay for Xabi Alonso and Fernando Morientes had they been of comparable quality and English, or already at Premiership clubs. Benítez was quoted £14m when enquiring about the availability of Jonathan Woodgate, the talented but injury-prone Newcastle centre-back who ended up moving to Real Madrid, and promptly spent the entire season injured. For an extra £2m Rafa procured both Alonso *and* Morientes. At the same time, Wayne Rooney went to Manchester United from Everton for a 'mere' £27m. Even if Liverpool had wanted Rooney, he was too expensive, and Everton would have sold the player to anyone but Liverpool. (The player himself would not have favoured the move, either.)

It is such a lazy argument — whether from Hansen or anyone else — to say "sign from the English market as you know what you're getting". You don't. You may know a little more (especially in the case of Houllier and Anelka, after the player had been on loan), but there are no sure things in the transfer market, full stop. Liverpool — from Shankly through Paisley to Houllier — have signed enough players from the English (or Scottish) league who looked good until they pulled on the famous red shirt (whether made of cotton or space-age synthetic fibres, undeniably *heavy with history*) and wilted under the pressure.

During 2003/04 Hansen was understandably sent into paroxysms of delight by Arsenal's glorious free-flowing football, and stated that while they weren't the "greatest ever" side from these shores (how could they be, without winning the European Cup?), they did play the 'best football' he'd ever seen in this country. Their historic achievement — in going a league season unbeaten — was duly noted and wholeheartedly praised. But how did Wenger achieve this success? Was it built on a core of astutely-assembled British purchases?

That couldn't be further from the truth.

There was Sol Campbell, the rock at the heart of their defence. But of course, he was a 'Bosman' transfer; had a fee been involved, there is no way Arsenal would have got him, given that Spurs would have sold to anyone *but* Arsenal, and Arsenal would have not been able to take part in any auction. (If only Campbell had instead opted for Liverpool in 2001 . . .) And that is it — the extent of Wenger's successful domestic purchases. One player in nine years.

Now look at the flops. Richard Wright — £6m well spent? Clearly not. Wright was soon sold to Everton at a big loss, after failing to impress at Highbury, and is now a reserve at Goodison Park. (He managed to get a game for Everton in May 2005, back at his previous club. He let in *seven*.) Talking of Everton, there was the £8m Wenger shelled out for that *sure-fire hit*, Francis Jeffers; less fox in the box, more mole in his hole. Matthew Upson hardly grabbed the bull by the horns while at Highbury. Then there was the £2m handed over to Notts County for the talented 15-year-old, Jermaine Pennant. He would go on to start just five Premiership games for the club in six years.

In fact, Pennant is the perfect example of the pitfalls in buying English talent. There is a kind of stupidity you so rarely get from overseas players. Speaking just two weeks after serving one month of a three-month sentence for a succession of driving offences, Pennant told *BBC Radio Five Live*, "I don't know whether it's because I'm English but Wenger brought in a lot of foreign players and they're playing and I got brought in and never played." As you can tell, there is a total lack of reality in such statements. What planet are these young English players living on?

It's like the dreary and nonsensical Lisa Stansfield song, *All Around The World*, where she spends the verses explaining how she mistreated her lover, letting him down and acting so very terribly, and then spends the chorus dumfounded as to why on earth he'd up and leave her. Pennant, with only marginally less melody, said, "If you play week-in, week-out, you've got to look at your life [and look after yourself]. I wasn't playing so I didn't have to worry about anything. I was in a big city enjoying myself."

And there it is, in a nutshell. Instead of knuckling down, he is admitting to losing interest, going off the rails, enjoying the lure of the bright lights, and failing to do his utmost to fight for his place in the team. How did he expect to displace Robert Pires and Freddie Ljungberg, two talented and proven *model pros*? And then he cries foul about it being all the fault of 'xenophobic' Wenger, who would rather ignore Englishmen. It would beggar belief, if such attitudes were not so common in young English players.

According to Hansen's logic, Wright, Jeffers, Upson and Pennant were the kind of players Wenger was right to invest in. Meanwhile, you can only conclude, Arsenal were wasting their time and money with Patrick Vieira, Robert Pires, Fredrik Ljungberg, Jose Antonio Reyes, Dennis Bergkamp, Robin Van Persie, Lauren, Thierry Henry, Francesc Fabregas, Edu, Nicolas Anelka, Emanuel Petit, Marc Overmars, Phillipe Senderos, Kolo Toure, Gilberto Silva, et al.

Why is this policy — top continental players — good enough for Arsenal and Chelsea, but not Liverpool? All Liverpool fans would rather see world-class local talent in the side ahead of average foreign journeymen. But ultimately, fans just want to see the best players playing with heart and pride, in the way Vieira and Henry do for Arsenal, and Pennant and Jeffers didn't.

The hypocrisy from the media is now in place again, of course, as suddenly Arsenal, after a slump in form, lack "British character" — no matter that the same set of players made history just 12 months earlier by coming from behind on numerous occasions to save or win matches. You don't go unbeaten in a 38-game league season without an extraordinary amount of character — if you did, they wouldn't have been the first team in 100 years to do so. It seems that whenever a top team struggles, it's down to a lack of '*Englishness*'. It is an attitude stuck in the 1970s.

The whole point is that no market — in itself — leads to conclusively better purchases. There are pros and cons wherever you shop, dependent on a myriad factors. Ultimately it is the individual player and his unique ability and temperamental make-up that count. Just as no one would tar Michael Owen and Jermaine Pennant with the same brush, then you cannot just lump together groups of foreigners as one 'type' or another.

To continue with the example of Arsenal, Wenger signed plenty of 'failures' from France and other European countries, too: Christopher Wreh, Gilles Grimandi, Pascal Cygan, Alberto Mendez, Jeremie Aliadiere (yet to deliver, but still has time on his side), David Grondin, Nelson Vivas, Luis Boa Morte, Moritz Volz, Sebastian Svärd, Igors Stepanovs, Oleg Luzhny, Remi Garde, Stathis Tavlaridis and Kaba Diawara — to name just a few 'luminaries'. (If you remember half of those, you're doing well.)

Wenger has signed far more average and, frankly, poor players than he has world-beaters. But it's those few great signings that have made all the difference, as they have proved truly exceptional talents. In time, and thanks to the success of the side, the dross has been forgotten. Similarly, Alex Ferguson has bought both well and poorly at home and abroad, in almost equal measure. All managers sign duff players, from Britain and from overseas. Wenger and Ferguson both made glaring mistakes in the transfer market — but especially early in their tenures, when making radical overhauls. Hell, even Shankly, Paisley, Fagan and Dalglish bought duds — mostly from Britain, where they supposedly 'knew what they were getting' (Hansen's logic). Souness and Evans also bought plenty of flops from these shores. I'm sure they thought they knew what they were getting when they paid a lot of money for Paul Stewart and Phil Babb. It didn't mean they ended up getting it. Meanwhile, no one but Houllier, Phil Thompson and Chief Scout Ron Yeats knew what the club was getting with Sami "who?" Hyypia in 1999, John Arne "who are yer?" Riise in 2001, or Milan "not even a household name in his own home" Baros in 2002.

It made sense for Benítez to initially shop in his homeland, given that he clearly knew Spanish football far better than English football, and that it would take at least a season to remedy that. If he came to England in 2004 and instantly bought Premiership players known to him only courtesy of his scout's recommendations, he would be sailing blind. However much he faith he had in Alex Miller (whom he chose as his British "eyes"), he would have needed to get to know Miller a whole lot better before he could trust him implicitly on such issues. There wasn't time for him to see these players for himself, as it was the close season, and by the time Liverpool would come to face them, the transfer window would be closed. That is no way to begin your tenure.

If you can buy the finest tailored suit, a bespoke fit and spun from the finest Italian silk, but won't be ready instantly, then surely that is better to wait for it to be perfect (with all the necessary adjustments, to get it *just right*) than plumping for some overpriced off-the-peg suit that might look fine initially, until it quickly loses its shape and frays at the seams? If Xabi Alonso, Luis Garcia and Fernando Morientes were all *Giorgio Armani* couture, then it surely made more sense to opt for such class ahead of three mass-produced well-known British High Street retailer suits like Scott Parker, Lee Hendrie and James Beattie? The difference is that in this case, the *Armani* suits costs the same as the far inferior English variety. That surely makes it a no-brainer?

If Benítez was pilfering players from the Ukrainian third division, then you could understand the criticism. But he was plundering what is often seen as the best league in the world. Four signings have been from *La Liga's* top three clubs. Just as Barcelona were reluctant to let Luis Garcia go, Real Madrid wanted to hold on to Fernando Morientes. Can someone suggest where Benítez could — in England — have spent £10.5m more wisely than he did on Xabi Alonso? In England you couldn't pay £20m in England for a player half that good and that young. After all, Kieron Dyer was recently rated at £20m by Newcastle — overrated, injury prone, and noted to have an unprofessional attitude.

That is the true comedy of the English transfer market. That is, to quote Alan Hansen, knowing "what you are going to get by shopping in the home market".

Shaun Wright-Phillips has been in stunning form for Manchester City for a couple of seasons now (having been fairly average up to the age of 21/22), but has no true experience of European football and just a handful of England caps (and in his most recent appearances, looked fairly awful as he struggled to cope with the pressure). And yet he's valued at £20m+ (or the combined cost of Henry, Pires and Vieira). There's nothing to say that Wright-Phillips, while looking like a fantastic player, would *definitely* make a smooth transition to a new club, with new expectations, and a gargantuan price tag hanging over his head. He may well leave City and do brilliantly in a better side, and clubs with the spare cash would be right to have a gamble on him, but there's no *guarantee* about it. And at that price, you'd like to hope for some guarantees, especially if it's 90% of your transfer budget. Even if Wright-Phillips does do well following a move, it might take him time to settle. You often find players who come through a club's youth system build their confidence brick-by-brick over a number of years — being eased into the side with little expected at first, and gradually improving month after month. A bad start at a new club — be it down to injury, a lack of understanding of the system, or initially being only a substitute — can shatter that confidence in one blow. Their entire support system is no longer in place, and instead of being the kid who exceeded low expectations, he is now the player unable to justify a massive price-tag. Sometimes expectations have to lower again, before the player can start from scratch, in order to come good. (This may happen with Djibril Cissé.)

If you have £20m burning a hole in your pocket, and no other, more pressing needs — then sure, Wright-Phillips is the kind of player you look for. But if Benítez had bought the Manchester City player for £20m in 2004 instead of Alonso, Morientes, Núñez, Josemi, Pellegrino and Carson (who, combined, cost the same amount), then of course the chosen route was a far better piece of business. (Just as Houllier had to opt for Henchoz, Hyypia and Hamann instead of paying over-the-odds for Rio Ferdinand in 1999.) Six players will cost a lot more in wages than one, of course, but if Wright-Phillips had broken his leg, he'd have been no use to anyone. All eggs would be in that one basket. Even with Alonso out with a broken ankle, Benítez could still call upon the other five players in the squad.

The final thing with Benítez' buying policy is not only does he know the Spanish market, but — and this is the key thing — it is there that his reputation is greatest. Did Alonso and Morientes want to play for Liverpool? Of course. But for them, Benítez was key to the deal — they trusted this man, having seen Valencia's quality at close quarters. Would they have wanted to play for a manager they didn't rate or trust, or at best, simply didn't know? Would they have been as desperate to play for Liverpool had the club been managed by Alan Curbishley, a man they knew nothing about? These players had other options, and playing for Benítez was cited as a big part of their decision to relocate to Merseyside. Other teams had — and will continue to have — more money to spend, so Liverpool have to rely on the reputation of the club, and the reputation of the manager. Where French, German or Italian players may know of Benítez, it is those plying their trade in *La Liga* between 2001 and 2004 who *revere* him.

"Worst Liverpool team in recent memory"

Words hurt. Fans of any club tend to be hypersensitive to criticism, and often need to stand back and take an objective view of their club and its strengths. They take barbs personally, as if their own kith and kin has been insulted. But that doesn't mean they should stand by and watch journalists or pundits rip unjustly into their club, or its players, *especially* when it is being done not in the name of honest insight, but because being outrageous sells newspapers and boosts TV ratings. (We all know that a number of ex-players are happy to be controversial in order to stay in a job; Rodney Marsh at *Sky* was one, until he was *too* controversial even for his job, and promptly lost it.)

Alan Hansen doesn't fit into this category, but he did overstep the mark when he claimed that the first half performance when losing 2-0 at Southampton in January 2005 was the worst by the club for 14 years, since he retired. A *Daily Mirror* writer went 26 years better, and dubbed it the worst by the club for 40 years. (Had this journalist seen every one?) You'd think Liverpool hadn't lost 3-0, 4-0 or 5-1 in away games since 1991 (or 1965 for that matter). In fact, you'd think Liverpool had *never lost a game*, or ever played incredibly poorly. While it was a dire showing at the St Mary's Stadium, and definitely down there in the bowels of displays not worthy of the club's great name, there has been a good collection of even more inept performances in that period of time, with far fewer extenuating circumstances. (The club's treatment room in early 2005 arguably contained as good a side as could be mustered from fit players.) For the sake of the media, it can't simply be labelled *bad*; it has to be 'the *worst*'.

If every vaguely inept or inglorious performance ends up labelled as the worst, then there can be no chance of honest perspective, no chance of balanced appraisal, and you end up bouncing from sublime to ridiculous and back, week after week. Liverpool's form was inconsistent, but not *that* inconsistent. Beating Olympiakos in December was compared to besting St Etienne in 1977. Little over a month later, and suddenly, following FA Cup defeat at Burnley and the Southampton reverse, the club was in crisis. A further three days later and Liverpool were in the League Cup final, while also awaiting to play (and of course, beat) Bayer Leverkusen in the last 16 of the Champions League. The club sat 5th in the league. In early 1993 — less than three years after Liverpool were last Champions, and with Manchester United still waiting to claim their first title for 26 years — Liverpool were out of all cup competitions, languishing in the bottom half of the table, and in danger of the unthinkable: being dragged into a relegation dogfight. So while the club has plenty of glorious moments to which comparisons are understandably made, there have also been many dark days in the last fifteen years. If Liverpool Football Club has fallen a long way since the halcyon days, then it has also more than stabilised since its lowest ebb of the 1990s: the patient still hospitalised, but out of intensive care.

Paul Wilson of the *Observer* went far further. Not content with singling out one shocking showing, he claimed in February, 2005, that Liverpool didn't deserve to qualify for the 2005/06 Champions League as it was "the worst Liverpool team in recent memory."

Of course there is no set definition of "recent memory". Amnesiacs, those with temporal lobotomies, not to mention goldfish (the literate ones, anyway) will of course already have forgotten what they read in the previous paragraph, let alone anything as far back as 1992, the year the Premiership came into being.

But even allowing for the grey area of 'recent memory', it was plainly a ludicrous suggestion. Had Wilson been comatose during the entire dire three-year reign of Graeme Souness? (Admittedly, most Liverpool fans were.) Was he out of the country during the early — or indeed, late — years under Houllier? Not to mention the early — or indeed, late — years under Evans? It is staggering to think that a squad (and it *is* a squad game) containing Gerrard, Alonso, Carragher, Morientes, Luis Garcia, Riise, Hamann, Kirkland, Cissé, Baros, Sinama-Pongolle, Finnan, Dudek, Hyypia and Kewell, whatever the personal form of those listed, could be described as the worst in 'recent memory'. Those names roll off the tongue with more than a savour of class.

Liverpool's league form did not improve dramatically after Wilson's piece (it remained inconsistent), but nor did the club's European form — after all, Benítez' men had already done extremely well in reaching the last 16 of the Champions League, so some signs of class were apparent. At the time he made the statement — with the club in the Carling Cup final — it still stood out as a grave error: yet another example of the club being unfairly damned. No one can pretend Liverpool had the look of definite Champions League quarter-finalists, let alone finalists, but the side Benítez inherited had crashed out of the previous season's Uefa Cup much earlier and, unlike the team of 2004/05, did not make a domestic cup final (or even come close). While Liverpool were still far from championship material, they were also *clearly* better than they had been twelve months earlier — and therefore, categorically within 'recent memory'.

Instead, we have to read about how poor Liverpool are, struggling to make headway in an increasingly poor league. The quality of the Premiership, outside of the top three, is easy to write off, and yet a team 5th and 31 points off the pace (Liverpool, in case you were wondering) found itself eliminating Juventus (Italian champions-in-waiting) and Chelsea (newly crowned Premiership champions) in order to reach the final of the Champions League. If the Premiership is so weak, why do promoted clubs perennially struggle, and bemoan the gap in class between the two divisions? If the domestic league is so poor, how can the runners-up from 2003/04 make the Champions League semi-finals, and a year later, a team radically off the pace go one better, after setting up an all-English clash? (And is the 'real' Liverpool the one that, Burnley aside, has excelled in cup competitions, or the one that has struggled in the league?) Both Middlesborough and Newcastle did fairly well in the Uefa Cup while having poor domestic seasons. Since Arsenal, for some baffling reason (most likely psychological, with a smattering of tactical troubles), fail to make a dent on Europe while still able to rip through teams domestically, it seems to be used as definitive proof of an intrinsic weakness in the league itself.

The influx of money into the Premiership, and the intrisically fair nature of the TV deal (when compared to other countries), has enabled even smaller clubs like Portsmouth and Charlton to fill their teams with international players. On their day, any team can give a side like Liverpool — with potential but in transition — a tough game. You only have to take a look at Bolton — a provincial club run on a relatively tight budget — to see how attractive the Premiership, as a whole, has become to the world's best players, or once-great players who are entering the final years of their careers. In the last two seasons they've fielded two World Cup/European Championship winners in Youri Djorkaeff and Vincent Candela. They've paired Jay-Jay Okocha with El Hadji Diouf — both winners of the African Footballer of the Year on two occasions. They've signed two Champions League winners from Real Madrid, in Fernando Hierro and Ivan Campo. One of their strikers, Stelios Giannakopoulos, played a key role in Greece winning Euro 2004. Meanwhile, Gary Speed had a league championship medal from his time at Leeds United, and holds the record for the most Premiership appearances. While approximately half of these players were past their best, they still represented a wealth of experience at the highest level.

Like Everton, they succeeded (relatively speaking) by being organised, and hard to beat — after all, it is easier to vandalise a Renoir with a razor blade than to try and create something as beautiful. At Liverpool, Benítez was trying to 'open up' Liverpool's football, to make it more expansive. But that needs to be balanced out over a period of time. The organisation and preparation was superb, but the players needed time to adapt. The defence, no longer protected by a defensive midfield, was exposed. An example of how difficult such a transition can prove to be was evident at Southampton. Under Gordon Strachan, the Saints were very well organised and kept things tight at the back. After a couple of management changes, they opted for Harry Redknapp with relegation threatening. Redknapp was famous for exciting, attacking, passing football while in charge of West Ham and Portsmouth. In the attempt to get Southampton's attack functioning and their football flowing, the same defenders who had looked so solid under Strachan now looked horribly exposed, and terribly limited.

Back at Liverpool, Benítez was trying to change the 'habits' of his players: the positions his defenders took up, the ambition of his midfielders, the movement of his forwards, and the intentions of his entire team when in possession. You can change certain things fairly quickly — in a matter of months, or weeks if you are lucky — but you cannot *perfect* them in such a short space of time. It needs to become second nature to the team, and at times being cool on the ball, and taking time to find the right pass, only looked natural to Xabi Alonso. Even Steven Gerrard needed to adapt his game. This was a team which had spent the previous five or six seasons looking for the early pass over the top, or the long ball from the back to the big centre-forward.

Everton and Bolton benefited from time during the week to prepare to stop the opposition, especially if facing teams in Europe during the week — Sam Allardyce never hid that fact. Both teams weren't afraid to just lump the ball into the box, although Everton played some good passing football at times, and Bolton had the skill and flair to vary their approach. It's easy to say the league is weak as such clubs were still in the hunt for 4th spot with just three games of the season left, but doing so ignores the stability regarding their managers — both in the job for a number of seasons — and the power for organisation that gives them. (A team with a long-established manager will always have an advantage with regards to 'drilling' his players. George Graham didn't fine-tune that late '80s Arsenal defence to perfection until three seasons into the job.)

If Liverpool really were so bad, how could Benítez, in his first season, take a clearly inferior (but improving) Liverpool side far further in Europe than Wenger had taken Arsenal *in his entire Highbury career?* It is one of the strange quirks of football that while any Red would swap Arsenal's recent history for Liverpool's, it was now the Gunners who were looking on with some form of jealousy.

Sometimes it is the weight of games, and the gruelling schedule, that counts against Premiership teams, bearing out French legend Michel Platini's assertion that the English start the season as lions, and end it as lambs. Middlesborough, who won a domestic cup in 2004, spent that summer making good purchases and looked in far better shape to push further up the league in 2005, but they simply couldn't cope with the punishing repetition of games. While professional footballers are physically fit enough to *get through* three games in a week, they are obviously going to be at a disadvantage when facing equally fit teams who have not had to spend their midweek playing a tough European game, not to mention the likelihood of having travelled halfway around the continent in the process. Not only that, but opposition not involved in Europe also get longer on the training pitch to prepare for the weekend's game, and to perfect their negating tactics. The more games, the more pressure, and, cumulatively, the more *mentally* draining the season becomes.

History? What history?

The most successful club in English football history, Liverpool had fallen victim to the re-writing of the history books; or rather, discovering that its achievements were writ in slowly-vanishing ink. Eighteen-times league champions — and yet, the world is frequently told, never winners of the Premiership. Four European Cups — and yet it was noted (prior to 2005), still to even make the semi-finals of the Champions League. The two biggest competitions, and Liverpool lead all other English rivals in both. That is, until the names were changed.

The early 1990s were unusual in that the game experienced blanket re-branding — to what was once the First Division, as well as to the European Cup — and almost overnight, *everything* changed. (Division Two then became the First Division, and now, in 2005, the third tier of English football is the level known as Division One. At this rate is will be only another six years before the Football Conference is known as the First Division, by which stage no one will have the slightest clue about which league — with the myriad different names and sponsors — links to which, and it will take a panel of experts to deduce promotion and relegation issues. Chaos will reign when, following an administrative error, the *Cock and Bull* Sunday League pub team from Skelmersdale will find itself replacing Blackburn in the Premiership, though of course it may be fully six months into the season before anyone notices.)

The 'modern game', which always implied the post-war years, now related to the post-Gulf War years (the first Gulf War, that is). It has always been very rare to hear statisticians refer back to when 'records began'. Even when Ian Rush was breaking all kinds of records in the 1980s and '90s, it was often 'post-war' or 20th Century milestones he was setting. Now there are a generation of kids growing up thinking Andy Cole (who even re-branded *himself*, insisting on being called Andrew) must really be something special, as the Premiership's *second-top all-time goalscorer*. Rushie's 'scoring boots' must be turning on their peg in the closet under the stairs.

Overlooking pre-war achievements is at least understandable, to a degree, as they belong to another time entirely — a different *world*. It was a game of five forwards and super-baggy shorts (long before super-tight shorts and, as the circle completed, super-baggy shorts once again), and a time of relative innocence compared to what was to follow. Football in its usual form ceased to exist during the war years — the professional game suspended, and replaced by wartime leagues — and so when the game resumed in 1945, it was after a very definite, six-year hiatus. The *game* had changed, not just the name.

The best thing about Benítez' achievement, in taking the team to Istanbul, was how it united two separate parts of the club's history. Suddenly the four European Cups could be linked to the Champions League. Everyone was reminded that it was, after all, still the same tournament, the same trophy on offer. It constructed a bridge, from then to now, from past to present, from an old history to a new one.

Chapter eight

The Spanish acquisitions – the star imports
"Ra-ra-ra Rafa Benítez, Xabi Alonso, Garcia y Nunez"

The Spanish prince

The first thing you say to yourself, watching Xabi Alonso in an early appearance at Anfield in the early autumn of 2004 as, without even appearing to look, he curls another delightful pass, with pace, to Luis Garcia's feet from 50 yards away, is *There must be some kind of mistake.* For once, the mistake does not relate to *Why the hell have the club wasted all that money?* (In fact, £10.5m looks instantly like a steal.)

The discrepancy appears to be with his birth certificate.

There is no way this man is a mere 22-years-old. *No way.* Everything about him, on and off the pitch, screams late 20s, early 30s: the poise; the composure; the air of experience; the maturity evident in his voice as he speaks in such good English during those early interviews. This is a man, not a boy.

The second thing you think, as he drops his shoulder and sends yet another opponent in pursuit of his shadow, is *Why the hell did Real Madrid pull out of a deal to sign him?* It was a question asked by none other than erstwhile Madrid legend Michel, who felt Alonso was a more complete footballer than Patrick Vieira. That's not to say the idea had no support at the Bernabéu, since Vieira's signing was backed by Alfredo di Stefano, although his double-edged assessment of the player ("Vieira plays well and he also kicks people"), may hint at the reason for divided opinion. The politics at Spanish clubs is truly something to behold, and it didn't stop there. José Antonio Camacho, the re-instated disciplinarian manager, back at Real Madrid to sort out the galácticos, had told Florentino Pérez that Vieira was more his type of player. Opinion was heavily divided: Jorge Valdano, the Director of Football, urged Pérez to buy Alonso at all costs, but the President was keen on placating Camacho, given that Camacho had previously walked out on the club over a lack of control over transfers. So while Madrid procrastinated over a Spaniard in trying to procure a Frenchman, Rafael Benítez stepped in like Alonso himself, when reading the play and cutting out a through ball. No longer denying Europe's most successful club league titles, Benítez was now snapping up their transfer targets. Vieira would remain at Arsenal, and score a fantastic goal at Anfield four months later; Alonso, however, was also on the field, in the red of Liverpool, and would score an even better goal: curling a shot into the top corner after a delightful move involving Finnan, Kewell and Gerrard.

If anything could soften the blow of Michael Owen joining Real Madrid it was the fact that, for the same fee, Liverpool picked up a 22-year-old genius who might otherwise have been playing at the Bernabéu.

Alonso was born into football: the son of Miguel Angel ('Periko'), a Spanish international who played for Barcelona, as well as Real Sociedad in their successive-title-winning side of the early 1980s, and who later coached the team (Xabi's brother Mikel is still part of the senior squad at the Anoeta). The Liverpool connection goes back to 2001, when ex-Anfield great, John Toshack — returning for his third spell as Real Sociedad's manager — recalled Xabi from a loan spell at Second Division Eibar. Periko, who had been caretaker up until Toshack's arrival, and was fearful of accusations of nepotism, sent his teenage son out to Eibar. The story runs that Toshack stormed into the office of the Director of Football, and yelled "What the fuck is Alonso doing at Eibar?" Suffice to say that within 24 hours the young Xabi was not only back at Sociedad but back in the side, and the club, 2nd from bottom of the *Primera Liga*, soon rose to mid-table safety. Within a year, the club (with new signing Sander Westerveld in goal) would be challenging for the Spanish title, eventually finishing as runners-up.

Acclaim

Xabi, the most talented of all the Alonsos, was an early contender for Liverpool Player of the Season, before his campaign was thought to have been curtailed in the home game with Chelsea, when Frank Lampard's clumsy late tackle resulted in a broken ankle. But there was a twist in the tale: Alonso was named as a substitute on April 5 against Juventus — he was still some way short of full fitness, but his mere presence on the Anfield bench was a massive boost to everyone at the club, and he would return to the starting XI just one week later, in the return fixture at the Stadio Delle Alpi.

At the time of his return, Alonso was still sitting clear in fourth spot in the voting on the club's official website for its player of the season, despite missing almost four months, and having only arrived at the end of August, four games into the season. (The voting also included the club's four pre-season games.) With fans and the site's journalists voting on the best five players following every game, in two separate polls, Alonso trailed behind only Jamie Carragher, Steven Gerrard and Milan Baros in each, while a fair way ahead of John Arne Riise and Luis Garcia. Within just three games, he was in third position, and the plaudits started arriving, thicker and faster than before.

Ian St John — so critical of Liverpool during the reign of Gérard Houllier — said Alonso had grown to become even more crucial to Liverpool's game than Steven Gerrard. It was a statement that, if made the previous summer, many would have found implausible: who could possibly be more influential than Gerrard? Whereas Luis Garcia had been prematurely (and incorrectly) compared to Kenny Dalglish, given the position he occupied early on in the season, Alonso was now being compared to Dalglish in terms of influence and passing ability. 'Anfield Iron' Tommy Smith said: "The performance of Xabi Alonso [against Juventus] was exceptional. You don't have to be a genius to see how good the young Spaniard is. He reminds me in many ways of Kenny Dalglish, having that rare ability to make time and space for himself to play his football. He never seems to give the ball away and his range of pinpoint passing is a joy to see. Alonso is pure footballing class and a real symbol of hope for the future at Anfield."

Rafael Benítez echoed those sentiments. "When I look at the best players in the history of the Premiership or at the top of the English game, the most influential are those with the most skill. You have Dalglish who inspired the great Liverpool side, Cantona at Manchester United, Zola at Chelsea and Bergkamp who was crucial at the start of Arsenal success. These are players who rely on skill more than physical play. For me, Xabi is the kind of player who can come into their category. Of course, you always need good players around someone like this which is why it's a shame we've had few opportunities to have Xabi and Steven Gerrard playing with each other. With both of them, we could do a lot better than we are."

Benítez clearly rued the loss of his influential midfielder between January and April. "It was a pity we lost Xabi for three months because if he'd been playing for the whole season, I'm sure we'd have more points. He makes our team play well. When Xabi plays we pass the ball a lot better. Our vision is to create a Liverpool team which passes the ball well across all sides of the pitch, and this is something which Xabi does very well. When we [the staff] joined Liverpool, Xabi and Luis Garcia were the players we knew we wanted to bring to the club with us."

Quarterback

The position made his own by Didi Hamann under Houllier was now Alonso's for the taking. (Although Benítez did opt for three in central midfield at times, knowing that no team could match that trio.) Whereas in previous seasons the job of Hamann was to shield the back four and to give the ball, simply, to a nearby player, it was now, with Alonso, the fulcrum from which attacks could be launched at all angles. The problem with Hamann playing that role was that his midfield partner — Gerrard, in most instances — often had to drop deep to collect the ball from the German, in order to start a move with a searching pass. Hamann had no long-range passing, and if he ended up giving it back to the centre-backs they then looked to bypass the midfield (often referred to by opposing fans as the 'hoof'), and it was a lottery for the forwards. At times, Gerrard, Hamann, Henchoz and Hyypia were standing within touching distance, and given that the full-backs and wide midfielders weren't always free to roam, options for the pass were few and *literally* far between. Either Gerrard gave it back to Hamann or Hyypia, or he looked for the 60-yard pass.

Alonso, however, was akin to an American Football quarterback. He dropped off the play to receive the ball, and then had the ability to find someone in space, in any part of the pitch. The change of emphasis in the role perfectly summed up the difference between Houllier and Benítez. Where it had been an almost-exclusively destructive one under Houllier, it is now a *starting point*. But that is not to suggest Alonso is some lightweight dilettante unprepared to roll up his sleeves, or dirty his kit. While he doesn't excel at the destructive side of the game to quite the extent Hamann does, he is still perfectly capable, given his innate footballing intelligence, of reading the play and breaking up moves by being in the right place at the right time. Just as Bobby Moore could defend expertly without a hint of pace — as Bob Paisley often noted, the first two yards are in the mind — so Alonso can patrol in front of the back four and obviate trouble in a fashion not too dissimilar to Hamann himself; it doesn't need a Paul Ince flying into bone-juddering tackles at 100mph. In fact, those players who can nick the ball away rather than go to ground can be more effective. (Often the reason blood-and-thunder types have to make those meaty challenges in the first place is due to their own poor control.) Salif Diao won some (rare) acclaim for his performance at Goodison Park in December 2004, and indeed won plenty of tackles. But almost every one involved conceding the ball to the opposition. A player who can anticipate the danger, and cut it off at the source (or indeed, to use the apt phrase from *Westerns*, 'cut it off at the *pass*'), might not *appear* to be winning the midfield battle, but will often be far more effective. In the British game fans love to see a thundering challenge, but some continental brainpower and nous can remove the need. Players like Hamann, and Hansen all those years ago, excel at the defensive side of the game, and yet neither has enough meat on them to worry even the slightest of attackers. By staying on their feet, they give themselves an advantage.

As well as being able to make a tackle, Alonso proved he could take a tackle, too. His full debut at Bolton was notable for the number of times he was clattered after he released his pass. But it didn't stop him wanting to get on the ball — always a sign of a great player — and he didn't moan at the punishment he received. Even after Frank Lampard's foul on New Year's Day, Xabi looked to carry on, despite what transpired to be a broken bone in his ankle. Sometimes special players are more at risk, as their speed of thought can catch lesser players out — the ball is there, so they try to win it, but like a conjurer the ball can be moved in a case of 'now you see it, now you don't'.

Pass master

It is possible to write a book about Alonso's passing alone. He is the team's metronome, getting the ball and dictating the pace of the game; an easy pass here, a long ball there, and a drilled pass to feet, or into space. Never predictable, but always in control, and nearly always picking the correct option.

It was the home game with Norwich which made the rest of England sit up and take note. (Admittedly not the greatest of opposition, but Norwich had, in the fashion typical of promoted clubs, made a fighting start to the season, and had been performing well.) Xabi shone like a beacon. The ball found him, and he found others with the ball: a magnet, but one which could turn from attraction to repulsion in a split second.

The Norwich manager, Nigel Worthington, remarked after seeing his side vanquished 3-0, "If I was a fan, I'd pay money to see him wherever he played. He and especially his passing were a different class." The BBC's Stuart Hall, interviewing Benítez after the match for *Radio Five Live*, suggested that Alonso was the best midfielder in Europe, possibly the world. Benítez, not wishing to single out an individual, stressed the importance of the team, but when pushed on the subject, conceded that Alonso "Is a very clever player. That makes everything easier for him." According to former Everton and Norwich midfielder Neil Adams — summarising for *Norfolk Radio* — Alonso's first half was "the best individual performance by a midfielder I can remember seeing".

Aged just 22 when he arrived in England, Alonso's passing and reading of the game already exhibited more maturity and composure than that of Steven Gerrard — whose range of passing was not expected to be equalled, let alone bettered, in this generation. Where Gerrard's game was almost exclusively about *adding* tempo, Alonso's was about *controlling* it. Alonso's arrival means more scope for Gerrard to get forward, and use his dynamic running and thunderous shot to hurt the opposition (as his goal tally suggested). While Gerrard was capable of hitting jaw-dropping long passes from deep, at times his decision making can be a little lacking.

Alonso is now, without doubt, the best passer of the ball in England; Jan Molby reincarnated, after a lengthy stint on the Atkins Diet. Alonso, like Molby, knows where, when, and *how* to move the ball to the correct option, without appearing to break stride or indeed break sweat.

Together, Alonso and Gerrard, given their age, talent and complementary skills, possess the potential to become the club's greatest-ever central midfield partnership — if it is allowed to happen. If debate rages as to whether or not Gerrard has surpassed Graeme Souness in terms of all-round game, it is hard to think of a previous pairing that offers everything Alonso and Gerrard can, and with both players still a long way from their peak years. Broken bones to both players — Gerrard in the autumn, Alonso in the winter — limited the times they were seen in tandem, given that for six months of the season either one of them was out. With the departure of Gerrard still a possibility (if no longer an inevitability), it is perhaps a partnership Benítez will never see flourish.

Weaknesses?
No player is perfect. Hustle and harry Alonso, and of course he looks a little less impressive — very few players can cope with the extra attention of being man-marked, or having two players detail him (although, as a result, it does allow others in the team more freedom). Xabi has enough clever turns and dummies to buy himself space for the pass, but he will receive more attention from opposition sides, now he has shown the damage he can inflict; the attention could be even more pronounced if Gerrard isn't around to occupy the opposition enforcers, and to drag players around with his forceful running.

Fitness issues remain Alonso's main concern. He is a natural footballer, but not a natural athlete. The brainpower, while it can compensate on many levels, cannot will his legs to run faster when a sprint is called for, or empower his lungs with the stamina of a Steven Gerrard.

John Toshack spoke about how his staff had to work to make Alonso more nimble, with all sorts of exercises designed to 'lighten' his feet. In his early months at Liverpool, Alonso was rotated more than other key players, and left on the bench in games where, in an ideal world, he would have started. (Fulham away being one such example: 2-0 down at half-time, Alonso came on at the start of the second half, and totally changed the game, scoring one and creating another, as Liverpool ran out 4-2 winners.) It could be argued that this is Benítez' way of allowing his most expensive signing to settle and acclimatise, but Luis Garcia, despite his small frame and some severe buffetings, tends to start games whenever fit. Alonso was mothballed for Champions League games, and it is a great testament to the club that it performed so well in the knock-out stages while he was absent.

The future

It's hard to make predictions in football, as so much can change in a short space of time. Issues outside of the game can draw a player back to his homeland, in the way Antonio Reyes, his compatriot at Arsenal, has reportedly been pining for a return to Spain. Anything can happen: heaven forbid, but too many more lates tackle like the one that broke his ankle, and Alonso may merit a mere footnote in the history of Liverpool Football Club; a 'what might have been'.

Alonso, an avid student of the game — always thinking about what both he and the team can improve — can become Benítez' 'manager on the pitch', in the way Gary McAllister performed that role for Houllier. "He is a youngster with the mentality of an experienced player," said Benítez. "Football has been his life because of his family and he analyses the game as well as he plays it."

The potential is immense, and maybe one day soon, with luck on his side, he will merit an entire book of his own.

Luis Garcia — Good Vibrations from the Beach Boy

Do not check your eyes as you read on — they do not deceive you:

"The ex- ones of Barça and Atle'tico, that add 8 already so many this season with 'reds' in all the competitions, emphasised the merit of a classification obtained in precarious conditions because of the numerous losses that the set of the Mersey drags."

Such sentences became all too familiar for non-Spanish speaking Liverpool fans searching the internet for translations to articles published in the Iberian press. Websites such as *Babelfish* offered an amalgam of apparent gibberish interspersed with words and phrases that, tantalisingly, made a modicum of sense. Luis Garcia, it became clear, was generating a lot of press back in his homeland.

While not a regular in Frank Rijkaard's exciting Barcelona side of 2003/04, this boyhood Barça fan was also far more than a bit-part player. The little Spaniard played in roughly half of the team's games that season — scoring six goals in 24 games. He had twice been called up to the national side, only for injury to curtail his dreams of becoming an international — dreams that would come to fruition in March 2005, when, as a Liverpool player, he made his debut for Spain, coming on as a 54th minute substitute in the friendly with China (and hitting the bar with a shot from the edge of the area).

Rijkaard was loath to let Luis Garcia leave, even though he had a glut of flair players to choose from, including the mercurial Ronaldinho, and new signings Deco and Ludovic Guily, the erstwhile creative lynchpins of Porto and Monaco, who had contested the previous seasons Champions League final, not to mention the considerable attacking talents of Henrik Larsson and Samuel Eto'o.

Liverpool agreed to pay Luis Garcia's £6m buy-out clause, and the player himself knew that however valued he was at Barcelona, he would be no more than a squad player — a talented understudy to the stars of the show. Joining Anfield's Spanish Revolution was an exciting prospect, not least because it meant teaming up once more with Rafa Benítez, the first man to show great faith in him when taking him to Tenerife on loan, and seeing rich rewards with 16 goals as they won promotion to the *Primera Liga*.

He started incredibly well at Liverpool — *too* well, if that's possible — so that when the inevitable dip occurred there was a backlash. Had it all been an illusion? Was he another lightweight foreigner who would flatter to deceive? In many ways he had set himself impossible standards to live up to: no player can maintain that kind of form over the course of a season, where *every* flicked pass or dragback turn comes off.

A hamstring injury in the opening minute of the fixture in Monaco at the end of November, coupled with the birth of his first child back in Spain (on top of which were the issues surrounding moving his family over and settling them in on Merseyside), was not the ideal preparation for the tough winter months in English football. Suddenly fans were questioning the wisdom of Liverpool signing him. The goals never completely dried up — witness the close-range tap-in at West Brom, and the sublime lob at Norwich — but he was missing lots of chances in home games, and going missing in away games, where the team as a whole struggled. Perhaps the warmer autumn and spring months were more conducive to this genuinely two-footed *beach boy*'s skills, but the English weather was so unpredictable it snowed in April. Even with deep winter enduring past Easter, Luis Garcia was well out of his hibernation.

There could be no doubt that Luis Garcia added something extra to the team in place of the undervalued — but ultimately expendable — Danny Murphy, the man he effectively replaced: quicker movement of the ball, and even more goals than Murphy managed. (Murphy's best tally was 12, but that included free-kicks and penalties.) Luis Garcia's stunning volley against Juventus at Anfield was his tenth goal of the season, all from open play, and, but for very poor linesman's decisions at Bolton and Middlesborough, it would have been his twelfth. But he wasn't finished there: there was another glorious goal at home to Spurs, turning inside his marker to curl a shot into the top corner (mirroring his Juventus strike); a powerful header away at Portsmouth, where he rose above (and like) Fernando Morientes to head home; and, of course, the winning goal in the Champions League semi-final. Nearly all of his 13 goals proved decisive.

Erratic

It is clear that Luis Garcia's finishing is somewhat erratic, and will probably remain so throughout his career — sometimes he misses implausibly easy chances that leave 40,000 people scratching their heads. He will never be like a top-form Michael Owen, when every chance was tucked away with apparent ease by the previous (and equally-diminutive) incumbent of the No.10 shirt. But when you play on the wing, as Luis Garcia did for much of the season, the important thing is to at least get into the positions to score — as you won't get many goals from the touchline. Less proactive players may keep their position as if part of a bar football table, stuck out wide, and more worried about getting caught out of position. (If every player stuck rigidly to his position, only forwards would ever score goals.)

Not so with Luis Garcia, who always anticipates the ball dropping his way. If he skies two and scuffs another, but scores the next, he might be labelled profligate, but he will still have affected the scoreline; a winger who stays out wide and never gets criticised for missing chances will not. Emile Heskey was the perfect case in point. When Houllier used him on the wing, it should have meant one extra forward getting into the box when Liverpool attacked — a possible clone of Gus Poyet (a player who, incidentally, Houllier tried to sign in 2002), where the tall and powerful Heskey should have been bursting into the box to arrive at the far post and score. But too often, when the cross came in, Heskey was nowhere to be seen. He occasionally scored goals when starting wide in midfield, but he had many of the attributes needed to be a goalscoring winger — just not that *proactive* urge. Heskey was a reactive player, who waited for things to happen for him, rather than going looking for them. The little Spaniard's goals — especially his three in the two games against Bayer Leverkusen — were from making a run either across, or in behind the defenders, and being so quick and alert when the ball came his way. The same can be said of his semi-final goal against Chelsea.

Luis Garcia scores poacher's goals, without ever appearing to be a *poacher*. He is closer to Freddie Ljungberg, the Arsenal midfielder who pops up to score with great regularity. As well as his goals, Luis Garcia's clever footwork and ability to pick a pass led to a number of assists. He made things happen. If Jamie Carragher was indispensable *en route* to the Champions League final for keeping the ball out of the Liverpool net, then Luis Garcia proved equally crucial at the other end, as the man *who put it in*. Five goals came in the seven games which followed the league stage.

The Mersey derby at Anfield in March 2005 helped move Luis Garcia into the realms of folklore. Not only did he score the winning goal (never the worst game in which to do so), he played the second half in considerable pain, aware than in so doing he would probably negate his chances of finally making his debut for his national side a week later, having twice before been called up, only to lose out through injuries. An unfortunate hat-trick beckoned, but as Benítez had been forced to use all three subs by the 40th minute, Luis Garcia had to spend the second 45 minutes hobbling about. Fortunately the player was finally able to get his first taste of international football.

It's all too easy to label small foreign players as lightweight with the (often inaccurate) assumption that they don't *care* to put themselves about — missing the point that it's not their game, and not why they were bought. When a 14-stone defender muscles someone like Luis Garcia off the ball it may look as if he is not trying, but there's really not an awful lot he can do about it, other than to try to use his fleetness of foot to deceive such players when the ball is at his feet. He cannot physically impose himself on games — he needs to do so with his skill, and for that he requires accurate passes to his feet; knock a pass into space, and it gives the defender the time to go shoulder-to-shoulder and barge him off the ball. It should not be overlooked that he still works hard, tracks back, and makes sliding tackles, but he'll never be one to go flying into 50-50 challenges. John Barnes — a far bigger, stronger player — was never castigated for not getting 'stuck in'. People were able to see that tackling wasn't his strength, and he was so good at what he did, frankly no one cared. Luis Garcia isn't yet at Barnes' level, and cannot use his physique to protect himself, but what he *can* offer far exceeds what he *cannot*.

Above all, Benítez' beach boy is a team player — never more clear than the joy and openness in his congratulations to others upon them scoring, greeting them with his broad beaming smile; or, once he has removed his thumb from his mouth (following the ever-more familiar goal celebration, in recognition of the birth of his son), the way he makes straight to the player who set him up, to offer heartfelt thanks. Some players can tap in from a yard after a teammate has done all the hard work — and then spin away as if *they* did it all themselves, ignoring the supplier as they flip and somersault towards the corner flag, their egos inflated with helium — but Luis Garcia is a far too magnanimous for that.

Few skillful imports have settled so successfully, so quickly. That is the greatest testimony following Luis Garcia's sparkling debut season.

'El Moro' - super player, not superstar
Given the circumstances surrounding his arrival, it will be 2005/06 before Liverpool fans get to see the best of Fernando Morientes — the *real* 'El Moro'. Having hardly featured

at all for Real Madrid in the first half of the season, the subsequent lack of match sharpness made settling into the ferocious pace of the Premiership that bit harder. Arriving in January, it meant there was no pre-season to acclimatise and get to know his teammates. Anyone doubting his quality, after an unremarkable first few months, should take this into account. This is not some journeyman clogger.

Players of the calibre of Morientes' are rarely found going begging on the transfer market, unless they happen to be out of contract, or nearing the end of their deal. Clubs just don't willingly release such talent. Unless, of course, that club happens to be Real Madrid.

One thing cannot be questioned as pen was put to paper on 13 January 2005: Liverpool FC had never previously purchased a player with the pedigree of their latest Spanish acquisition. Those at the club in the 1970s and '80s went on to procure a litany of honours, but all arrived at the club as relative unknowns, or as men of little prior success — at least by comparison to *El Moro*. Players in possession of a Champions League winners' medal had signed for the club in the previous decade: Karl-Heinz Riedle, winner with Borrusia Dortmund in 1997, and Jari Litmanen, architect of Ajax's success two years earlier. But neither came close to matching Morientes' experiences.

El Moro had played in four finals, three for Real Madrid and one for Monaco, and won all three with the Spanish giants. His only failure in those showpiece occasions — during his one season on loan at the French principality — saw him attain the consolation of being the tournament's top scorer, with nine goals in 12 games. In the 38 internationals he had played for Spain at the time he joined Liverpool, he had amassed an incredible 25 goals — all the more remarkable given that he only started 29 of those matches. Other goals and achievements too innumerable to list here were on his overcrowded CV, and yet still he had some question marks hanging over him.

No longer a regular for Real Madrid following Ronaldo's arrival, he was pushed further down the pecking order by the signing of Liverpool's Michael Owen. The emergence of young and exciting forwards, such as Fernando Torres, put Morientes' position in the national side in question, despite having one of the best strike-rates in world football at that level. Morientes is one of those players whose face never quite fits; not seen as glamourous or graceful: the essential glue that no one appreciates when considering a beautifully constructed piece of furniture. It is impossible to resist the theory that if Real Madrid had purchased him, for the very first time, from Monaco in 2004, he would have been seen as a 'galáctico'. As it was, he arrived much earlier, as a 21-year-old from unfashionable Real Zaragoza on the back of two 15-goal seasons, having made his league debut as a 17-year-old at even-less fashionable Albacete.

There are superstars. And there are *super players*. It is notable that Real Madrid have stuttered since Ronaldo arrived in a hail of glory and, given his waistline, in a limo with reinforced suspension. The Brazilian was unquestionably the world's most gifted striker, having just completed a successful World Cup where, for once in his recent life, he looked fit and sharp and hungry (in the football sense — as he'd clearly left the pies untouched), and scored eight goals as Brazil trailblazed their way to glory. But the Ronaldo who has represented Real Madrid has rarely looked quite the same proposition. The more 'galácticos' arrive at Real, the less successful the club gets. Fantasy footballers on the team-sheet do not necessarily result in fantasy football on the pitch.

Given a straight choice, most people would take Ronaldo over Morientes every time. But maybe not Benítez (not that such an offer was ever on the table). Ronaldo has God-given genius, truly sublime talents, but Morientes is from the Kevin Keegan school of hard work. No one can envy Ronaldo the attention and hype he's had to deal with since he was 18 (who can forget the 1998 World Cup final, and his supposed seizure?), but sometimes you buy the sideshow as well as the player, David Beckham being a case in point.

Sometimes you only discover how valuable someone is to a club in his absence. Just as Valencia imploded following the departure of Benítez, the statistics back up Morientes' importance to Real Madrid to dramatic effect. If it is mere coincidence, then it is a startling coincidence. Perhaps Madrid's enduring failure in Morientes' absence is also *symbolic*. As the team shifts from an honest, hard-working ethos to hype, glamour and superstars, it falls flat on its face year after year.

In 1998, after a 32-year wait, Real Madrid finally won Europe's elite trophy — which had been *theirs* in the competition's early years. It just happened to be Morientes' first season at Real Madrid, and he played a full part in the success, scoring four goals in ten games on the way to defeating Juventus 1-0 in the final at the Amsterdam Arena. (He also scored 12 in 33 La Liga games.) If that wasn't coincidence enough, Madrid repeated the trick in the 2000 final at the Stade de France, as El Moro scored the first as Real beat pre-Benítez Valencia 3-0. (A game in which a certain Steve McManaman also scored, and was named Man of the Match.) Another two years, another Champions League trophy, this time defeating Bayer Leverkusen, Liverpool's conquerors from the quarter-finals, 2-1 at Hampden Park. Morientes had been at Real for six seasons, and the club had experienced its first, second and third European triumphs since 1966. Each time Morientes scored goals *en route* to the final. The league was only marginally less fruitful: two championships in those six years.

It makes you wonder what the powers that be in Madrid were thinking. The expression 'If it ain't broke, don't fix it' must not exist in Spanish. All teams find it essential to strengthen when at the top, in order to stave off complacency. But Morientes is not a complacent footballer — an accusation that could possibly be levelled at Ronaldo, his direct replacement. Having won that trophy in 2002, Morientes was then cast into the shadows, as the Brazilian arrived to take his place.

Pérez's approach was that of the middle-aged man who discards his loving, faithful and attentive wife for the head-turning charms of the new temp in the office pool: giddied by glamour, he loses exactly the person who knows him best. Pérez discovered that the latter will turn more heads, but she won't be there for you when the skies turn grey. In the three seasons since the glamourous Ronaldo arrived, the club have failed to get past the semi-final of the Champions League. In fact, they have fallen a hurdle earlier in each successive season: the semi-final in 2003, losing to Juventus; the quarter-final against Monaco in 2004, and then, most recently, at the "Round of 16" stage to Juventus once again, in March, 2005. They have just one league title in those four seasons.

By contrast, the two clubs Morientes has played for since — Monaco on loan in 2003/04 and Liverpool in 2004/05 — have both got further than Real Madrid, making it to the final of the competition. Morientes couldn't actually represent Liverpool in Europe in his first season, but even so, he clearly remains a very potent lucky charm.

Often the men who run clubs don't understand the *power of the team*, the immeasurable benefits of understanding and mutual trust — the kind long-term *amigos* Morientes and Raúl experienced (they became friends in the Spanish national youth team). Chairmen and Presidents often only understand the cult of the individual, of the 'star'. Unity and concord between two strikers is possibly the most important element to a successful team. It's not just a balance of styles, it's a harmonious relationship, where they look out for one and other, and supply the pass when the pass is on, or take the shot when the shot is on. Strikers have the biggest egos, and it is they who carry most of the hopes of the team. It is no use having two fine individuals who both want to be top dog, and refuse to pass to each other. Is it any coincidence that Raúl's star has dimmed considerably since being separated from his erstwhile strike partner? They were two superb players who, united, exceeded the sum of their parts.

Raúl was one of the players who came out in vehement support of his strike partner when Morientes was ostracised after Ronaldo took his place in the team. The then Real technical director Jorge Valdano hawked Morientes around — to Internazionale and Barcelona (as shocking as that sounds) — without the player's permission. Vicente del Bosque, the manager, was ordered to omit Morientes from the squad for the European Super Cup final. Raúl wore his friend's No.9 jersey beaneath his own as a gesture of support. Raúl, Morientes and the captain, Fernando Hierro, argued bitterly with Pérez and Valdano in the lobby of the team's Monte Carlo hotel late that night. But Morientes' career at Real was effectively over. You wouldn't treat a dog so shabbily.

The greatest twist of fate was when Morientes, now exiled to Monaco for a year, scored what appeared to be a mere consolation goal at the Bernabéu at a time when Monaco were trailing 4-1, and was roundly applauded by the home fans, with whom he remained a firm favourite. Morientes' scored again in the return leg as Monaco won 3-1 — and the 5-5 aggregate score meant the game was decided on the away goal rule, and thus El Moro's strike at the Bernabéu knocked his 'permanent' employers out.

Morientes had just experienced the best season in his career (before or since) at the point when Ronaldo arrived to supplant him. On six occasions the Spaniard had finished with between 15 and 20 goals in a season, achieved while representing three different clubs (Real Zaragoza, Real Madrid and Monaco). But in the Champions League-winning season of 2001/02 he scored 21 domestic and European goals, and, incredibly, also provided a phenomenal 18 assists — so that he had a direct hand in 39 of his team's goals.

That is the kind of quality Rafa Benítez will be looking to, once the player settles in. But as Morientes approaches his 30s, is the hunger still there? Is the fire still in the belly? Some champions never lose that — wanting only to return for more, as if failure is a personal affront to them. Benítez sent his spies (in trenchcoats with dark glasses?) to watch Madrid train, in order to gauge El Moro's attitude, as the player — now back at the club and behind Owen as well as Ronaldo — looked to win his place back, against the odds. The report that came back suggested he was the best trainer, and the most committed. Benítez had no doubts. "Morientes is a winner, he has the right mentality. He has won lots of trophies and has finished as top scorer in the Champions League, but he is really hungry, and that mentality will be vital for this club. The young players can see the way Morientes is, a player who has such a professional approach. He has done everything in the game, but he never says, 'I'm the star, I won't do the work'. Other transfer targets were spoken to, but none impressed as much as the man who was surely Benítez' prime target. "In the transfer window, we had been talking with some important players, and you get a feel from that of whether they are hungry or not. With some players, they get in there and the talk is just, 'my contract, my contract'. With Morientes he had just one thing to say: would he play. That is all he was interested in."

So far his contribution for Liverpool has been sporadic and fitful: a superb left-foot goal at Charlton; a prodigious header at home to Fulham; a tap-in at Portsmouth; the 35-yard volley that lead to the winning goal in the Anfield Mersey derby; and the sublime cross to John Arne Riise that, for the following 80 minutes against Chelsea, appeared to have won the Carling Cup. Beyond that, it's been a nice touch here, a good pass there, but allied to a distinct ring-rustiness.

But given time, class inevitably shines through.

Chapter nine

Steven Gerrard: Scouse heart?

If one player dominated — even overshadowed — the 2004/05 season, it was Steven Gerrard; just as he had the season before. On the pitch — but mostly off — his was the name on everyone's lips. Much of this was down to the sensational transfer to-ings and fro-ings over the summer of 2004, when he came within hours of joining the Abramovich revolution at Stamford Bridge, right in the middle of Euro 2004. From the point he admitted it had been an extremely close call, he became fair game for the press to speculate — *ad nauseam* — about it being only a 'matter of time'. In February, 2005, the *Mail on Sunday* ran an apology for stating that a deal with Chelsea had been in place since the previous June, and that Rick Parry accepted it was inevitable Gerrard would leave.

In March, the player himself was driven to speak out: "There has been a lot of rubbish written about me this season and it's getting ridiculous. There are people out there whom I've never even met assuming they know what I think. Sometimes I feel I'm in a no-win situation. If I say nothing, then you'll have some fans saying 'Gerrard hasn't denied it, so it must be true'. On the one hand I want to put the record straight and let the fans know they shouldn't believe everything they're hearing about me. On the other, I know everything I say is being interpreted to mean one thing or another. It gets to the point where you wonder if you should do interviews, but I've always been honest in everything I've said. If I responded every time a rumour was printed about me I would spend all my time denying I had decided to go. How many times do I have to say it?"

His attempt to quell the rumours was about as successful as trying to put out a forest fire with an empty watering can. The speculation was out of control, burning wildly across every newspaper back page. Even Gerrard himself could not douse the flames, only inadvertently fan them.

So what of the player's future? At the point of writing it is still unresolved. Things quickly change in the world of football. The latest, in May 2005, is that he will sign a new deal at Liverpool, with it being rumoured that Chelsea are either losing interest, or — realising Gerrard was now going places with the Reds — trying to save face by pursuing other targets. But nothing is crystal clear. Will Parry and co. choose to cash in? If so, will it be sooner rather than later? Will Gerrard demand a move, and run the risk of serious contempt and enmity on Merseyside? (Less of a risk, more of a cast-iron guarantee. The more a player is loved and identified with, the greater the rejection and disillusionment felt by fans, and the more hostile their reaction when they feel 'betrayed'.) Although it seems less likely now the season has concluded — when at times it had seemed like a cast-iron certainty — the possibility of Gerrard leaving remains.

What would selling Gerrard mean to the future of Liverpool Football Club? And even if he stays, will it merely be a *matter of time* in the eyes of the media? Or has the speculation ended once and for all? By the time you read this, you may already have your answer.

There can be no doubting that Gerrard would prefer success at Liverpool than anywhere else. It would clearly mean more — as was clear in his delight when lifting the European Cup in Istanbul. West London and Madrid may offer more obvious chances of sustained success, but Michael Owen can attest to how there are no certainties in the game when it comes to trophies. While Chelsea deserve praise for the way they spent their money — especially in the summer of 2004 — and for the quality of the team two successive managers helped create, it remains a fact that to a large extent they 'bought' the title. Every season there will be a club whose finances mean it has the most to invest in its team, but once a club has the ability to spend *three times as much* as any of its closest rivals, it is the money doing the talking. Where is the fun in joining something like that, where the advantage is so unfair it's akin to fielding a 14-man team every week? In the time between beating Liverpool in extra-time during the Carling Cup final, and their previous trophy, Chelsea had spent £278m, £213m of which had been invested since the summer of 2003. If Gerrard wanted to join Arsenal, where success has been built with skill, not money (Wenger balancing the books to startling effect while garnering trophies), it would be easier to respect his decision to leave, should he opt to do so. There is something slightly hollow about Chelsea's success, and the more extravagantly they spend, the less impressive any subsequent success will be. The situation hasn't been helped by the accusations of tapping-up top players levelled against the club.

There is no getting away from the fact that selling Gerrard before the final year of his contract (which currently runs until 2007) could lead to the arrival of four or five top quality players (if the money is invested as prudently as it was with Alonso and Luis Garcia). As good as Gerrard is, he is not a team in himself. The statistics suggest that the team actually does no worse without Gerrard than it does with him. Of course, that doesn't take into account the level of difficulty of the games in question. But in the course of this season's Champions League campaign, Gerrard missed the impressive away victory against Deportivo La Coruna, the destruction of Bayer Leverkusen at Anfield, and the odds-defying 0-0 draw in Turin. Whatever the statistics, it's fair to say that any manager, given the choice, would choose to include Gerrard rather than opt to omit him.

For all his talent, and all his worth, one serious injury and Gerrard is out of the equation. So would it better to sell in order to bolster the strength and depth of the squad? Of course, the problem with selling one world-class talent, to replace him with a handful of new players, is that only one of them can go into the team in direct replacement. Five 'decent' players do not necessarily strengthen the team inasmuch as a manager can't field 15 men. If the player who goes into Gerrard's central midfield role is not as good as Gerrard (and, barring miracles, he wouldn't be), then the quality of the starting eleven is instantly diluted. The key is getting the other replacements to improve areas of the team where there are weaknesses, be it goalkeeper, left back or centre-forward. Adding depth to the squad is one thing, but you need to continually improve the first eleven. Big squads are essential in the modern game, where injuries — despite the advances in medical procedures — are more commonplace, given the increased pace, ferocity and athleticism. But it is still the strongest first XIs that tend to win the big trophies. No team can have reserves as good as its star players, as world-class players don't hang around at clubs where they are consigned to the bench.

Clearly the chance of success in Liverpool's future does not rely on Steven Gerrard — but it would be a big benefit if he was part of it. Examples of a team's best player leaving and the team going from strength to strength are ample, the most obvious examples coming very close to home. Ian Rush left Liverpool for Juventus in 1987, for £3.2m. The three men who came in — for a combined fee of roughly that amount — were Peter Beardsley, John Barnes and John Aldridge (who arrived shortly before Rush's departure, given the club knew one year in advance that the Welshman would be leaving). The following season saw arguably the best football the club had ever produced. You can argue about it all day long, and eras are notoriously difficult to compare to one and other, but it was certainly up there as something special — no lesser judges than Sir Tom Finney and Michel Platini were full of glowing adjectives for the team that season. A new dimension had been added to the play. The supposed hammer blow of losing legendary marksman Ian Rush was instead — paradoxically — the catalyst for improvement. But it's not easy to sell a truly outstanding player and replace him with three, four or five great ones. A manager cannot afford mistakes when spending that precious money, as it is hugely symbolic. Whomever it was spent on would forever be known as the man/men bought with the *Gerrard money*.

Everton are another obvious example. Even though they had been unable to instantly spend the £27m they received on Wayne Rooney, the team gelled in his absence, and suddenly a collection of mediocre players were an over-performing unit. Rooney was no longer overshadowing Everton.

A final example can be found by looking into Rafa Benítez' past. In 2001 Valencia sold their prize asset, Gaizka Mendieta, to Lazio for nearly £30m. By 2002 Valencia, under Benítez' guidance, were champions of *La Liga* for the first time in 31 years, despite hardly re-investing any of the money. Clearly it is not the selling of your best player, but the manner in which you replace him, and how the balance of the team is affected. And on that front, it will always be a gamble. One fact with all of the aforementioned transfers is that the players were not sold to close rivals who possessed the same ambitions. Rush and Mendieta went abroad, and Rooney joined a club with totally different objectives, despite the subsequent ascendancy of Everton. If Gerrard were to leave, much would depend on where he opts to move to. Go abroad, to Real Madrid, and he'll merely be following in the footsteps of Kevin Keegan, Rush and Owen. (And, of course, the unforgettable Phil Babb.) Such a move would not be completely devastating to Liverpool fans, as they've seen it before.

A move to another Premiership side, however, would be a first in the modern history of Liverpool, as it would be the first time the club had sold its best player to a rival. Robbie Fowler was sold to Leeds — then in a very similar league position — for £11m in October 2001, but although that was very shocking, he was no longer Liverpool's best player, and history shows that Anfield had already seen him at his peak. As it stood, Owen was about to be named European Footballer of the Year, and Gerrard had also elevated himself above Fowler, for whom injuries had taken their toll. Fowler was expendable. He had become a bit-part player, whose cameos were growing ever less frequent. Losing Gerrard to Chelsea would be like losing Robbie Fowler to Manchester United in 1996, or Michael Owen to Arsenal in 2001.

Selling Gerrard to a rival would confirm the relegation of Liverpool from the elite — albeit largely because Chelsea have established a new tier in English football, where they stand alone in terms of finance. Chelsea can't buy the kind of rich history Liverpool possess, but their money can go a long way to buying a similar level of success; no team in the history of the sport has ever had such financial backing. Many clubs have had generous benefactors, but none to whom money seemed literally no object. Even Manchester United look like poor relations by comparison.

While Liverpool could recover from a blow like losing Gerrard, it is hard to say what lasting damage it could cause. The name (or *brand*, if you are so inclined) of the club remains very strong; people don't forget the might and pull of teams like Liverpool, Juventus, Barcelona and Real Madrid during lean times. But with Owen already departed, it would conceivably be harder to attract quality new acquisitions without Gerrard at the club — he is a player others aspire to play alongside. Fortunately Benítez' stock is currently riding higher than ever across Europe, and top players will always want to play for clubs that retain a special cachet, especially those managed by a figurehead they can clearly recognise as a special talent.

One-man team

The most inaccurate declaration of 2004/05 was the assertion that Liverpool were a 'one-man team' — as spot-on as calling helium-chested glamour model Jordan a 'one-man woman'.

While patently not true in a factual sense (even 'Stevie G' would struggle to beat teams at a ten-man disadvantage — although you know he'd give it a go), it was also an insult to his teammates. At times some of them may not have seemed deserving of sharing the same pitch, but not many opposition players looked fit to be in such close proximity, either. If you are comparing anyone to Steven Gerrard — be they teammates or opponents — then they will inevitably be cast in a poor light. You will always have a best player, the one whom the media feels you cannot do without. It was Owen in the late 90s, Ian Rush in the mid-80s. In 2003/04, Liverpool were deemed a one-man team — Gerrard FC — even when Owen was also in the line-up.

In recent seasons other clubs have had players who have stood out from the crowd. In going unbeaten throughout the 2003/04 season Arsenal had many great performers — but no-one came close to Henry. He was head and shoulders (and a fair bit of upper torso) above the rest. Did that make Arsenal a one-man side? Of course not. Other players performed key roles in winning the title, but Henry was often still the difference between Arsenal and whoever they were playing.

It is rather ironic that these claims are made about Gerrard when another player was excelling in Liverpool's midfield, putting in consistently brilliant performances. Xabi Alonso wowed fans and the media alike with his skill and sublime passing. Yet those same pressmen, when not extolling the virtues of the new Spanish midfield maestro, were — rather hypocritically — calling Liverpool a 'one-man' outfit. And Gerrard wasn't even the club's player of the season — that was Jamie Carragher, although even he might have been usurped had Alonso not missed four months of the season. (Gerrard himself missed two months.) Elsewhere, John Arne Riise, Steve Finnan, Luis Garcia, Sami Hyypia and, fitfully, Milan Baros, all made telling contributions.

Perhaps it is Gerrard's versatility and apparent omnipresence — seeming to be in several places at once — that makes him seem like a one-man team. He can — and does — do so much, that as spectators we are acutely aware of his every contribution. (That these contributions — be they passes, shots, or tackles — are rarely anything less than spectacular also draws your attention.) That said, he can be guilty of overdoing things, and at times teammates, rather than grow, seem to wilt in his presence. He can seem a little overbearing, taking the ball off the feet of certain players, as if he doesn't trust them, and in so doing, undermining their confidence. Then again, is that his problem, or *theirs*? Roy Keane and Graeme Souness inspired and even bullied those around them, but were also surrounded by players capable of taking on the responsibility themselves.

Complete

It is hard to believe there has been a more complete player in the history of the game — not just in England but in any part of the world. That may seem like an incredibly bold statement, and a case of hyperbole. There have been *better* players, of course — Gerrard is not even the best in Liverpool's history. At Liverpool, it would take a special player to usurp 'King' Kenny Dalglish as the club's greatest-ever player, while Billy Liddell is still revered by fans with longer memories. John Barnes — winner of the Football Writers' Player of the Year twice in three seasons — was a quite sublime attacking force, creating chances and scoring goals with panache in abundance. And in the midfield, Souness' shadow still looms large. Souness was the consummate competitor, a fearsome character (in an age when you could still intimidate the opposition) who controlled the tempo of matches, sprayed passes around and scored goals. (All the while managing — somehow — to look inordinately hard whilst sporting a silly perm and a moustache: perhaps his greatest achievement.)

Terry McDermott, a man who played alongside Souness at Liverpool during the halcyon years, told the club's official website: "I've gone on record about this before and I'll say it again, Steven Gerrard is possibly the finest midfield player ever to play for

Liverpool Football Club." The key difference between the two was outlined as follows: "Stevie can get up and down the pitch, whereas Graeme couldn't!" It is Gerrard's pace and athleticism, as well as his height, that mean he is such a phenomenal all-rounder. Souness, while the undoubted paragon of central midfielders, could not match Gerrard's all-round effectiveness, in that the Scot could only really play that one role, whereas his Scouse successor has played — and won rave reviews — in nearly every position for the club.

Bryan Robson, himself a pretty decent all-rounder, said of Gerrard: "He scores great goals, pressure goals, he's good in the air and he's quick. Stevie can also ping a pass 40 or 60 yards straight to a player's feet. He has got everything that anyone would want in a central midfield player. I think he is right up there with the very best midfielders in the world." Robson previously described Gerrard as a better player than himself at his prime.

Gerrard has a bit of everything; he is like a celestial experiment conducted by Messrs. Shankly and Paisley, to create the ultimate modern footballer: a hybrid of Souness, McDermott, Dalglish, Lawrenson, Barnes, with a little bit (if not all) of the magic of each. There have been better passers of a football, but few who could also tackle like Gerrard. There have been better tacklers, but none who could also pass over long distances like Gerrard. There have been taller players who were better in the air, fractionally quicker players, tougher players, more skilful players; there have been players (but not many) with a better shot; some players may have had better levels of stamina, and covered more ground, although it's hard to think who. Better crossers of the ball have graced the game. There have been midfielders who have scored more goals.

But have all these talents ever before been bound up in one man? Has a player ever been able to not just play but excel in every aspect of the game, and every outfield position?

Gerrard does have weaknesses to his game, but they are more slight flaws than glaring imperfections. He cannot slow a game down as well as some of his legendary forebears (or Xabi Alonso, for that matter). He still makes rash tackles, although the nasty two-footed type appear to be a thing of the past. His left foot isn't anywhere near as good as his right, but he still uses it when called upon, and it's not merely for standing on.

In his younger days, Gerrard was seen as a potential centre-back, given his physical attributes. It's easy to see him being quite superb there, although for the senior side it's a sight we've yet to see; maybe that's where he'll end up in later years, when the legs start to wane a little. Of course, goalkeeper is the least likely destination for Gerrard, but he's certainly tall and agile enough, and you wouldn't put anything past him (including the ball, no doubt). With the exception of these two positions, he has played everywhere else. And not just played there, but been quite sensational.

During one game in 2000, he was forced to move to emergency left-back at Villa Park. It was as though he'd played there his entire career. In the 1999/00 Mersey derby at Anfield, he played right back, with quite stunning results at both ends of the pitch. For both England and Liverpool he has played left and right midfield, and on the right his superb crossing ability has been abundantly clear; on the left he still manages to be hugely effective, cutting inside but never at the obvious moment. Under Benítez he has even played as a striker, either on his own (late in games) or, more frequently, with a licence to roam behind the main forward. This ploy worked to great effect at home to Arsenal, when he was sensational in the 2-1 victory.

Of course, he is almost certainly wasted anywhere other than central midfield (or in a more progressive role behind the main striker). He needs to be in the heart of the play, the epicentre of the action. From there he can flit out wide if the opportunity arises, but he is not stranded. If he starts out wide, there is less scope to move around.

A favourite maxim of Gérard Houllier was that a manager does not omit a player on account of what that player cannot do — but instead plays him because of what he *can*. Almost any major talent in the history of the game can be criticised as having at least one major flaw: John Barnes, like Maradona, Cruyff, Pele and Platini, was no hard-working tackler; Kenny Dalglish and Bobby Moore had next to no pace; and so on. Houllier was right — you would not opt against any of these players on account of their weaknesses. Given their match-winning strengths, you would simply surround them with players who compensate, to make the perfect blend.

As hard as you look, you cannot find a single reason to omit Steven Gerrard on account of what he *cannot* do.

Badge kissing, and loyalty

Against Everton in the Anfield Mersey derby in March, 2005, Gerrard stood poised to blast the free-kick that Didi Hamann was about to roll his way. A false start when the wall encroached, and then, as the Everton players broke towards him for a second time, Gerrard changed his mind and stroked a gentle side-footed shot into the corner of the net. Delirium ensured.

Perhaps to avoid the accusation of being a 'badge kisser' he decided to instead heartily *bite* the club crest as he ran towards the fans in the Lower Centenary. (Was this a 'love bite'?) Maybe it will lead to the start of a new trend, where full digestion of the club crest becomes the *only* way to prove your affection and affinity? Time will tell. (Expect to see Wayne Rooney and Alan Smith ingesting the three-course meal of Manchester United shirt, shorts and socks, before promptly leaving to join Real Madrid.)

While in some respects Gerrard should be free to choose where he plays his football (when his contract expires), it is also true that certain players have an added responsibility to stay with their current club, especially those who, as locals, have made a large play on their affinity with the fans. If it really means that much to them, they need to *prove* it, and not leave at the first opportunity. There comes a time when every player reaches a crossroads in his career, but Phil Thompson, speaking in the summer of 2004, said Gerrard owed Benítez at least two years, and it was hard to argue with such a statement. There was almost no point in staying for the transitional season, if only to leave at the end of it.

The most shocking example in recent times was Leeds-through-and-through Alan Smith, who left to join Manchester United, their most hated rivals. Smith thought that what he was doing was okay as Leeds were relegated — therefore they were not rivals anymore. So in other words, just when every Leeds fan feels like he's lost his job, his house and his life savings, the girlfriend he adores goes and dumps him for the neighbour he detests. Oh, but as a goodwill gesture, she says she won't take the fondue set.

Nice.

A little sensitivity wouldn't go amiss. Foreign players get accused of being mercenary, but what rankles more with fans than an action like this? If players talk the talk, they must then walk the walk. The Elland Road fans really did see Smith as so much more than just another Leeds player. He was chairlifted around Elland Road after the final game of the season following the club's relegation. Smith's comment "I'd like to move abroad so I can return and play for Leeds one day," became laughable once he signed on the dotted line at Old Trafford. Manchester United almost certainly provided Smith with the best financial offer, along with the best chance of silverware. It is his career. But there has to be a thought spared for the fans that adored him for so long. Old Trafford wasn't the only destination on offer. But it was the only destination that would skewer Leeds fans' hearts.

Is glory everything, or should an enjoyable career replete with *respect*, and being valued by everyone at a club, be more important? Are trophies the only way to 'fulfil' a career? Is Alan Shearer viewed with any less respect for only having won one trophy in his 20-year career, compared to Emile Heskey's six? Will Phil Neville, in possession of a clutch of medals, or David May, European Champions' League winner, be remembered longer than Matt Le Tissier, who won nothing? Who had the better career? Do people still talk of the German World Cup-winning side of 1990? And yet fans still revere the beaten Dutch finalists of 1974 and 1978. Of course the sport is all about winning, but it's also about glorious *efforts*. If players are at mediocre clubs going nowhere, or where their international careers are visibly harmed, you can see why, after a while, the feet become itchy. But Liverpool, even when not at its best, has never been a mediocre club heading nowhere. At times it resembled a giant who had taken one too many sleeping pills, but it has never become irrelevant.

Teams like Liverpool, even during fallow years, still *matter*. They never disappear from view for long. Since 2001 the club has reached six cup finals, winning five — not to mention the Community Shield and European Super Cup won under Gérard Houllier. It has also had three Champions League campaigns, two of which were very successful (one spectacularly so). It might not be *everything*, but it's a long way from nothing, and it is testament to the club's ambition that even this isn't enough. As Jamie Carragher said, in a not-so-thinly veiled manner, winning the Premiership title once with Liverpool would mean as much to him as winning it four times with another club. And he grew up an Evertonian.

The Champions League success of 2005 might just tip the scales for Steven Gerrard. In a season when Emlyn Hughes, the first captain to lift the European Cup for the Reds, so tragically died of a brain tumour, it had to be more than coincidence that the latest all-action Liverpudlian found himself hoisting the imposing trophy above his head. As Liverpool captain, Hughes returned to lift it 12 months later. Perhaps it is too much to ask for Gerrard to do the same; but it would be nice to see him try.

Chapter**ten**

The Champions League - dream time

Surreal remains an apt word. *Unlikely*, and its cousin, *unexpected*, are two more apposite examples. *Glorious*, of course, is equally valid. Most often used when describing the culmination of Liverpool's efforts in the Champions League was *unbelievable*.

How did Liverpool Football Club find itself back in a European Cup final? How did the team end up winning the trophy from a position way beyond lost hope? If there was a script to the action, it was of *Oscar*-winning quality. And the award for Best Director goes to Rafael Benítez, unassuming mastermind who remained happiest behind the camera. Working with only a couple of stars of world renown, he had to rely on a succession of understudies, and trust the ensemble playing. It turned out to be the big summer blockbuster.

Under Gérard Houllier there had been such a steady progression, season upon season (at least until 2002/03), that reaching the quarter-finals in 2002 made sense. This time around, nothing was expected — to the point where even the unexpected was not a possibilty. Could Liverpool upset the odds? No one even contemplated it, as the team faced Grazer AK in the qualifying round, especially as it was evident Michael Owen — the man who had dug the side out of a myriad holes — was about to depart.

It wasn't even a case of *not daring* to imagine such an eventuality; it literally never crossed anyone's mind.

Tradition

Going into the season, only two teams had won the European Champions Cup — in its various guises — more times than Liverpool: Real Madrid and AC Milan. Ajax and Bayern Munich sat alongside Liverpool with four wins each. These were the five teams who had dominated the competition to the point where the next best teams had just two successes each from the 49-year history of the tournament. The years 1977, 1978, 1981 and 1984 remain the four high points of Liverpool's history. Add Liverpool's three Uefa Cup successes — from 1973, 1976 and, most recently, 2001 — as well as its European Super Cup victories, and you have a very rich European tradition. But tradition doesn't win you trophies. Or does it?

One man who felt justifiably proud of Liverpool making the final was Gérard Houllier. The semi-final had been won with a starting XI containing eight of his signings (two of whom — Traoré and Biscan — were seen as amongst his worst), while he gave Gerrard his debut and Carragher his wings. Two of the three subs who featured were also his recruits. While it required the superior tactical acumen of Benítez to take the side all the way to the final — with the key recruits of Luis Garcia and Xabi Alonso adding a dimension previously absent — Houllier can only have felt vindicated at the legacy he bequeathed. "With Liverpool," he told *L'Equipe* in May 2005, "I [as manager] played 57 European matches. We only lost seven. That means there is a European culture. This team is not at that level by chance. There is a very high level of experience. That is important. I explained that history to the players. They still have improved their experience. That is why they can achieve a great final. In one match, everything is possible."

Despite the memorable Uefa Cup success of 2001, and the run to the quarter-final of the Champions League a year later — two seasons when Liverpool put itself back on the European map — 57 games still reads as a surprising amount. That is the equivalent of exactly one-and-a-half Premiership seasons: a lot of football. That the Reds were undefeated in 50 of those games is equally surprising — a wholly remarkable statistic (and Houllier did like his statistics). That is the same as losing four games in a 38-game Premiership season: championship consistency. He was right: the Reds *do* have a European culture, and it is not confined to the glory years of the 1970s and '80s. (It is apposite, then, that the city itself will be the European Capital of Culture in 2008.)

Speaking ahead of the semi-final with Chelsea, ex-Red Gary McAllister talked about the club's unique standing among its English peers, and what a special place Anfield was. "Macca", who in his two years at Anfield become an undoubted folk hero, had also apparently become a Liverpool fan — it was suddenly *his* club. In his media appearances he speaks with an affection for the club usually reserved for those who played their entire careers at Anfield. He had been starting out as a player at Motherwell at the tail-end of Liverpool's European dominance, and the respect he held for the club's heritage was clear. He ended his top-flight career, in 2002, with the club back in the continent's biggest competition, reaching the quarter-finals. A year earlier he had experienced the might of a European semi-final at Anfield — and that was 'just' for the Uefa Cup. He felt Liverpool's tradition would see them through. It's a strange concept, given that the youngest player during the club's last European Cup success, back in 1984, was now in his mid-40s — therefore leaving no connecting factor between the playing or backroom staff of the two eras. None of the current side had even reached his teenage years at the time of that victory in Rome, and many were still babies or pre-school toddlers. How can a 'club' have the ability to transcend its current position — to elevate its players — so as to raise them to a level comparable with previous successes?

McAllister felt that there was something almost magical about Liverpool — as a club — and as such, the team would win through to Istanbul. Whereas clubs like Arsenal and Chelsea had never made a European Cup final, Liverpool stood on the brink of their *sixth*. Domestically, Liverpool had not even come close to matching the brilliance of Arsenal in their recent title-winning seasons, or the Chelsea side that was turning the Premiership into a cakewalk. But in Europe, McAllister reasoned, a special power hoisted the Reds above mere mortals.

He wasn't wrong.

The "Champions" League

Or, as it could of course be known, the *Misnomer League*. Going into the season, Liverpool were a long way from champions — 30 points, no less, and as such, closer to relegation in those terms — and yet still the club qualified for what was once the 'Champions Cup'. Not that anyone connected to the club was complaining about the change in qualification criteria. It was embarrassing, to a degree — to be so poor in all competitions in Houllier's final season and yet still make it into the elite of European football, but the back door was open, and the invitation was there.

Fans were happy at the arrival of Benítez, but that didn't erase the memory of two years of mediocrity, or in any way cloud the issue of the massive rebuilding programme required. In the previous season, even the Uefa Cup had proved a monumental struggle.

The format of the Champions League — forever being tinkered with — had reverted back to a single group stage (it had been two group stages on Liverpool's previous visits since the word *Cup* had been replaced with *League*), followed by the final 16 teams entering into two-leg knockout ties.

"The best teams don't always win the Champions League," Jamie Carragher said in March, 2005, with more than a degree of truth. It is a cup competition, and as such, much depends on who you are drawn against. However, unlike one-off games in the FA Cup, the two-legged format means that the better teams can have a bad day and still prove their class in the return fixture. Playing both at home and away decreases the chance of lesser teams winning through on the back of one outstanding display in front of an intimidating home crowd, in the way lower division teams 'level' the playing field in domestic cups.

To return to Carragher's point, it is equally true that to win it more than once, and in quick succession — four times in eight seasons, as an example (and a completely random one, *of course*) — is definitive proof you're the best. You can get lucky once, perhaps — favourable draw, fortunate decisions, no injuries (Alex Ferguson noted how fortunate United were in terms of injuries when they won the trophy in 1999 — not one major casualty; how different to Liverpool's attempts six years later). But the only true and accurate marker of greatness is *consistency*. Because even the flukiest team on earth cannot ride their luck indefinitely. Going back and doing it again, and again, *and again*, is what counts. 'One-offs' are still noteworthy achievements — especially unexpected victories from unfashionable teams with low budgets (such teams tend to be unable to repeat the success, as they tend to be stripped of their prize assets by the big clubs), or those against whom adversity is mightily stacked — but to become *legendary* takes more. It was why Ferguson couldn't retire in 2002, as previously planned. He knew that whatever people's opinions on who was the greatest, the record books show:

Bob Paisley, European Cup Winner *three times in nine years.*

Alex Ferguson, Winner just *once in twenty.*

Within ten months of his arrival, Benítez had become only the second manager in 20 years to take an English club to the final of the competition that the country once believed it *owned*. Not only that, but he led Liverpool to the most unexpected of victories. It was a remarkable parallel to his first season at Valencia: taking the Spanish club to its first league title for 31 years.

A major accomplishment was the manner of the victories along the way, and the two distinct ways of playing. In most home games, Liverpool tore into the opposition. Monaco were well beaten, and Olympiakos held all the cards at half-time before the Reds swept them aside with the necessary three-goal salvo. Bayer Leverkusen were put to the sword both home and away, and Juventus could not live with Liverpool's tempo and commitment. At Stamford Bridge, Benítez' team came closest to scoring, and took the sting out of Chelsea by keeping the ball throughout the second half. But when the requirement was to keep things tight in the second leg of a tie, the Reds excelled with equal effectiveness. The amazing rearguard action at the Stadio Delle Alpi reduced Juventus to an impotent attacking force, while the return match against Chelsea, this time at Anfield, saw waves of Blues' attacks flounder on the twin rocks of Carragher and Hyypia. Last, but not least, the way the team responded to adversity in the final, to yet again score three goals in a second half. For a team labelled defensive, it was a remarkable feat against the meanest back four in the competition. There was now a tactical flexibility about the Reds that meant they could alter their approach to suit the situation.

That the run to the final came about in the face of such adversity — crippling injuries, poor refereeing decisions (in the earlier rounds), losing Owen, being unable to procure Morientes until he was cup-tied, the scandalous suspension of Xabi Alonso for the semi-final — made it all the more remarkable. The history books will not necessarily say as much (as they deal in the 'black and white' of results and not the wider context) but just making the final was one of Liverpool Football Club's greatest triumphs.

Defying expectations

In his first season, Benítez had taken Liverpool further than Arsene Wenger managed in his first nine years at Arsenal. It didn't mean Liverpool were a better side than the Gunners, especially the 1998, 2002 and 2004 vintages (oh how Liverpool fans would like a couple of league and FA Cup doubles), but it did suggest a style and approach more conducive to the continent's premier competition — or at the very least, a little more tactical flexibility. Arsenal, for all their attacking flair, were accused of having only one way of playing; that they couldn't be 'boring' (or, if you prefer, 'smart') and keep things tight when required. They also seemed to have too many hang-ups in Europe.

Wenger, speaking three days after Liverpool made the final, told of how the Champions League had become like a standard cup, which anyone could win. "The priority has to be the Premiership. If the Champions League goes well it goes well, but the Premiership has to be the most important by miles. The Champions League is too much of a surprise cup now."

It's hard to imagine him saying that should Arsenal actually *get somewhere* in the competition. The European Cup has always had 'surprise' teams in the final. It has always involved a knock-out competition, in one form or another. But it was impossible to say that Liverpool hadn't earned the right to be there in 2005. If the competition was devalued years earlier by opening it up to teams who finish 4th in their domestic leagues — from which Liverpool clearly benefited — Benítez' team at least proved worthy finalists with their performances in the competition. While there was a modicum of truth in Wenger's assessment, his statement that the Premiership was more important by "miles" was laughable, and indicative of a man under pressure in the Premiership (from Chelsea) and needing to disguise his own shortcomings in the Champions League.

Perhaps, given the changes to the competition in the last decade, there is more pressure on the *actual* champions than on those teams who qualify for the competition via the back door — and for whom it remains some kind of 'bonus'. (It is one of those strange quirks of football that Benítez' hardest task will be repeating the success when fans don't so much expect it, as demand it.) When Liverpool scraped into the Champions League for 2001/02, following its last-day win against Charlton, the club progressed, with some style, to the quarter-finals, coming within just eight minutes of a spot in the semi-finals. A year later, having amassed 80 points in the Premiership, and having qualified comfortably — and as such, suddenly being taken seriously — the subsequent Champions League campaign was a disaster: outclassed by Benítez' Valencia in both fixtures, and despite beating a poor Spartak Moscow home and away, ultimately eliminated by lowly Basle following draws at Anfield and in Switzerland.

National champions have to defend their own league title the following season — always more difficult than winning it in the first place (according to ex-players) — while concentrating on doing very well in the Champions League, which they are expected to do (if from a major European league). This intensity — and pressure — leaves the door open to mediocrity, both in terms of qualifying (and Liverpool *were* mediocre in the league in 2003/04), and in the tournament itself. While Liverpool were in no way mediocre in the Champions League (with the exception of the early away performances), they were still rank outsiders, and as with the previous season, the semi-finals contained teams not expected to progress beyond the group stages.

And so, with another inglorious, last-ditch qualification behind them (feeling nowhere near as sweet as in 2001, when it felt like winning another trophy), the club had a superb season in the Champions League. Playing brilliantly in Europe, both as an attacking force and, when required, a stout defensive unit, the club didn't have the wherewithal to repeat the intensity of their performances domestically. (Understandable, of course, given the reasons listed elsewhere in this book.) Had Liverpool also been in the title race, then it would perhaps have been to the detriment of their European campaign. What was noticeable about Arsenal's failure against Chelsea in the quarter-finals in 2004 was that the games were sandwiched in between an FA Cup clash with Manchester United, and a league game against the same rivals.

Fear of failure is the greatest barrier to success that exists in sport. If you are scared to lose, inhibition hinders your chances of winning. It is why teams often play better once they go behind in a match, especially at home: once there is nothing left to lose, they can try to *win*. However, being the underdog only works until you have an advantage in a match — and then the situation reverses (once you are leading, you often become the favourite). A gambler visiting a casino can happily bet, and lose, £100 of his own money and still leave in good spirits, without any great sense of loss. However, if he walked in and was given £1m by the manager, the express condition that he has to bet it all on ten consecutive spins of the roulette wheel, he will start to feel pressure if he is in profit on the eighth spin. If the last spin is 'all or nothing', he will feel sick inside — even though, should he lose, he will not be losing any of his own money: just the money he *could have won*. That very situation occurred in the 2005 Carling Cup final — Liverpool were clear underdogs, but after scoring a matter of seconds into the match, with Riise volleying in superbly from Morientes' pin-point cross, it was suddenly the Reds' fortune *to lose*. As a result, Liverpool, having come out of the traps flying, were suddenly nervy and uncertain; unsure (and I'm aware this is a mixed metaphor) of whether to stick or twist. A similar scenario arose against Chelsea once again, in the Champions League semi-final, but this time the Reds clung on to the 4th-minute lead Luis Garcia had given them. Once that goal had gone in, Liverpool had to play the remaining 86 minutes (plus six minutes of injury time) as the *favourites*.

Whatever the advantages regarding a lack of pressure and expectation, Liverpool's passage to the 2005 final was not easy, nor was it lucky. Along the way Benítez men overcame the finalists of 2002 (Bayer Leverkusen), the finalists of 2003 (Juventus), the finalists of 2004 (Monaco), plus two semi-finalists from 2004, Chelsea and Deportivo La Coruna, while facing the winners from 2003, AC Milan, in Istanbul. Only Olympiakos did not have serious recent form in the competition (but many of their players featured in Greece's amazing Euro 2004 success).

Group of life, September - December, 2004
Come the autumn of 2004, there wasn't much 'smart' money on Liverpool progressing to the knockout stages, especially following the dreadful display against Grazer AK in the second leg of the qualifying round. With the team virtually assured of progress, the Reds strolled through the game at Anfield with a casual, lackadaisical air, losing 1-0 in the process.

The opening match of the group stage saw Liverpool host Monaco. This time it was a thoroughly professional performance, with no shortage of style. The previous season's runners-up were dispatched with goals from Cissé and Baros, as the Reds turned on the style, winning 2-0 but unlucky to not triple that margin. Monaco's shell-shocked manager, Didier Deschamps, said: "We could not get into the game and lost out in all areas of the pitch. We were put under pressure sometimes last season in this competition, but I do not recall us being forced to defend as much as this." Luis Garcia was in sublime form, and his attacking combinations with Gerrard, Alonso, Cissé and Kewell were a delight to behold.

The second game proved the complete opposite. The Reds were lame in Greece, losing 1-0 to Olympiakos without much fight, spirit or quality. Teething trouble with the zonal marking system from dead-ball situations allowed Stoltidis to rise above Sami Hyypia in the 17th minute, and Liverpool had nothing to offer going forward. The form was rediscovered at home to Deportivo La Coruna in October, but unfortunately the Reds suffered from a combination of poor finishing, bad luck and inspired keeping from José Molina. After the match Benítez said: "I'm not happy with the result but we played very well. I was happy with the way we played and we had chances with Cissé, Baros and

Luis Garcia but the keeper Molina played very well. The result was disappointing but we deserved to win the game in my opinion. For me this is the best Liverpool have played this season against a very good team. We kept the ball well, pressed well and had many opportunities."

Fortunately the goal that proved so elusive at Anfield arrived at the Riazor two weeks later, in what was billed as a 'must win' game. This time luck was on the Reds' side, with the game settled by an own goal from Jorge Andrade, following a surging Igor Biscan run. Biscan fed John Arne Riise, whose cross would have fallen to Milan Baros had the Spanish side's defender not done his job for him.

Suddenly there was optimism on Merseyside again. But a 1-0 reverse in Monaco, courtesy of Javier Saviola's blatant use of his arm to control the ball before scoring, left elimination from the competition as the likeliest outcome. The group was still exceptionally tight, with Liverpool vying with both Olympiakos and Monaco for the top two spots going into the final round of games. Depor subsequently threw in the towel at home to Monaco, losing 5-0 (the game was as good as over by half-time), and Liverpool needed a miracle against the Greeks at Anfield, not least because the Reds were trailing 1-0 at half-time following Rivaldo's low free-kick which crept through the defensive wall. With just 45 minutes remaining, Benítez' men needed to score as many goals as they had in their previous five-and-a-half Champions League games, while keeping out any further Olympiakos attempts.

It turned out to be one of the great nights in Anfield history, and instantly voted, as is the current trend, as the 'best ever result in Europe' by the club's official website. (As will always be the case when hysteria is still reigning amongst fans, many of whom were not old enough to remember more incredible achievements, such as St Etienne — the same result, against opposition far superior to Olympiakos.) While clearly not the best — as only the passage of time can dictate such decisions — it was still right up there, along with the victory over Roma from 2002. The game hinged on Benítez' substitutions. First, his decision to send on Florent Sinama-Pongolle at half-time: within two minutes, the score was 1-1, and Liverpool had a fighting chance. Good work down the left wing resulted in Kewell pulling the ball back, and the little French forward poked home from close range. Suddenly the Greeks' half-time team talk meant nothing. Next, on came Neil Mellor with just fifteen minutes remaining, and yet again there were almost-instant dividends. The lively Sinama-Pongolle was again involved, twisting and turning on the right of the area before sending a deep cross to the back post, which Antonio Núñez headed powerfully towards goal. Nikopolidis pulled off a stunning reflex save, but Mellor was on the spot to poach another close-range finish. Belief poured down from the Kop, as the Reds stood just one goal away from crowning a famous comeback.

As remarkable as the revival had been, it appeared time was running out — fractionally too little, and arriving too late. There were just four minutes left on the clock when Jamie Carragher chipped the ball towards the area, and Neil Mellor rose to flick the ball in the vague direction of Steven Gerrard. The Liverpool captain stepped up and unleashed a fulminating drive that was, to quote the cliché, 'in from the moment it left his boot'. Nikopolidis never even saw it — he just heard the Kop erupt behind him. Minutes from elimination, the Reds were now in the draw for the knock-out stages.

After the match, Benítez said: "A game lasts 90 minutes and I knew we could do it and I told the players that at half time. We were 2-0 down at Fulham earlier this season and we came back to win 4-2. I have never experienced a result like this in the Champions League, we did something like this against Celtic at Valencia in the Uefa Cup, but this result is very special to me and the whole club. It is one of the proudest nights of my career. The players ran hard all the time and you see how much it means to the supporters, it is a great night. I felt that the difference between the sides was really our supporters, I cannot thank them enough."

Nor, it seemed, could they thank him enough in return. Despite stuttering domestically, Benítez was putting the club back on the map in European competition. The Reds would resume their Champions League campaign in the New Year, although as rank outsiders in the competition.

Chapter eleven

Shocking luck: who ran over the black cat?

It always sounds a bit tame, a little pathetic — desperate, even — when a manager finds excuses for his team's failings: blaming referees and bad luck with injuries; possibly even railing against the wrong type of grass, the size of the football, (or — perish the thought — the wrong shade of shirt). Even the alignment of the stars is not beyond reproach, with Jupiter rising in the 3rd house putting the Brazilian right-back at a distinct disadvantage when facing a Piscean winger. It sounds like sour grapes, inevitably, but there has to come a point when, as a manager, you look at what's happened, and it becomes fair to say things *have* gone against you to a quite ludicrous degree. Do you laugh, or do you cry? Staying sane would appear to be the greatest challenge. At what point is it acceptable to bemoan your luck? What if your entire squad falls ill with the bubonic plague? And if so, why would that be more acceptable as an excuse than a dozen unrelated injuries and illnesses?

To his great credit, Rafael Benítez avoided making excuses, choosing to instead extol the virtues of those still fit and able — or in the case of poor refereeing, a shrug of the shoulders and perhaps one passing comment about how the ref, while clearly making a mistake, was only human. Benítez pointed out, when the time was right, the problems he had to contend with, but never laboured the point. He had a right to ask how he could produce his best results without his best players, and when — certainly in the first half of the season — his side suffered some bizarre refereeing decisions, to say the least.

Injured souls

Are injuries down to bad luck, or bad preparation? Perhaps you can argue that more could be done to prevent muscle strains. (In some cases this is possibly true, although a perfectly fine and a thoroughly-stretched muscle isn't immune to sudden damage: witness the awkward fall of Michael Owen at home to Arsenal in 2003/04, and the over-extension of his calf muscle.)

Bolton's Sam Allardyce made a snide comment, after his side lost at Anfield in April, about Bolton working in a way that doesn't result in as many injuries; and yet he manages a side that doesn't have all the extra Champions League games to contend with. He could rest the majority of his team during international breaks, while Liverpool's were travelling all over the world playing games. As mentioned before, teams like Bolton get more opportunity to keep their players fresh. It's why big clubs need large squads for the modern game, and why Benítez' hands were tied by the lack of options: at times he was selecting from only half a squad.

If muscle strains can occasionally be avoided, the same cannot be said of freakish fractures. Three broken limbs in three-and-a-half months must be some kind of record. It is also worth pointing out that the most serious — a terrible leg break — was to the club's record signing, Djibril Cissé, and a £14.2m investment was removed from the equation in October. This came after the man regarded as the club's best player, Steven Gerrard, broke a metatarsal bone in an innocuous-looking incident at Old Trafford. The third fracture was to Xabi Alonso, the club's best passer, and the man whose responsibility it was to control the tempo of games. With four months of the season left, Rick Parry must have been double-checking all the players' insurance policies, and inviting any willing witch doctors to Anfield to remove any curses and hexes bestowed upon the club.

How can any manager be expected to deliver consistency in these circumstances?

The task Benítez faced this season was hard enough without the slings and arrows of outrageously bad fortune. Nearly all of the injuries befell Liverpool's best players, or beset 'lesser' players when they were experiencing their best run of form. Benítez could not make a new side gel without the ability to select his best players.

On top of those three fractures, there was a series of muscle problems: hamstring trouble for Baros and Luis Garcia, causing both to miss a succession of games, and Harry Kewell was in and out of the side all season with lingering calf and groin injuries, and seen less and less as the season progressed. Josemi missed games from a stomach-turning clash of heads, and then picked up another injury. Kirkland's back started causing him trouble again, not long after he'd looked to have made the goalkeeper's position his own (albeit far from convincingly, given that he was struggling to even get out of bed in the morning without experiencing excruciating pain). An operation followed, and he duly missed five months of the season — an all-too-familiar situation in Kirkland's case, but at least the operation represents hope of a permanent cure. Igor Biscan, in the best form of his Liverpool career, fell into the advertising hoardings in the Carling Cup at White Hart Lane and wasn't seen for weeks. Djimi Traoré, Steven Warnock and Fernando Morientes also missed a few games here and there. Even Anthony Le Tallec, out on loan at St Etienne, missed a couple of months at the start of the season.

Knees appeared to present the greatest problems. Within a day of his arrival in England, Antonio Núñez fell awkwardly and damaged his knee, which delayed his debut by almost four months; his compatriot, Josemi, missed five months with a knee problem. Vladimir Smicer's chances of earning a new contract were all but destroyed by missing the first six months of the season following surgery to his knee. Prior to the quarter-finals of the Champions League, Didi Hamann's knee ligaments gave out on him in the Mersey derby. Florent Sinama-Pongolle's knee injury in January, when in the best form of his Liverpool career, meant he would not be rehabilitated until the summer. Neil Mellor, finally making some headway and scorer of some crucial goals, suffered tendonitis — in both patella tendons — and as such underwent surgery on both knees at the start of March, ruling him out for the rest of the season.

The Bermuda Triangle had relocated to L4. (Although thankfully there was no accompanying Barry Manilow song.)

According to the club's doctor, Mark Waller, Liverpool experienced four times their expected meniscal tears, and three times the amount of fractures. Chondral lesions — damage to the back of the cartilage — were also three times as prevalent. All managers can accept — even expect — injuries. But for Benítez to have so many bad injuries when trying to put his stamp on the club, and to construct a coherent plan, smacked of desperate bad fortune. That the club managed two great cup runs — especially the European campaign — was testament to the manager's organisational skills, in having the ability to shuffle his pack, often at late notice. While there were notable disappointments in the league, and some dire away performances — not all of which can be excused — the season provided a valuable lesson to Benítez. He got to learn a lot about the demands of the English game, and in so doing, a lot about his entire squad, from the stars to the lowest-ranked reserves. Even the tea lady was pencilled in for the subs' bench in the Champions League at one stage.

It got to such ludicrous levels that even *dental* problems threatened to derail the Reds' Champions League campaign. Just hours before the semi-final first leg, Steven Gerrard — who wanted to be at his best to gain 'revenge' on Chelsea — had to undergo emergency surgery on an abscess. He played the game with a swollen face, and his body still recovering from the local anaesthetic, while pumped full of antibiotics, but understandably was not his usual ebullient self.

If luck is on his side, Benítez' second season as manager should be markedly more successful. If he has a fit side for most of the season, and doesn't have so many key refereeing decisions go against him, there will be far less scope for excuses; no longer in a transitional season, he will have to start delivering on the considerable promise he, and his players, offer.

"The referee is prone to bouts of onanism, the referee is prone to bouts of onanism."

Let's start with the old cliché: *Decisions even themselves out over the course of a season.*

Clearly they do not.

Such a supposition assumes that there is some cosmic fairness at work — that a higher power is overlooking the world of football, and redistributing the wealth of good fortune with the aid of his godly Equitable Scales.

Unfortunately, such a concept — also known as the Law of Averages — doesn't have to apply. Life simply isn't fair. If you flip a coin, and it's heads, the Law of Averages suggests the next flip will be tails. But the next coin flip has no memory of the preceding one; it starts again with a 50-50 chance (in other words, it doesn't say to itself *I landed heads last time, better land tails this time because the Law of Averages says so*). The previous flip has no bearing on the subsequent flip. Quite conceivably you could flip ten coins in a row and have them all land on heads.

In any given match, the referee (unless an amnesiac) has a 'memory' of the decisions he has made. He knows that if he's given an unpopular decision (and refs know when they are wrong, they just rarely admit it), he can always 'even it up' later with a generous award. Had another handball occurred in the Chelsea box on New Year's Day, you can bet Mike Riley would have been looking to give Liverpool a penalty, once Jamie Carragher and co. made the extent of his error clear to him. Referees know from the reaction of the players if they've made a monumental cock-up. The officials like to think they treat every decision on its individual merits, but we all know that what has gone before colours their judgment.

The problem Liverpool faced was different referees giving them bad decisions; so as with the flip of a coin there is no 'memory'. The first half of the season saw some quite incredible decisions go against Benítez' men: Javier Saviola's handball before scoring for Monaco (which the ref said he saw, but surreally claimed was 'ball-to-hand'); Newcastle's ten-yard offside goal; Tiago's blatant punch; Muzzy Izzet's goal-line save; Luis Garcia's 'onside' goals wrongly disallowed at Bolton and Middlesborough; the Grazer AK player, Rene Aufhauser, who was booked for the second time at Anfield with 20 minutes to go, and still not sent off; the clear foul on Gerrard in the first game of the season at Spurs, or when he was tripped by Kolo Toure at Anfield, or the blatant trip on the Liverpool captain in the Carling Cup final, where a penalty might have meant a 2-0 lead to the Reds, and possibly *game over*; Aston Villa away, where the home team equalised from a free-kick won by Gavin McCann's blatant dive (he instantly apologised to Jamie Carragher, but by then the free-kick was given); Manchester United's goals at Old Trafford coming from a corner that should have been a Liverpool goal kick, and a wrongly-awarded free-kick; Baros taken out at Bayer Leverkusen with the latest tackle the Champions League has ever seen; the booking of Alonso that ruled him out of the Champions League semi-final second leg, when Gudjohnsen dived; or Carvalho hauling back Carragher in the penalty box, in yet another penalty denied Liverpool against Chelsea; Gattuso not dismissed for his foul on Gerrard in the final. And so on.

While the occasional slightly debatable decision favoured the Reds, there was nothing close to divine retribution — the only clear-cut mistake to favour Benítez was the goal Middlesborough had chalked off in the Carling Cup tie at Anfield. Much was made of the winning goal in the Champions League semi-final, when Luis Garcia's shot was cleared off (or from over?) the line. And yet even then, the Chelsea players didn't complain as they knew they were getting off lightly: Petr Cech had fouled Baros in the lead-up to the goal, and as such, the award of a penalty and a red card from Slovakian referee Lubos Michel would certainly have followed had the advantage not fallen Liverpool's way. Michel told the *Sunday People:* "I believe Chelsea would have preferred the goal to count rather than face a penalty with just ten men for the rest of the game. If my assistant referee had not signalled a goal, I would have given a penalty and sent off goalkeeper Petr Cech." Michel added: "Roman [Slysco, the assistant referee] beeped me to signal the foul by Cech, but I didn't know that till later. It was the noise from the crowd that stopped me hearing it. I have refereed at places like Barcelona, Ibrox, Manchester United and Arsenal. But I've never in my life been involved in such an atmosphere. It was incredible. I did not need the signal from Roman, though. I had already seen the foul and played advantage. There was no doubt in Roman's mind about the goal and he was in the best position to see. I chose him to be part of our team and I trust him. He is a heart surgeon and mistaken decisions are not allowed in his job."

Most of the grievous errors listed above cost Liverpool the points in games they drew or lost. A magazine published a Premiership league table based on 'what if' the correct decisions had been made by referees. While not allowing for cause and effect that shapes the game *after* a bad decision, it was still an interesting and amusing guide to the vagaries of fortune. It had Liverpool seven points better off, and Everton three points *worse off*: a ten-point swing in Liverpool's favour. In fact, all the teams above Liverpool would have been worse off, and no team in the league could match Liverpool's misfortune with regard to refereeing decisions. Even Manchester City would have finished above Everton.

It was therefore "official" — Liverpool were the unluckiest side in the league, both in terms of injuries and in terms of decisions. However, by the end of the season much of this was forgotten or overlooked in the reviews of the campaign.

When a team like Crystal Palace can get three times as many Premiership penalties as Liverpool, something has to be wrong. No disrespect to Crystal Palace (ah heck, of course I mean *plenty* of disrespect to Palace), but Liverpool, without a shadow of doubt, will have spent more time in the opposing box, with more skillful players outfoxing defenders. (Interesting that Baros won his only two penalties *against* Crystal Palace — both clear-cut — but was still denied an obvious third in the same game.) Whereas the direct-running Englishman Andy Johnson got a penalty every time he tumbled (and set a new Premiership record for most converted penalties in a season: eleven), Milan Baros — never proven to be a diver, and one of those strikers always more concerned with scoring rather than falling over — could have been assaulted with a meat cleaver in the other 37 league fixtures and still not won a penalty. If Hannibal Lecter were in the opposition defence — mutilating and then devouring Baros — the referee would look across at his linesman and then wave play on. (Afterwards saying "I felt he clearly played the ball before eating the man.") Baros' entire style is one that invites bad tackles — running at defenders with the ball under tight control — but that still wasn't enough. The same applied to Gerrard, who occasionally fell a little theatrically, but was still denied several clear penalties. It took *two* Spurs players to simultaneously up-end him at Anfield in April before he finally won one.

Maybe Benítez was paying for the good fortune of 2000/01, when Liverpool, despite suffering some questionable decisions themselves, benefitted from some favourable refereeing, not least the penalty against Roma that miraculously became a corner kick. Benítez will be praying that whatever the reason behind the ill fortune, his luck will change.

From now on, only white cats are to be allowed near Anfield and Melwood.

Chaptertwelve

Disappointment: the Premiership campaign

Had Liverpool's league form matched two of its three cup campaigns, then it would have represented something of a miraculous season. As it was, that was clearly too much to expect — and too soon to expect it. But fans obviously hoped for better than what they ended up witnessing in the Premiership, especially away from Anfield. The final league position of 5th was nothing short of disappointing, but it still did not represent a nadir in recent times: in 1998/99, Gérard Houllier's first season (and Roy Evans' last) the Reds finished 7th, and in Graeme Souness' last (and Roy Evans' first, as he took over late in the campaign) the final position was 8th.

Why was Liverpool's league form the 'Mr Hyde' to the team's Champions League 'Dr Jekyll'? The season turned out to be a case of the Great, the Good, the Bad, the Ugly, and the Downright Dowie. (Was it true that the more hideous the opposition manager, the more ugly Liverpool's display? Certainly, performances at Crystal Palace, Birmingham, Everton and Southampton — all managed by men too ugly even for a horror movie casting call — had not been pretty on the eye, and as such, suggest a possible correlation.)

The league and the FA Cup failures upset the traditionalists. (It upset everyone, of course, but the traditionalists more so. Losing in the FA Cup still somehow leads to more hysteria than losing in Europe, despite the different value clubs now assign to those competitions.) However, the Carling Cup and the Champions League campaigns were *exceptional* in the circumstances. The kids got the club to the semi-finals of the Carling Cup, beating Millwall, Middlesbrough and Spurs, (from which point the senior players took over), while European progress came in the face of a plethora of problems for the manager: not so much selection headaches, as migraines. While the cup successes to a degree shielded Benítez from (most of) the hostile criticism managers receive, they also made people question why there were two distinct sides to his Liverpool team. The good only accentuated the bad. Had the team been knocked out of all the cups fairly early (but not *too* early) and trundled along in a plodding, methodical manner to secure 4th spot in the league, then maybe that would have pleased some people, as it would have ticked the 'minimum criteria' box and left little excitement or pleasure — or anticipation — in the process. The season was to prove more interesting than that.

The league campaign had the consistency of curdled milk — smooth and clear in parts, lumpy and unpalatable in others, not to mention hard to stomach. Inconsistency, while far from ideal, is usually par for the course in a manager's first year, unless there are exceptional circumstances. (Such as at Stamford Bridge — at any other club, the previous manager, Claudio Ranieri, would not have been sacked after taking the side to its highest point for 50 years. Chelsea seriously strengthened its staff, both on and off the field, at the point the club was already on the rise. New managers usually inherit a team that is in decline.)

There are greater problems a manager could face in his initial season, such as lacking great players — Liverpool clearly had a nucleus of top-class talent to build around — or simply being *consistently average*. To use a musical analogy, it's better to be a patchy Beatles album, with some throwaway tracks, than the most consistent effort the Stereophonics could wish to produce. While top-class talent undoubtedly still needed to be added, there was the spine of a great side there, and the best performances were scintillating. Benítez could never have been expected to produce his *Revolver* or his *Sgt Pepper's* at the first attempt — only in time. (Although perhaps the Champions League success of 2005 was his *Rubber Soul*.)

109

It was a strange kind of inconsistency, as it changed from game to game, not month to month — there were no lengthy unbeaten runs, and no periods when the club couldn't buy a win for weeks on end. It was consistent inconsistency. Gérard Houllier often commented that great teams don't lose two in a row. On that logic, you could extrapolate it to mean very good sides don't lose three in a row, and only once during 2004/05 did the team suffer three consecutive defeats. Not ideal, but at least Benítez proved able to arrest any slump before a deep rot set in; it was just not long enough until another defeat came along. The more common pattern, in all competitions, was two or three wins, followed by a draw or a couple of defeats; gentle undulations of form, when looked at on a graph, rather than a sweeping rollercoaster.

Contrast this to Newcastle United, who, under Graeme Souness, lurched from long unbeaten runs into stretches that included five or six defeats on the bounce. Such patterns are more alarming, as they involve big strides up the league table (everyone gets excited) followed by sinking like a stone, and being unable to reverse the losing trend. Whereas Liverpool always knew they'd end up in the top six, having spent most of the season there, Newcastle flirted with relegation, then the European places, and then relegation once more. They also had a new manager, and they too had a fairly expensively assembled squad (as well as an expensive, troublesome striker sent out on loan). While they could never match Liverpool in terms of history, they did share similar ambitions going into the season. The 52,000 fans they can cram into St James' Park (almost 10,000 more than at Anfield), whose presence confirm Newcastle as a 'big club', must have been despairing at their team's antics on and off the field.

Souness, despite some misfortune, also never suffered the level of injuries with which Benítez was having to cope (nor did Newcastle have to sell their top striker on the eve of the season), and yet Newcastle still ended up in the bottom half of the table, and after fairly good cup runs were dumped out of the Uefa and FA Cups by humiliating 4-1 margins — not all Souness' fault, of course, given that he was still new to the position, and the depth of the problems he inherited. However, for those who felt Liverpool erred by looking overseas to procure a top European coach, and in buying a collection of cultured continental players, here was a club managed by its second successive British manager (who knew the Premiership inside out), with a group of largely British players, suffering the almost exclusively 'British' problems of ill-discipline (not least when Craig Bellamy called his manager a liar live on TV, or when Lee Bowyer and Kieron Dyer, who had already refused to play for the club earlier in the season, stopped playing and started punching each other during the 3-0 home defeat against Aston Villa).

While Benítez had an unsuccessful first season in the league, it could have been a lot worse. But that provides scant consolation.

Not good enough
One third of the Reds' league campaign was simply not good enough. Some performances were too inept for words — nearly all of them away from home: eleven league defeats came on the road. Benítez was livid with some of the displays, and promised changes ahead of 2005/06. But he also announced that the club — from top to bottom — would be better equipped to deal with the domestic schedule. He knew that, after a year of initiation rites, he would begin the new season knowing far more about the English game.

It's hard to pinpoint what the exact problem was — if indeed it was confined to one thing — but 'tempo' seemed to be an issue. At Anfield, the pace was often intense, and — give or take the odd blip — teams have been played off the park with a fast, fluid passing game. It is the kind of form title contenders produce, and it should only get better in the coming seasons, as better players arrive (if Benítez' major purchases are anything to go by) and the team understanding — as well as the *team's understanding of what the manager wants* — becomes more pronounced. The home form compared favourably with that of Chelsea, Arsenal and Manchester United. In the Champions League, Anfield proved a fortress.

The major problem was clearly the Premiership away form. At one stage it was the away form, full-stop, but the European travels got steadily better, and proved that, given time, the manager was capable of rectifying things. It just proved easier to do in a situation he was more familiar with.

Like players, managers also need time to settle. They need to understand what is required, and get used to the idiosyncrasies of the English game, which is like no other. Football is universal in its main themes — pass, move, tackle, shoot, head, etc. — but the specifics need tweaking, honing and fine-tuning. That the manager's tactics have worked so much better in Europe tells its own story, relating to what he understands. It is the situation he knows best, but anyone who has already proved his tactical ability, in the way he has in Spain and in European competition, can *learn*. English football offers no great secrets to which only the initiated can be privy. Effective methods simply need to be discovered, through trial and error, experimentation and time. Benítez is a football obsessive, and spends hour upon hour thinking, plotting, studying and planning. In his heart he will feel that the attention to detail will start to pay off.

Teams like Bolton, Everton and Crystal Palace pose problems very different to the more tactical, sophisticated fare from *La Liga*. These teams all played some fairly decent football, but they also knew how to 'mix it', both in terms of roughing up the opposition, and in terms of getting the ball into the 'mixer'. It is hard to believe that there is someone on the continent who shares Duncan Ferguson's approach to the game, and the kind of wars he wages on central defenders.

The physical — and sometimes over-physical — nature of the English game was noted by Benítez on several occasions, but it was never a case of sour grapes, or 'how dare they?' There were times when he clearly felt his team deserved more protection from the referee, and others when he wasn't impressed with opposition tactics — but he never suggested anybody had gone so far as to be cheating or seeking an unfair advantage. It was interesting to hear him note that he was told, upon arriving in England, that he needed tough, burly players (and possibly why he signed Josemi first, who certainly fits that bill). But towards the end of the season, he felt, having witnessed the success of Alonso and Luis Garcia, that the solution was simply to be too *good*, too *skilful*, for the cloggers. Despite acknowledging that Luis Garcia needed to toughen up a little, it was also clear that the little winger had been a success in English football. It was the same at Arsenal, with Robert Pires — as 'tough' as wet tissue, he was crucial to two league titles at Highbury on account of his skill, and because he applied himself with hard work, if not hard *tackles*.

The converse is someone like Salif Diao: a great athlete, tall, strong, powerful, good in the air, able to tackle, and as such, surely perfect for English football? Well, no. A lack of any real skill on the ball meant he couldn't cut it at the top; while he is a very different kind of player to Luis Garcia, given the choice in 2002 of whose game would be more suited to the Premiership (before either had played in it), you'd have picked Diao every time.

The key is to match hard-working teams in terms of effort, and let quality win the day. Benítez will need to find a way to keep the team playing at a high tempo all season long. Rotating the players obviously plays a key part in this, as it involves fresher personnel, but it also requires a squad with depth. It also needs the reserves to understand what is required of them.

Highlights - it wasn't all doom and gloom

Sometimes a moment within a game of football takes on an other-worldly aspect — a magic, a super-realism — and the action appears to decelerate, so it feels like you are already watching a slow-motion replay as events unfold; that you have already seen into the future, and so 'real time' feels like déjà vu. One such example was the moment the ball left Neil Mellor's boot in the 92nd minute of the home match against Arsenal, and the Kop, as one, foresaw the arc of the ball's trajectory — and knew, before it had travelled more than a few yards, that it was in. The gasp was already in the air, and the collective intake of breath drew the ball into the back of the net. It was the third of three great goals in the game and, happily for Liverpool fans, the Reds' second.

Xabi Alonso's goal at the end of the first half was one of the real gems of the season: a diagonal cross-field pass by Steve Finnan, and the cushioned header by Harry Kewell into the path of Gerrard, who released a sublime 15-yard pass with the outside of his right foot, curling the ball into the chasm — created by Mellor's run across the box — on the edge of the area, where Alonso arrived to curl a powerful side-footed drive into the top corner. It was one of the best pass-and-move goals seen at Anfield since Terry McDermott finished off a stunning move — also at the Anfield Road end — in a 7-0 rout of Spurs in September 1978. It summed up everything that was good about Benítez' Liverpool. Such heights are impossible to hit game after game — moments like Alonso's goal are the high-water marks any great side would be proud of during a season — but it was exhilarating to see a move of such quality against what was, at the time, such a defensively sound unit.

Away from home, there were some highlights in amongst all the gloom. The 5-0 thrashing of West Brom was more like a shooting practice session for John Arne Riise, and wins at Charlton and Portsmouth came about from extremely good all-round displays. But the best moment away from Anfield came at Craven Cottage where, with Fulham leading 2-0 at half-time, the Reds, who had been abysmal, emerged for the second half with Xabi Alonso replacing Salif Diao (akin to *Krug Clos du Mesnil* champagne introduced in place of a £1.99 bottle of supermarket *Liebfraumilch*). For the first time since 1991, the Reds reversed an away half-time league deficit, as they put four past Fulham to no further reply — despite Josemi seeing red for a second booking with the score at 2-2. While the Reds had usually done very well away under Gérard Houllier, it was the recovery from going behind that his teams could never muster. Unfortunately, there weren't too many further highlights away from home, but at least that match proved what the team was capable of, and was used as an inspiration point for the Olympiakos game in the Champions League.

The Reds' home form was infinitely superior, in terms of consistency. The Reds found similar levels to that late-November Arsenal display on New Year's Day, at home to Chelsea, but this time only bad luck and poor refereeing denied the Reds a win. Of the major home games, only the display against Manchester United disappointed. Everton were soundly vanquished in March, in an exciting, and rather physical match which left four Reds hobbling from the pitch during the first half, the last of whom — Luis Garcia — had to play in the second half as there were no substitutions left open to Benítez. The Reds totally outclassed the Blues, but the game turned on its head with the sending off of Milan Baros for a late, high tackle. It was a little harsh on the player, if only because he'd received some brutal treatment himself — much of which went unpunished — and because Tony Hibbert's tackle on Luis Garcia in the first half was even more reckless, and yet he escaped even a caution. At least Gerrard converted that free-kick, and Luis Garcia was able to head in the second, after Nigel Martyn could only tip Fernando Morientes' dipping 35-yard volley onto the bar. A late Everton goal proved meaningless, and some pride was restored to the Red half of Merseyside.

But only temporarily.

Spanner in the works

Of course, the one inescapable factor of the season — the spanner in the works — was the form of Everton. Had Liverpool's local rivals not been flying so high, everything would have seemed a fair bit rosier in the red garden. It was typical of the luck Benítez endured in his first season: Everton finally making a fist of things, when in recent seasons — with one exception — they'd not been anywhere near the European places. Somehow Everton managed to rouse themselves from perennial strugglers to take control in the pursuit of the 4th Champions League spot. They were the pacesetters in a 10,000 metre race who fail to drop out as planned, while the favourites, realising this all too late, can do nothing to claw back the advantage. Once Liverpool failed to beat Arsenal at Highbury on May 8th, Everton were confirmed in 4th spot.

The situation on Merseyside was intensified by a lack of clarity over who would get that fourth Champions League spot. With Everton looking clear favourites in late April, it appeared Liverpool's best avenue back into the Champions League was by winning and then defending the trophy. Except, there was no provision in the Uefa rulebook for such eventualities. The Champions of Europe, it seemed, were not guaranteed entry into the Champions League, but certain 'also-rans' were. Where's the rewarding of champions there? Or was it a case of misunderstanding the mandate? The rule ran as follows:

1.03 At the request of the national association concerned, the Uefa Champions League title-holders may be entered for this competition, as an additional representative of that association, if they have not qualified for the Uefa Champions League via the top domestic league championship. If, in such a case, the title-holders come from an association entitled to enter four teams for the Uefa Champions League, the 4th-placed club in the top domestic league championship has to be entered for the Uefa Cup.

That rule states that 4th place was never guaranteed entry into the Champions League. Such beliefs were merely assumed. The frequent talk, in the media and from those connected to Everton, tended to consist of "the rules can't be changed half-way through the season", but the rule was never set in stone. It was open to interpretation, and the decision was ultimately left to the national FA to decide. The English FA had an unequivocal statement on its website, in a news article dating back to the previous season, in which it stated that in such a situation, the 4th place team would be entered for the Uefa Cup. As soon as this was discovered by the media, the news item suddenly vanished from cyberspace.

The debate raged on, with conflicting views emerging from the Uefa hierarchy, and the suggestion of a possible fifth place. Benítez said: "Common sense says that if you win a trophy next year you need to defend this trophy." Everton chief executive Keith Wyness countered: "It's also common sense that the domestic league, which is 38 games as opposed to a cup competition which probably is about 16 or 17 games, should also take priority. [He ignored the fact, rather conveniently, that the cream of Europe contested this 'cup'.] I understand the thought that the cup winners want to defend their trophy but nevertheless I do believe that the domestic league is the cornerstone of football." So league mediocrity should take precedence over league mediocrity *combined* with European brilliance? Even Howard Kendall was wheeled out from cold storage, to moan and gripe about 1985, Heysel, and the banning of English teams from Europe. "I coulda been a contender", he apparently came close to mumbling.

Liverpool found allies all across Europe. Milan director Umberto Gandini believed that Liverpool would deserve a place in next year's tournament if they were successful in Istanbul claiming it would be "unthinkable" for the winners to be denied the opportunity to defend their trophy. "It must be paramount for the title holder to be in," said Gandini. "They will have won the right to defend their title on the pitch. If it happened in Italy, the fourth-placed team would go to the Uefa Cup, it's very simple." Indeed, the Spanish FA were faced with the same dilemma in 2000, and opted to allow European Cup holders Real Madrid — who finished fifth in the Primera Liga — to defend their title and entered 4th-placed Real Zaragoza in the Uefa Cup, without much fuss or hysteria. At times Uefa seemed to be pushing the English FA towards Everton, especially when a spokesman claimed 4th spot in a domestic league was more worthy. The precedent, however, lay in Spain.

Martin Samuel, writing in the *Sunday Express* in May, said Liverpool weren't even the best team on Merseyside. This is a form of logic that is really hard to understand. Over the course of a league season, Everton finished marginally higher — a mere three points, having won one more game. No one can argue with that fact. Meanwhile, in the Carling Cup, Liverpool progressed to the final — a notable achievement, but of course not one the Reds would crow about, given that it is still seen as 'small beer' for a club as big as Liverpool. The key factor to the season is that Liverpool also produced a truly remarkable run in the Champions League. How do those three points elevate Everton (who finished with a negative goal difference!) above Liverpool in terms of *all-round* quality — as a team — for the season across all competitions? After all, if you are a better team, it doesn't just apply to the Premiership. The Carling Cup is fairly meaningless in comparison to the league — that is well understood. But the European Cup is not, and it's laughable to suggest otherwise. Could Everton have beaten Monaco, Deportivo La Coruna, Bayer Leverkusen, Juventus, Chelsea and AC Milan? And could they have done so without it affecting their league form?

While it was a great achievement for the Blues, you'd have thought they had won the league given their reaction; however well they feel they did, they still only came 4th, 34 points behind Chelsea. David Moyes, speaking two weeks before the Champions League final, said: "There's no denying Everton are the best team in the city this season."

It is hard to tally with the facts. What next? Birmingham claiming to have proven they were a better side that the Reds by beating them both home and away? While Everton may have had the better season *comparatively*, when held up against their expectations, Moyes was saying that being Champions of Europe (should Liverpool go on to succeed in Istanbul) counts for less than a small points difference in the Premiership. How bizarre is that? Everton clearly deserved to finish above the Reds — but why were they so excited about getting into the Champions League? Wasn't it to dream of making it to the final, possibly even winning it? How could 4th place domestically be elevated above the possibility of lifting the most important trophy in club football? Surely 4th place + nothing in Europe = less than 5th place + Champions of Europe? It's a simple sum.

No one was saying Liverpool were not the best team in Europe in 1981 when the club won the European Cup, but only finished 5th in the league (in a season when they also made the League Cup final, winning it for the first time). The concept that they wouldn't have been able to defend their title in deference to West Bromwich Albion, who finished 4th in the old First Division, would have been met not so much with derision, as with the arrival of straitjackets.

Unlike 1981 however, this was only the start of a project. Winning the Champions League wouldn't provide conclusive proof that Liverpool were the best team in the Europe — they would have needed to ally this to some form of domestic domination, or repeat the feat in subsequent Champions League campaigns — but it would have meant that they were the best team in European competition that season, and that, as such, was an achievement far more deserving of a return invitation.

An unlikely story

Everton had a number of things working in their favour in the race for 4th. They found unity in the sale of a star player — which should of course have been poor fortune — when everyone was anticipating collapse. Not exactly a stroke of luck, but it stopped one player overshadowing the club, and focused minds; Everton no longer had to suffer the kind of nauseating speculation that surrounded Steven Gerrard week in, week out, and disrupted Liverpool's preparations to many games. Losing Rooney lifted a weight from the rest of the squad. Unlike Gerrard, Rooney was never particularly effective at club level — clearly a great talent, he made only fleeting impressions. (It was actually the departure of unglamorous midfield enforcer Thomas Gravesen that would affect Everton's form.)

Low expectations helped Everton's cause, as did David Moyes' ability to work with the same squad he had the season before; a squad which lacked an abundance of ability and numbers, but contained the commodity of understanding. They were not beset by serious injuries. The manager was in the third year of his reign, and therefore at his most potent: he had a well-oiled machine that reeked of effectiveness, if often lacking real style. They worked hard, and ground out a series of 1-0 wins in games that could have gone either way.

It comes back to the issue of how gruelling the season is. Making no impression in either domestic cup competition, Everton had plenty of time on the training ground to prepare for league games. Teams who set out to negate the opposition — as is their right — can always make more use of the extra preparation time. It becomes a 'leveller'. And without European competition, there were none of the extra games and gruelling travel schedules that other teams faced. The Champions League is a big drain on a club's energy. Even the teams in the Uefa Cup saw their league form severely disrupted. Middlesborough were many people's outsiders for a Champions League spot, having invested shrewdly in the summer of 2004, and given they were entering the campaign on the back of winning the League Cup. But trips back from Europe meant that their league form following every game on the continent was severely disappointing — only improving again once they were eliminated from the competition, from which point they moved up the table again. Bolton manager, Sam Allardyce, attributed much of his team's success against the top sides to facing them on the back of a midweek European game. George Burley, the former Ipswich manager, uttered a cautionary tale: bringing to mind the Tractor Boys' relegation the season they competed in the Uefa Cup — having finished 5th the previous season. He told of how his team could not cope with the extra games, and they only played six times in the competition. Teams who don't compete in Europe have it easier domestically.

A league is intrinsically *fair* — a meritocracy — once everyone has played each other home and away, but it doesn't take into account all the other issues surrounding a club *outside* its league campaign. The Reds ended up playing 23 cup games, only two less than in 2001 (when, for the first time in its history, the club contested every game possible in a season on their way to Treble success). The difference then was a manager who had been established in the job for three years, and as such had assembled his own large squad, and who never had his hands tied by having to regularly pick a team without its best players. If Everton won the marathon — and as we all know, a league is a marathon, not a sprint — then it was because Liverpool were running two simultaneous long-distance races. (Liverpool's Champions League campaign amounted to 15 games — just over a third of the amount in the Premiership — but involved playing superior opposition, and travelling far greater distances. The second half of the season also involved two Carling Cup semi-finals, and the final which went into extra-time at the Millennium stadium.)

Over the course of 2004/05, Bolton and Everton played significantly fewer games than Liverpool: 17 and 16, respectively. Add internationals (given many of the players at those two clubs had never represented their countries and were unlikely to do so, or were no longer considered for international duty) and that was another six or seven games for Liverpool's first team and a number of its reserves.

Of course, the largest clubs have big squads in order to deal with such circumstances, and if a club has the 'best' players then it must accept it will lose them on international duty. But that's the problem Benítez encountered: he effectively only had *half* a squad. While he would have wanted all the additional games, he would also have wanted the resources to deal with them. He didn't have the depth of squad usually associated with big clubs, due to unforeseen circumstances.

First of all, he offloaded a lot of the 'dead wood' and problem players on loan deals (Bruno Cheyrou, Salif Diao, Gregory Vignal and 'bad boy' El Hadji Diouf), as no club was willing to pay the asking price for permanent deals. Trimming the excess from the squad was wise, and none of those let go — with the exception of the troublesome Diouf — could have offered much to Benítez on the pitch. These were Gérard Houllier's 'mistakes', and their presence when Benítez arrived disguised a lack of true depth to the squad. There were plenty of bodies, but a fair few were not good enough to be at the club.

Second, Michael Owen and Emile Heskey were effectively on their way out before Benítez arrived — Heskey was already sold, with Cissé due to replace him, and Owen had yet to commit his future to the club. Meanwhile, Danny Murphy was deemed by Benítez to be a mere squad player — a fair decision, retrospectively, given the impact of his replacement Luis Garcia (who would have arrived regardless of what happened with Murphy). Murphy, while he would have provided experience and versatility as cover, preferred first-team football — he wasn't forced to leave Liverpool, but he was told his chances would be limited, and so he opted instead to move to Charlton. It's fair to say he would have helped plug some of the unexpected gaps during the season, and that maybe his chances would have been less limited than either he or the manager envisaged. The same can be said of Heskey: while his time as a first choice was rightly up — given his overall underachievement — it transpired (with the aid of hindsight) that the manager could have used the player given the injuries to his strikeforce (unless, of course, Heskey stayed and got injured too). His strength and power may also have helped in some of the more British-style games, especially away from home, and provided a temporary physical buffer as the club changed its style of play. Everton had a lot of success throwing on Duncan Ferguson late in games to make a nuisance of himself, and it's role Heskey could have played, albeit in a more muscular, less aerial manner. (Whether he would have wanted to stay as a reserve is another matter, but he did love the club.) Heskey was often at his best for Liverpool as a sub, and his style was different to anything Benítez had to call upon, and as such, handy, if only as a last resort. While Murphy and Heskey had no long-term future at Anfield, their presence may have helped for 12 months, during the difficult transition the club suffered in the league.

(Benítez will benefit, in the long-term, from the time his new overseas players spent acclimatising to the Premiership, even if on occasions they patently struggled. Time playing in the English league was 'experience' they wouldn't have garnered as much of had Murphy and Heskey been kept, and deployed more than sparingly. If fans accept that the club needed a radical change of direction — from predominantly 'long ball' to a pass-and-move style — then they must also accept the difficulties of a transition. If they don't accept that, then the alternative was keeping decent English players who needed no introduction to the vagaries of the British game, but who were never going to take the team forward while regular first team starters. There is an eternal pressure on Liverpool to do well both domestically and in Europe, and as such, the club needs to possess 'international' players. As a result, everyone has to accept a period of adaptation.)

Add to these Anthony Le Tallec and Alou Diarra, who were on long-term loan deals — not to get them off the wage bill, but as part of their education — and the manager's options were limited yet further. Le Tallec, who had asked to leave on loan in a fit of pique at being fifth choice, was called back at the first opportunity of both Liverpool and St Etienne agreeing to it, and that was the winter transfer window. Little did Le Tallec or Benítez know, that within two months of going on loan, Liverpool would have lost Owen to Real Madrid, and Cissé to a Lancashire hospital.

Third, an unprecedented amount of injuries decimated his options. Any team would struggle without its best players, especially when they are missing *simultaneously*; something that often gets overlooked with the 'the squad should cope' argument. No club can have reserves as good as its first team — after all, no other team in the world has a player like Thierry Henry, so how could a team like Arsenal have one sat in its reserves? It's the same with Gerrard and Alonso at Liverpool. You could argue that the Liverpool squad wasn't good enough to deal with the absences, but at times — certainly up front — the manager simply ran out of fit bodies. At one point he even joked about dusting down his boots.

It has been widely noted that Chelsea coped well without Arjen Robben for large chunks of the season (although in his absence they often appeared to lack inspiration, tending to merely 'scrape' victories, as they had done before he made his belated debut). Elsewhere, Didier Drogba's absence for a couple of months in the autumn proved in no way catastrophic. Otherwise their serious injuries were to full-backs (and no full-back, no matter how good, makes the difference between winning or losing a title), and to midfielder Scott Parker, who was not even close to the first team at the time. If you look at Chelsea's best players — the only four awarded 10 out of 10 by The *Observer* newspaper for their contribution to the title success — it is noticeable that they never had to deal with the loss of Frank Lampard, John Terry, Petr Cech and the often criminally underrated Claude Makelele, described by the Chelsea staff as their most important player.

Had the injuries instead occurred to those players, it is highly likely they would have struggled to win the league. Would Robert Huth have adequately deputised for Terry for several months? Would Tiago have filled the void of Lampard, or Alexei Smertin that of Makelele, for lengthy periods? Even with a squad as strong and formidable as Chelsea's, and as expensively assembled, there were certain players they could not afford to be without. Liverpool's injuries, centre-back excluded, were to players at the heart — the spine — of the side: central midfielders, centre forwards, and in the case of Chris Kirkland, first-choice 'keeper (as he had become).

While it's impossible to say precisely how much effect this had on the league results, it's clear that it must have had *some*. Most missed was Xabi Alonso, who managed to start just half of the league games, due to the broken ankle sustained just as he was fast becoming the team's key player. Given so many of Liverpool's defeats were by a single goal — and no one beat the Reds by more than two goals all season — it is abundantly clear that the margin between success and failure was often tight. Even if a team doesn't play well, it needs to be able to win games — doing that very thing is apparently the sign of a good side. (When poor sides play poorly and win, they are 'lucky'; when good sides do so, they are 'great'.) And it is the best players who tend to prove capable of creating such moments: a sublime pass, or a goal out of nothing. Most of Liverpool's injuries occurred to its magicians: the players there to 'pull something out of the hat': Gerrard, Cissé, Alonso, Luis Garcia, Baros, Sinama-Pongolle, Kewell, and even Mellor, who had scored some crucial goals in big games. As well as Carragher and co. played, if they conceded one goal away from home — no disaster in itself — there was a shortage of fit 'special' players to turn the game around.

Benítez' rotation policy, which worked so well in Spain, had yet to reap dividends in England. It hadn't helped that the players he was rotating 'out' were often replaced by men who would otherwise be the manager's third or fourth choices. He was like a dealer shuffling his pack, only to discover half the cards were missing. If a player needed resting, then it meant throwing in someone who was perhaps not up to, or not suited to the task. At Valencia there was also a core of players who were so important they played almost every game for Benítez; at Liverpool, Jamie Carragher was one, but Xabi Alonso and Steven Gerrard — two of the players most affected by injury — would surely have fitted into that category. Rotation, in moderation (in other words, not Claudio Ranieiri's notorious "Tinkerman" tactics at Chelsea, where he made eight or nine changes from game to game), can help keep a team fresh. Too many changes and consistency suffers. For Benítez, Lady Luck was doing some heavy rotating on his behalf.

The Premiership proved a tough lesson for Benítez, but no one learns much from an easy education. The forewarning of 2004/05 will be the forearming of 2005/06.

Chapter thirteen

Home improvements

If Gérard Houllier's failings as a tactician, and the shortcomings of his style of football were underlined by the arrival of Rafael Benítez, then at least the Spaniard partially restored his predecessor's reputation in the transfer market. Players previously thought to be duds soon looked anything from half-decent to downright sensational. In some cases, this may have been luck, or good timing: Steve Finnan, for instance, had suffered injuries during his first season at Liverpool, and there was always the likelihood that he, like many other players at clubs all around the country, would settle into fine form after the upheaval and difficulties of a debut season, where trying too hard can be as lethal as not trying hard enough.

Other improvements were less easy to explain. Djimi Traoré, while never inspiring *complete* confidence (and never will, with his gangling style), improved beyond all recognition at left back; an error, you still sensed, was only one touch of the ball away, but only the atrocious piece of defending which cost the Burnley FA Cup tie stands out. His reading of the game still left a little to be desired at times, but the great pace, allied to the best recovery tackle in the game (courtesy of those telescopic legs), meant even when he was caught dozing he could still get back to make amends. Some of his last-ditch tackles were truly stunning.

Traoré, close to joining Everton for £1.5m in the summer of 2004, was kept on by Benítez as the player had been injured throughout the pre-season, and he wanted to get a good look at him. Whether or not he turns out to be the long-term solution at left-back remains to be seen, with John Arne Riise an option, and the emerging Stephen Warnock — another to make an impression under Benítez — likely to improve yet further in the coming seasons. Each has a doubt of one kind or another hanging over him (Riise's defending, Warnock's inexperience, Traoré's tendency to err) while also possessing several benefits. Maybe an entirely new player will secure the berth, but at least Benítez has options.

Eeeee-*gor*

Another whose days at Anfield looked distinctly numbered, but who received an unexpected stay of execution, was Igor Biscan. Told by Benítez that he was free to leave in the winter transfer window, Igor opted to stay, rebuffing Southampton in the process. He vowed to fight for his place, which he duly won following a succession of injuries; and did so well he then won the offer of a new one-year contract extension. "In that situation," Biscan claimed, discussing the moment Benítez broke the news of being released, "you need to think about your future but I never thought about leaving. Even though I wasn't guaranteed first team chances, I didn't want to go. I wanted to stay until the end of the season to do my best if games did come along for me."

If every club needs a talisman, an enigma, as well as a cruelly underrated player, then it also requires its cult hero — not good enough to be a hero *outright*, but to whom fans can but warm. There can be no doubt that Igor Biscan became that man at Liverpool: arriving for a large fee and, over the course of five years at the club, spanning the sublime and the ridiculous, the composed and the comical; as likely to drift past three opponents on a mazy run as trip over the ball. His elevation to cult status came about due to a number of factors: the dozy just-awake expression and its associated sleep-ruffled hair; the easy chant of "Eee-*gor*, Eee-*gor*" which arose on his debut at home to Ipswich — and which he instantly applauded, and would applaud for the next five years; culminating with the full-frontal photos — usually a public offence order — as Everton's Lee Carsley, pulling the big Croatian's shorts in an effort to dispossess him in March 2005, exposed more than any shortcomings in Biscan's game. The expression "big tackle", previously reserved for Steven Gerrard, was momentarily Igor's.

Igor was one of many players who found new levels of form and consistency under Rafael Benítez' tutelage. He turned in a sublime performance in helping the kids overcome Millwall 3-0 at the New Den (a deceptively tough game, in a very hostile atmosphere), and then proved he could do it a higher level when, in Spain, he topped an imperious display against Deportivo La Coruna with the storming run that led to the winning goal. He repeated the feat against Bayer Leverkusen at Anfield, jinking through the German midfield before delivering an inch-perfect pass for Luis Garcia, who put the Reds 1-0 up with a sweet finish. In fact, in the space of five months he trebled his Liverpool goal tally of five years — admittedly from just one to all of three — with a fine strike against Fulham at Craven Cottage (one that he greeted with an apparent bemusement which only served to further his cult status), and the match-winning late header against Bolton. The confidence flowing, he was shooting from anywhere, and finally looking far more like the complete midfielder, rather than the complete buffoon. He began to show that he *really was* worth £5.5m (or at least in the region), and that a previous club manager in Croatia, Ossie Ardiles, hadn't taken irrevocable leave of his senses when comparing the player's style to that of Ruud Gullit (even if there remains a gulf in terms of talent which Igor can surely never bridge).

It's clear that Igor falls behind Steven Gerrard and Xabi Alonso in terms of quality, and doesn't possess the canniness and experience of Didi Hamann, but it appeared he could give the German a run for his money, given his extra pace, surprising skill on the ball, and ability to thread a clever pass. He may opt to leave in the summer, as offers from decent clubs won't be thin on the ground. But the Liverpool squad would be a weaker place without his presence.

Meeee-*Lan*

It's hard to argue that the money Gérard Houllier spent on Milan Baros was anything other than a shrewd investment. While doubts remain as to just how good he is, and whether or not he offers the quality needed to push for the title, he has still been a valuable player to the club in the last three seasons — the first two as a bit-part player, and most recently as its figurehead striker. If ever sold — and the rumour-mill suggests he will be sooner rather than later — the club will surely recoup far more than that £3.2m outlay.

It's fair to say that the last two years of Baros' career have oscillated between the polar extremes. Finally having ousted Emile Heskey from the starting line-up at the start of 2003/04, and having partnered Michael Owen in a 3-0 demolition of Everton at Goodison Park (where Baros was superb), Milan was only one game away from a freak collision with Blackburn's on-loan Liverpool defender, Markus Babbel. His ankle broken, Baros would not play again until 2004. Upon his return to the side, he scored a wonder goal at Elland Road in the 2-2 draw with Leeds, but was soon frustrated by a lack of regular games, failing to score during several bit-part appearances, and he later admitted he had been close to calling it quits before Houllier was sacked.

Fit and fresh, but lacking the competitive edge regular football brings, he went to Euro 2004 with a point to prove. He came away with the Golden Boot — following five well-taken goals, all from open play. Suddenly he was on top of the world — or the top of Europe, at least. Rumours surfaced about interest from Barcelona, and the player stated that it had always been his dream to play for the Catalan side, without going as far as to suggest he was angling for a move. He started 2004/05 in similar vein to previous seasons at Liverpool: the occasional goal, lots of hard running, but still failing to play like he did in a Czech shirt. Then it all clicked into place, and in the autumn and early winter he raced ahead of the competition to join Thierry Henry at the top of the goalscoring charts. He finally looked the player who has scored a staggering 25 goals in just 35 internationals. Like all top strikers, Baros can look a shadow of his usual self when his confidence is low, but he is clearly a natural striker, in that he has the correct instinct: never afraid to shoot when half a chance presents itself. When on form, he can look devastating, and while much improved, it is his consistency which provides the main problem.

Just as 2004 was proving to be Baros' year, he sustained a hamstring strain while on duty with the Czech Republic, three days after his first Premiership hat-trick, against Crystal Palace. His rhythm was broken by weeks on the sidelines, followed by games when not fully fit, followed by further spells on the sidelines as the injury flared up again. What was looking like being a great season for the striker turned into more disappointment, and having been well on course for 20-25 goals, got stuck in the early teens. His stop-start Liverpool career was stopping at starting once again, like a car with an eternally faulty idle control valve.

Baros retains more than his fair share of critics, most notably because he's not as good as Michael Owen, the man he effectively replaced. (Who himself had more than his fair share of disparagers.) The main gripe with Baros remains his 'head down' approach, and there's no denying how frustrating he can be when the blinkers are on. But at the same time, it's all part of his desire to take the ball and head upfield with it — never the worst crime in a striker who excels at running fast with the ball under tight control, and who can turn people inside out. He puts defenders on the backfoot. He has a wonderful knack of going past people in incredibly tight spaces — his goal against Monaco seemed to involve him passing *through* the French defender. He goes around defenders by almost edging into them and burrowing his way past. Hugely positive in everything he attempts, awareness of his teammates, however, is not his strong suit: in that respect he is more Ronny Rosenthal than Kenny Dalglish. While no one has ever come close to matching the sublime vision of the latter, Baros is clearly a far better player than the former, with the amount of ground he covers in a match closer to Ian Rush at his peak.

The arrival of Fernando Morientes casts some doubt over Baros' role in the side. The two failed to strike up a convincing partnership, although their different styles should have complemented one another — in theory at least. But Baros is clearly a difficult player to partner, as he's so intent on going it alone, not to mention spontaneous and off-the-cuff. Benítez often opts for 4-2-3-1, and Morientes would get the nod on most occasions. If opting for two strikers, the second berth could well be taken by Djibril Cissé, whose awesome pace is a very potent weapon. Florent Sinama-Pongolle is another whose extra speed would be perfect alongside Morientes — the young Frenchman was coming on in leaps and bounds before his season was ended by knee ligament damage. Of course, there could be new additions to the front-line over the summer of 2005: names as diverse as Raúl and Peter Crouch have been mentioned.

The second half of the season proved a barren time in terms of scoring for the Czech, but his contribution to key goals in the Champions League cannot be overlooked: the persistence that led to Petr Cech fouling him against Chelsea, when Luis Garcia followed up to score, and in the final, the sublime flicked pass to Gerrard that resulted in the penalty, which Xabi Alonso converted at the second attempt.

At 23, Baros is still young enough to learn, and to continue improving, but this summer, with just two years left on his contract, might be the right time for the club to cash in. While it could be argued that Liverpool could do better than Baros, given his flaws, it is equally true that the club could do a lot worse.

John Arne Riise

For a while, there was a distinct pattern. Liverpool would win a free kick on the edge of their opponent's area, and the cry would go up from the Kop: "*John Arne Riise... I wanna know how you scored that goal*". Television commentators would speak in hushed tones, reverential of a great free-kick exponent at work, mentioning his ability to score from dead-ball situations. And then the cuprous-haired Norwegian would stride forward and, with ferocious venom and eyes closed, strike the ball as fiercely as a cannonball and as straight as a die — right into the wall. His accuracy was amazing — assuming, of course, that he was *aiming* at the defenders stood with hands cupped over their family jewels. (Maybe "Hit the Wall" was a popular Norwegian fairground challenge?)

In the three years Riise played under Houllier he scored only one free-kick for his manager. *That* free-kick, which seared past Fabian Barthez like an Exocet. Truly one of the greatest free-kicks Anfield has ever seen. You hear comments about a shot leaving the ground if the net hadn't been there to stop it; that shot would have left Liverpool.

And that was it. It seems an apt metaphor for his career at Liverpool, pre-Benítez. Lots of flattering to deceive, in amidst some very effective moments, but a player whose apparent lack of subtlety left him looking doomed once the Spaniard enforced a much-needed change of style, and had his players getting the ball down and passing it, rather than aiming to put snow on it. The leather-lunged, long-ball-lashing Riise was all energy and directness — too often of the headless chicken variety — and Benítez would surely look to aesthetes, magicians, and artistes to take the team further.

Riise's one hope appeared to be left-back, where — if he could learn to read the game a bit better — many felt he could yet flourish. But a remarkable transformation took place. Riise was pushed into midfield in Harry Kewell's prolonged absence, and, over the winter months especially, put in some storming performances. He added subtlety to his game, and an ability to slip seamlessly into the pass and move groove. Benítez, knowing a good thing when he saw one, ordered that Riise adopt a shoot-on-sight policy. Sometimes there's nothing quite as effective as giving the ball a good belting from 30 yards. The game against West Brom at the Hawthorns included one of the greatest displays of power shooting these shores have seen: eight fulminating drives, two of which resulted in goals, with the other six coming desperately close.

Riise's fitness and durability remain his main strengths, but are now allied to a more balanced, thoughtful approach. He has played 200 games for the Reds, in just four seasons. That kind of reliability and endurance make him a valuable commodity in today's frenetic game.

The transformation from long-ball merchant to all-round talent was completed — symbolically, at least — in the home tie with Bayer Leverkusen: instead of trying to decimate the wall like a cannon taking out a fort's defences brick by brick, he opted to curl a relatively gentle but joyously accurate shot *over* it (who'd have thought?), and into the back of the net.

(Even more surreal, in the same game Didi Hamann later did the same thing: and he had spent *five years* under Houllier blindly belting the ball from free-kicks.)

But Riise was not the most-improved player during Benítez' debut season: it was true that he added elements to his game, but his first two seasons at the club showed too much promise to make his success too much of a surprise, and his goal tally was in keeping with his early days at Liverpool.

The award of most-improved player goes to . . .

Elsewhere, Neil Mellor, after a far from promising start under Benítez, finally began to transfer some of his reserve-side form into the first team. However, he was fortunate that injuries to Cissé and Baros, and the sale of Owen, meant Liverpool were suddenly short of strikers, thus allowing him a chance he might not have got in other circumstances. The other striker to benefit was Florent Sinama-Pongolle, who, again after a shaky start under the new regime, emerged as a player of real quality, flair and devastating pace. Having only just turned 20 at the start of the season, and having already shown moments of class in his debut season, there was every chance 'Flo' was maturing in a way he would have under any manager.

Jamie Carragher, of course, was much improved. However, he was in a new role at centre-back, which, given his maturity may have now suited him more — and let's face it, he was pretty good to start with, not to mention unerringly consistent.

Which leaves the most improved player — on previous Liverpool performances — as Steve Finnan. As stated earlier, there may have been some perfectly plausible reasons for him finally discovering his true form — the form that once made Alex Ferguson table a bid, and that led Finnan to be voted by his peers as the best right back in the Premiership in the PFA XI of 2002 — the fact remains that he was a player transformed from his debut season. At worst he was merely good and reliably consistent; at best, he was superb: a two-footed attacking full-back who also would keep players like Thierry Henry and Damien Duff tucked up in his pocket. There was a worrying tendency earlier in the season for Benítez to opt for Josemi, who, after a fairly good start, began to look utterly dreadful; as a result, Finnan was either left out entirely, or played at right midfield, where he performed admirably, if not exceptionally. Benítez obviously rates his fellow countryman, but when Josemi missed several months with injury, Finnan really showed his worth and, you would think, cemented his place.

Chapter**fourteen**

Kewell, the enduring disappointment

A football club would not be complete without its enigma. Every side has its *if only* player — the man who has the talent, but somehow can't manage to translate it into consistent performances. With Emile Heskey moved on to Birmingham, and Vladimir Smicer nearing the end of his contract, Harry Kewell without doubt became that man. Fortunately for the Australian, Benítez had been a big fan from the player's time at Leeds, and he knew he was a special talent. (He spoke very effusively of the time, in 1999, when Kewell, playing as the lone striker at Old Trafford, ran Jaap Stam ragged.) If the manager's patience was tested to breaking point over the course of 2004/05, given Kewell's range of injury problems, at least Benítez knew the benefit of a *fit* Harry Kewell. It's always better for a manager to try and find the solution to getting the best out of an outstanding talent than to dismiss him too quickly, as special players are not easy to come by — there is no conveyor belt. But at the same time, you cannot give the benefit of the doubt on an indefinite basis, and just as Gérard Houllier's proclamations that Emile Heskey "just needs to believe in himself" started to wear thin after three years of the player's deep-rooted lack of self-belief, then so too will the make-or-break time arrive for Kewell.

First of all, it was rightly seen as a major coup when Houllier fought off competition from Alex Ferguson and Arsene Wenger — which speaks of Kewell's quality — after the player announced he would be leaving Leeds. It was a controversial move, in the sense that Kewell's agent, Bernie Mandric, appeared to take an improbably large cut of the transfer money, as did the player himself, at a time when Leeds — seriously in debt — needed all the money they could get. As with Michael Owen a year later, Kewell was about to enter the last year of his deal, so the fee itself — reported to be £5m — was far lower than Leeds would have liked, especially as Kewell was spoken of in the £25m bracket a few years earlier. But Mandric maintained that he was asked by Leeds to find a new club for Kewell, in return for a larger than usual cut of the deal. Whatever the true facts behind the rancorous deal, the publicity did Kewell no favours at all. Leeds fans cited Alan Smith as an example of a player who would "live and die for the Leeds' shirt", and a year later they chair-lifted their local hero around the Elland Road pitch when they were relegated. (Smith promptly left to join Leeds' most-hated rivals, Manchester United.)

It all started so well for Harry Kewell at Anfield. A Liverpool fan as a boy, he had finally *arrived*. The goals flowed, as he raced towards double figures for the first half of the season, and looked like the bargain of the millennium. But then he got injured before Christmas, and never recovered his full form or fitness. He was on high wages, and didn't appear to be earning his weekly pay packet.

His second season, now under the stewardship of Benítez, saw him paired with his fifth manager in just two years, and asked to perform in yet more different styles and positions. His early season form wasn't too bad, although that didn't stop criticism from fans who'd lost patience after a poor second half to the previous campaign: his cards were marked, and nothing less than exceptional form would be tolerated. Kewell was playing his part in the improved pass-and-move style the side was displaying, and it is worth noting that he remains a very intelligent passer even when not dancing past opponents on the wing: capable of a quick give-and-go, or a perfectly-weighted 'killer ball'. In tight spaces he wasn't beguiling opponents with tricks or pace, but he was still finding teammates with the ball. But then came more injury problems, and his form dipped so disastrously it became truly painful to watch. He was visibly struggling to do *anything* right.

He was caught in the awkward position of being unfit, and hampered by injury, but not so unfit as to not be considered for selection. A succession of niggling injuries impaired his performances, and in some ways — as bizarre as it sounds — he'd probably have been better off with a broken leg. If that sounds perverse, consider this: he'd have seen his reputation grow in absentia, as everyone pined for his return, while his crutches and plaster cast made it clear he was in no way fit to be considered for selection (something that is not so evident with 'invisible' muscle injuries).

Benítez, lacking options throughout his team due to a crippling injury list, was forced to call on Kewell when the Australian wasn't even close to match fitness, in the hope — more than the belief — that the wing wizard could pull a rabbit out of a hat. The wizardry wasn't there — all Kewell could conjure in the winter months was a selection of turkeys in time for Christmas. Finally he started to find some form in the new year, but then injury struck again, and his season was all but over.

In March 2005, Benítez explained his reasoning for persevering with a player so patently lacking sharpness and confidence: "Harry knows our ideas. He's not 100% but when you talk about good players sometimes 80% is enough. Sixty per cent of Harry is a good player, 100% a fantastic player. He is still in pain, we know that, but we have been talking with the doctor and he knows he will have to play with the pain. With pain some players play better and others find it more difficult. His main problem is with his groin but he suffered a different problem in Cardiff, he took a kick on the ankle."

Kewell had been playing games in discomfort, in an effort to help the team, but only suffered personally as a result, by further damaging both his reputation and his body. Interference from the Australian national team didn't help, with their insistence that he travel halfway around the world to play for them when he would be better served resting. Holland-based physiotherpist Andre van Alphen, who had treated Kewell, believed recuperation to be the best cure. "My opinion is for a good treatment period so the body gets time to heal and recuperate," Van Alphen said. "This will take about three months to full fitness. It is impossible to recover while playing football."

Liverpool almost certainly concurred — feeling that once 2004/05 ended, rest could take place during the three months of the close season. In the meantime, injuries to other players — who could not be hurried back — meant Kewell was needed whenever, as Benítez stated, he was just 60% fit. Only when the problem got too severe was Kewell removed from the first team picture.

The whole injury saga was not helped when Benítez was misquoted — or rather, *misinterpreted* — in the press, maybe as a result of his developing fluency in the English language. (While he could get his point across to a degree, the finer details of communication were what the manager claimed he wanted to be able to better explain.) "One day Harry is okay and the next he says he is unfit," he said. "We don't know exactly what the problem is. It changes each day. One day he says it's the groin, then it's the ankle. Another day he says he can play."

That was leapt upon as Kewell *inventing* problems: saying he is okay, then changing his mind, and announcing another fictional problem — as if he simply couldn't be bothered to play. Benítez, however, was almost certainly saying that Kewell had a number of injury problems, affecting different parts of his body, and when one was cured, another flared up. The manager said: "The player wants to be fit and we want the best for him and we are working together. We are happy with the situation and are working towards finding a solution to his problems. I don't have any problems with Kewell. Our relationship is good. We talk and there is no problem. I just want the best for him and he knows that. Harry is frustrated because he wants to play and he wants to be fit. I had an email from his agent today to say there are no problems. The most important thing is he is fit. He is a key player for us. He is having injections in his groin now and at the moment the situation seems under control although we will only know more in a week or two."

There are definitely some double standards at work in the treatment of Kewell by the media, and indeed by many Liverpool fans. When Kewell was forced to limp out of the Carling Cup final, after a kick to the ankle, he tried to play on — and for a while seemed to be moving freely enough — but eventually asked to be taken off. The critics were clear: Kewell should *want* to play in a match of such import, and by leaving the field he couldn't have wanted to play. Then in the Mersey derby, Stephen Warnock — who no one in their right mind would accuse of being a 'lightweight', after recovering from two serious leg breaks as a teen — received a kick on the ankle in a challenge with Tim Cahill. Same situation as Kewell at Cardiff. When Warnock, having given it his best, asked to be substituted ten minutes later, halfway through the first half of his first taste of local hostilities, there was only sympathy. Kewell was lambasted for walking out of a match he should want to play in; Warnock was excused. Ultimately, if you are injured *then you are injured.*

The same applies to Chris Kirkland, who has had a succession of injuries that have limited him to an average of 11 appearances per season since his move from Coventry (although Dudek's form in 2001/02 was never going to help Kirkland get a game that season). For all his injuries, and the 100+ games he has missed while sidelined with one ailment or another, he is never called a 'mercenary' and never has his attitude been questioned — and rightly so. And yet, in less than half the time, Kewell has played nearly twice as many times for the club.

Stephen Warnock has rightly earned a reputation as a player no fan would ever doubt — one of those where, if he stays down, you know it's serious — but it's all too easy to cast aspersions on the character of a flair player, especially if he is a good looking lad. Fans will always have more trust in a player who is scarred, and whose nose is bent at a 90° angle. In his autobiography, John Barnes notes that Jamie Redknapp suffered the stigma of being cast as a playboy not overly committed to football, despite Redknapp being an incredibly dedicated trainer. Contrast this to Neil Ruddock, whose drinking games and lack of professionalism made a mug of Roy Evans, the club and its fans, but because he was a good old-fashioned plain-looking 'hard bastard' centre-half who kicked people on the pitch and never bottled a challenge, he was seen as *dedicated.*

Similarly, Michael Owen's good looks perhaps contributed to him being viewed a little sceptically by a large section of Liverpool fans — his life was too 'perfect' for fans to empathise with the way they could with Robbie Fowler, whose flawed behaviour on and off the pitch made him more human. Would Fowler have been as adored by the Kop had he possessed male model looks? The image of the player counts towards how much leeway he is granted. Had he been ugly, Harry Kewell still wouldn't have had it easy from the fans, given his poor form (no one escapes in that situation). But it would have helped him be viewed less suspiciously had his face resembled a bag of spanners.

Another point is that not all players can be hardened fighters and battlers — John Barnes, for example, bottled plenty of tackles and never tracked back. Of couse, it helps if you're the best player in the country at the time. Some players *look* like they are working hard; some don't. Steve McManaman covered more ground than any Liverpool player during the 90s, but he still suffered the accusation of being lazy, due to his languid style.

Kewell might not be as brave as Stephen Warnock, but I'm sure both would want to play in a game when they were fit to do so. As Kewell himself later hinted at, why on earth would he want to walk out of the first cup final of his professional career, playing for the team he supported as a boy, and when his side were leading? (If Liverpool were losing 5-0 and getting humiliated, it might have been a different matter.) It's impossible to see why someone who'd dreamed his whole life of playing for Liverpool would suddenly lose interest once that dream was achieved, and he was turning out regularly at Anfield. Despite what many fans think, footballers desperately want to play matches. Having a few good games in the shirt before coasting was surely never Kewell's intention — players don't train that long and hard for years on end simply to screw up their long-term future at the club they love, unless they are very stupid, and there is no evidence to suggest Kewell is lacking brain cells.

Also, if Kewell knew he was struggling to run and kick the ball properly, it is surely in the team's interest if he leave the pitch, to let a fit player take his place? Or would we rather a half-fit player limp around doing nothing *but looking brave*, merely to selfishly remain in the limelight as he doesn't want to miss out on all the glory, while a fit replacement waits on the bench? It's a different way of perceiving the same situation. At Cardiff Kewell made way for Antonio Núñez, and Núñez scored the extra time goal that gave Liverpool a brief lifeline.

In the Mersey derby a few weeks later, Luis Garcia was rightly praised for playing the second half in similar circumstances, but as Warnock, Hamann and Morientes had already been forced off there was simply no alternative, other than the side coming out after half-time with just ten men. Had Luis Garcia hobbled around when a fit replacement sat on the bench, it would surely have been irresponsible.

Fortunately there is nothing at present to suggest Kewell has any permanent fitness problems, and before the string of injuries while at Liverpool, his appearance record had been fairly exemplary: he played his 300th professional game by the age of just 25. He had never previously been known as a 'sicknote' in the way players like Jamie Redknapp, Duncan 'tampon' Ferguson and Darren Anderton could never stay fit for more than a few weeks at a time before picking up yet another muscle strain. Kewell may well end up that way, of course, if his problems aren't resolved. The other worry is that his confidence has been irreversibly damaged by the last 18 months. He certainly won't have a patient Kop willing him to succeed, should he get a third year at Anfield. He deserves credit for working hard at his rehabilitation, and for paying some of his own money towards getting fit. Six months of injury problems came to a head in the Champions League final when the groin finally snapped. Half a year spent in the hope the problem would right itself without surgical intervention was time wasted, and finally Kewell underwent the surgeon's knife days after the season's end.

The re-emergence of John Arne Riise on the left of midfield will put further pressure on Kewell, but in fairness the Australian did his level best to avoid making excuses for his poor form, and continues to talk a good game about wanting to do his best, and needing to prove he is good enough.

If still a Red, Kewell owes the fans, the staff — and himself — a big season in 2005/06. Such is his talent, Benítez will surely opt to give him one more chance. A teamsheet with the midfield of Kewell, Alonso, Gerrard and Luis Garcia just *looks* right — arguably as good as any in world football. The Australian, when on his game, also provides a lot of invention in the 'hole' behind the main striker. In this role at Leeds he scored a lot of goals, and he is also deceptively good in the air.

Other than Kewell, there weren't too many disappointments during Benítez' inaugural season — certainly not amongst those players the manager inherited, and who were already established in the squad. (Excusing those signings of his that didn't settle quickly, who deserve a season's grace.) There were lots of indifferent or poor team displays in the league, with nearly every individual suffering his fair share of 'stinkers', and with a fair few having a longer-lasting slump in form at some stage of the season (or failing that, a period laid up with injury). Was Milan Baros' form until December a pleasant surprise, or his form thereafter a crushing disappointment?

Anthony Le Tallec's decision to go out on loan rather than stay and fight for his place was disappointing, but he had already been told he wasn't one of the manager's first four strikers. He returned, and ended up facing Juventus in the Champions League quarter-final. Salif Diao continued to look out of his depth, but no one expected much from him after his first two seasons, when he just didn't look a Liverpool player.

Inconsistency was the main disappointment, but in the circumstances — new manager, new coaches, new players, radically different tactics (defending higher up, possession football, using the width of the pitch), a plethora of injuries, and the constant unsettling influence of the Gerrard saga following so soon after Owen's exit — perhaps inconsistency was all that could be expected. In his second season, Benítez can expect a more settled situation, and as a result, an improved consistency in his team's performances.

Chapter fifteen

Jeepers 'keepers

Many experts feel that the difference between winning and losing a league title often rests with the man between the sticks, dressed in green or yellow (or, for that matter, orange and pink with lime chevrons, cyan stars and purple polka dots. In other words, a *Mr Blobby* suit).

Was there really that much separating Manchester United and Liverpool in the mid-90s? Is it possible to argue that the difference between the sides would have been reversed if David James and Peter Schmeichel had swapped places? Or is that too fanciful? One thing is for sure: nearly all title winners have a great goalkeeper.

At the start of 2005 Liverpool had three high-quality goalkeepers, and yet you could make a sound case against each, for varying reasons.

Chris Kirkland appeared to suffer from the same condition as Samuel L Jackson's character in *Unbreakable*: bones of glass. Jerzy Dudek, on the other hand, had been accused of having bones of butter: *butterfingers*, to be precise. Scott Carson arrived in January 2005, with a very bright future ahead of him in the game, but with less than a handful of first-team games for Leeds to his name. Experience was not something he could call upon, and that was no surprise — he was, after all, still just 19. However, he was not bought to be third choice: something will surely have to give, and it will be either Dudek or Kirkland.

It is important that a football club has a set goalkeeping hierarchy. The best teams have a clearly-defined — an undisputed — No.1, and his *understudy*. The No.1 (even if his shirt says No.87) has to have the total faith of his manager, and in return, prove his reliability. All goalkeepers make mistakes — just as all outfield players err — but it is the frequency of those errors that matters, and how the 'keeper bounces back. Arsenal and England stalwart David Seamen made three or four really high profile mistakes in his career, for which he was disproportionately ridiculed. But he made very few others, and rarely made mistakes in successive matches. He had bad games, never bad months.

The problem with the lack of a clearly defined structure — having two top 'keepers fighting it out for No.1, for example — is that you merely heap pressure and uncertainty on both, when what you need to do is make the situation less tense. Two nervous 'keepers are no use to anyone. A top 'keeper needs stability in order to be at his best.

It tends to be the case at successful clubs that the number two is either a competent older pro (such as Steve Ogrizovic, Bob Boulder, Mike Hooper, and latterly, Pegguy Arphexad during Houllier's Treble season), happy to take his place on the bench of a top team — for a handful of years, at least — rather than play regularly in a lower division or at an inferior club (something to which they inevitably succumb, in the eventual desire for first team football). Failing that, he is an upcoming rookie — someone like Scott Carson — happy to be a reserve on the basis that his opportunity will come if he bides his time, knowing full well that his best years are well ahead of him. In his four seasons at Anfield, Steve Ogrizovic played just four games between the ages of 20 and 24 — a clear average of one per season. After being sold to Shrewsbury Town, he later enjoyed a long and distinguished career at Coventry City, where he played 600 first team games, but of course never came close to matching the success he was witness to during his time at Liverpool. Like most professional footballers, there came a time when playing games — and not merely watching them — became the main motivation.

In the 1960s Tommy Lawrence — 'the flying pig' — was the main man; then Ray Clemence took care of the entire 1970s, and all the glory that went with that decade. In 1981 Clem made way for Bruce Grobbelaar, and he produced the most famous moment of goalkeeping in the club's history: the 'wobbly legs' routine in the successful European

Cup penalty shoot-out against Roma, played out in the Rome side's home stadium. Grobbelaar was the custodian for the next decade and more; meaning (give or take the odd brief interruption for injury) three 'keepers in three trophy-laden decades. Consistency of selection led to consistency in performances. Grobbelaar was seen as a bit of a clown, and he certainly differed from Clemence in his approach (and Lawrence in his physique), but he was still a top-class 'keeper, and undisputed No.1 at the club. That was until Liverpool slipped from its perch. Since last winning the league, in 1990, Liverpool have had over twice as many first choice 'keepers as in the preceding thirty years: Grobbelaar, David James, Mike Hooper, Brad Friedel, Sander Westerveld, Dudek and Kirkland.

A precedent was set at Liverpool in the early 1990s for how *not* to deal with goalkeepers. Graeme Souness rotated the ageing Bruce Grobbelaar, the new starlet David James, and the 'Steady Eddie' reserve, Mike Hooper, who suddenly found himself as outright first choice for a short period of time. Instead of increased performance from each — under the basis of intense competition — it merely made nervous wrecks of all three. Goalkeepers, unlike outfield players, cannot be proactive to influence a game; when they attempt to be, trouble usually ensues.

Goalkeeping is a purely *reactive* occupation, like firefighting. Just as you don't want pyromaniacs in the fire brigade, you don't want 'fire starters' (twisted or otherwise) in goal. 'Keepers can only make good headlines on account of what the opposition do. If there are no shots at goal directed at a nice height to make saves, or catchable crosses, then they cannot do a lot to justify their inclusion. If they keep a clean sheet without having made a save, they have not 'earned their corn' but will get an extended run in the side if that streak continues (and as individuals, they should be happy with nothing to do). If they concede four unstoppable goals, they will still not be exempt from criticism; somehow they must be *partially* to blame, as the scoreline makes them appear culpable.

The temptation for a goalkeeper, under pressure to keep his place in the side, is to get himself noticed. That was arguably the main failing of David James: he never seemed content *doing nothing*. The best 'keepers are those with no concept of boredom; those who are happy to not have to dirty their padded shirt. Grobbelaar was equally erratic, equally prone to moments of madness, but he played much of his career behind the best defence in Europe, and while he put the team at risk, it was usually able to dig him out of his hole. It also helped that he was a remarkable shot stopper. David James had no such luxury; Phil Babb wasn't going to bale him out. Nor did Grobbelaar, for that matter, once Hansen and Lawrenson retired, and such luminaries as Nicky Tanner and Torben Piechnik ended up in the Reds' defence.

The problem starts when your custodian begins coming for crosses he has no chance of reaching. Or doing fancy drag-backs, nutmegs, stepovers, and dribbling the ball out of his area. (Having said that, it is hard to not be in awe of that South American goalkeeper who, possessed by who-knows-what, brought the ball out of his box, outfoxed a couple of players on the wing, advanced over the halfway line, shimmied past a couple more opponents, before cutting inside a centre-back and unleashing an unstoppable shot into the top corner. Somehow you can't see a British-based manager applauding such behaviour, even though it was one of the greatest moments the sport has ever seen. Less well documented, however, are the 137 goals his team conceded when he was caught in possession doing fancy flicks and 'Cruyff turns' in the centre circle.)

A team needs its goalkeeper to be brave, and that doesn't just mean physically. He has to be prepared to deal with problems falling under his remit, and not rely on others. That is what let down Sander Westerveld. When the Dutch goalkeeper received criticism for missing crosses, he subsequently opted to remain rooted to his goalline, and left everything for the defenders to deal with. However tall a defender, and however high he can leap, he will never be able to soar to the height of a goalkeeper's reach. (A goalkeeper, with the added advantage of a three-foot arm span, has to take the ball at its highest point; once it drops below that, a tall striker has a chance of winning a header.)

While you may not want a goalkeeper taking crosses on the edge of the area (as David James did with heart-stopping regularity), you do want them to at least command the six-yard box, and a small way beyond. It's all about decision making, and goalkeepers under pressure may find their thinking impaired. A goalkeeper worried about losing his place may end up playing it too safe — from a purely personal point of view — so that if goals are conceded, he can say it wasn't directly his fault. (When it was merely *indirectly* his fault.)

When Gérard Houllier signed both Jerzy Dudek and Chris Kirkland on that remarkable transfer deadline day in August 2001, it was fairly clear that the experienced Pole would be first choice, with Kirkland, the promising 20-year-old rookie who had excelled in the Coventry first team, prepared to bide his time. In that first season, the situation rang true: Dudek was as good that year as any Liverpool 'keeper in living memory. He was like some kind of Superman between the sticks, doing absolutely everything right, and looking so calm and assured you half-expected him to be smoking a cigar when the ball was up the other end of the pitch. It all made sense: you could see why the legendary Dutch manager, Leo Beenhakker, claimed Dudek to be the best 'keeper he'd seen for 30 years, based on Jerzy's time at Feyenoord. Before the 2002 World Cup, Polish keeping legend Jan Tomaszewski — the man who broke English hearts by denying them a place in the 1974 World Cup — heaped praise on his countryman: "Liverpool contacted me over Dudek's transfer and I told them they had made a fantastic deal. All he needs to gain is the goal-line savvy and experience of Fabien Barthez and Oliver Kahn and he will be the world number one." Alas, that never transpired — although Andrei Shevchenko may beg to differ.

Ever since the demarcation between Dudek and Kirkland grew more blurred, neither 'keeper has managed to cover himself in glory.

Pressure points

Goalkeepers at the bigger clubs, and with the major national sides, will always be under more pressure, as they are often caught like rabbits in the spotlight's glare. They are on TV far more, including all those extra high-profile Champions League games, and any errors will make back-page headlines, rather than inside-page footnotes. There is also far more to live up to: legends who helped their teams win all the major honours. Away from the headline writers' cruelty, David "Calamity" James' career continued in fairly impressive fashion at Aston Villa, West Ham and Manchester City. It was only once he was thrust back into the spotlight again, as England 'keeper, that the serious criticism returned. The pressure revealed cracks, and the mistakes were magnified.

At least the goalkeeping errors under Benítez' goalkeeping coach, Jose Ochotorena, put to bed the tiresome suggestions-cum-conspiracy theories that Joe Corrigan, his predecessor, was to blame for everything from David James dropping the ball to President Kennedy's assassination.

A goalkeeping coach cannot be responsible for all of a 'keeper's mistakes once his charge crosses that white line. Is the manager at fault if his star central midfielder mis-controls a pass? A goalkeeping coach can work on technique, help with tips on concentration, do his best to prop up his charge's confidence with all the psychological tricks he knows, but one freakish, inexplicable error can undo all this good work if it preys on the 'keeper's mind. That is not to say that the goalkeeping coach might not himself be flawed, but you cannot condemn him for the irreversible weaknesses of the player himself. He can only work with what he has, and in the case of Sander Westerveld,

David James and Jerzy Dudek, that included faults of one kind or another, for all the natural talent.

The top clubs really need exceptional 'keepers, as the pressure is so incredibly tense, and yet these men are in short supply: Schmeichel and Seamen are the most recent 'greats' to retire and leave gaping chasms. (The one at Old Trafford also known, in late 1999, as 'Massimo Taibi'.) Arsenal have already had two No.1s since Seaman retired, and United have currently gone through a staggering *ten* keepers in five years. Is it a coincidence that United have now gone two seasons without winning the league — something that wasn't happening throughout most of the 90s — and that their one Champions League success was in Schmeichel's final season?

Chelsea appear to have it right: Petr Cech arriving as clear first choice, even though they already had a pretty special 'keeper in Carlo Cudicini. Cech is a quite exceptional young custodian, and one of few under 25 — such as Iker Casillas at Real Madrid and Gianluigi Buffon when he arrived at Juventus — who have appeared capable of handling the task of keeping goal at a top club. (Cech was the youngest goalkeeper in an English title-winning side since 1968.) But Cech has yet to experience a rocky patch, and much of a goalkeeper's infallibility comes from the feeling that he is invincible, and simply *will not* drop a cross or mishandle a shot. Cech also has the luxury of playing behind the league's best defence. But that should not disguise the fact that he is a special player, whose handling, so far, remains faultless — all the more remarkable given that football is now a sport designed to coax mistakes from goalkeepers: the *football itself* is now designed to coax mistakes from goalkeepers. Even legends as recently retired as Schmeichel didn't have to contend with a football whose movement through the air is more akin to a toe-punted beachball — or a burst balloon, even — in the way it zigzags a haphazard path, swerving left and right, up and down, without warning. Good goalkeeping practice has had to evolve, to the point where catching the ball (from a shot, at least) is no longer the preferred option. Ten years ago we were still laughing at 'keepers who opted to punch everything; now the continental style is the norm. Maybe that's why Cech looks so good: like Kirkland, he opts to catch, and does so successfully, rather than parry. Kirkland, if he regains the the No.1 jersey, has to match the Czech's standards, as many believe him to be capable of.

Dudek's dark days

Dudek's deterioration began in the late autumn of 2002, and his descent to despair was complete in December 2002, when a terrible mistake gifted Manchester United joke figure, Diego Forlan, the most simple of goals. Dudek then failed to make a decent fist (or rather, palm) of a saveable second for the Uruguayan. *Diego Forlan, Dudek Forlorn.* It was the worst possible game in which to make his first really serious howlers, and Dudek knew it — any other game, and he may have brushed them off. From that point on, he would be haunted by those ghosts. In the next two Anfield games against United, Dudek was at fault for the goals that ensured defeat, none worse that Wayne Rooney's daisy-cutter in January 2005: a shot so tame even the most fragile of daisies remained undamaged.

Games against United aside, Dudek hasn't exactly been a walking disaster zone. He has not started conceding sloppy goals left right and centre — he hasn't completely crumbled — but the cool, calm and collected customer of his debut season remains but a memory. Doubts suddenly existed in his mind, his confidence newly fragile. 2004/05 saw other mistakes: the sloppy piece of handling that allowed Nicolas Anelka to score during the first home game of the season; the unfortunate parry that fell onto Lua Lua's head in the last minute of the home game with Portsmouth, at the cost of two points; and, most notably, the fumble in the last minute against Bayer Leverkusen, which made the second leg less of a formality. On top of these, there were a number of goals where you felt he could have done better, such as when being beaten at his near post by Jermaine Defoe in the opening game of the season at White Hart Lane, but where you could equally argue that a lot of 'keepers would have struggled to make a save.

Dudek bounced back from his Leverkusen fumble to produce a Man of the Match performance against Chelsea in the Carling Cup final, including playing on with a gashed shin that would need ten stitches at full-time.

And of course, he was outstanding in the Champions League final. That shows the character of the man — the product of a tough upbringing in a Polish mining town, in whose collieries he was about to follow his father and begin work, when he was offered his first contract with local team Concordia. (If only more English players had such experiences to put their luxury lifestyles into perspective.) But too often, even though he bounced back with commendable courage, another mistake followed if not immediately, then at least *too soon*. Perhaps the game in Istanbul sums up his career at Liverpool: in amongst the brilliant saves, two inexplicable handling errors that could have proved so costly.

Enter Kirkland

Did the development of Kirkland — and the subsequent clamour for his inclusion — hasten Dudek's decline? Was Kirkland impressing in training to the degree it made the Pole wary of losing his place? Dudek will also have been aware that Kirkland was England's great new hope, and while fans like to see foreign superstars (if they are indeed 'super'), nothing can beat a home-born lad.

As football fans, we always want to see the kids thrown in, *as they can't do any worse, right?* But of course they can. A few mistakes, and they too are castigated. Following on from the success of players like Michael Owen and Steven Gerrard, if instant impressions aren't made by teenagers, doubts are voiced. Players develop at different paces, in different ways. Some are early impressers; others late bloomers. The key thing with all young players is that their age is taken into account. Even old pros admit to still learning about the game; but never is the learning curve as steep as in a player's incipient years. And never is that more important than in goalkeeping.

Kirkland has only ever received his chance in the first team by default. At no point did he have total, unswerving faith put in him, at no point was he clearly defined as the No.1. He merely got into the team because Dudek had erred or was injured. Kirkland always seemed to be on trial: here you go, here's five games, see how you do. The first three games may go well, but the pressure then grows as the trial nears its conclusion. A top 'keeper should be able to handle such pressure, but it hardly makes his life — already difficult enough — any easier. It would always be a big ask, given that Kirkland was still a kid himself (in goalkeeping terms, where, but for the odd exception that proves the rule, most first team custodians in the top leagues are 25-38). While Kirkland never made the handling errors that blighted Dudek's copybook, he failed to save (or apparently even see) three shots within eight days — including the galling losing goal at Goodison Park. He seemed ponderous in getting down to shots.

Kirkland's biggest problem remains his fitness — as it has been since first arriving at the club. Some of his injuries have been freak accidents: most 'keepers break fingers in their careers, and the clash with Dele Adebola in the FA Cup at Crystal Palace was one of those unfortunate collisions that would have curtailed the season of any player. Others have been more worrying: a litany of osteopathic traumas, perhaps relating to how his body has struggled to cope with the growth spurts of his teenage years, when this young boy suddenly found himself standing at 6' 6". (Steven Gerrard had a similarly tough time until extensive chiropracty at Gérard Houllier's behest set his body back into alignment.) Neck and back problems are always worrying, as the spine is such a difficult area to deal with.

It's hard to know exactly how much Kirkland's back problems affected his form in December 2004, but it was clear something wasn't right — as the subsequent operation confirmed. Playing with injuries can affect players not only physically, but psychologically. Said Kirkland, once back in training in late March: "I hope the problems I have had will now be over. Before the operation it wasn't just playing that was the problem, it was getting out of bed in the mornings and it was everything in general so I thought the best thing was to have the operation. I am fine now and can't feel anything which is great for me." Everyone connected to the club must be praying this is a 'cure all' for his perennial problems, and that the fans finally get to see more than sporadic evidence of why so many who have worked with him — from Gordon Strachan to Sven Goran Eriksson, Houllier to Clemence, Ogrizovic to David Platt — insist he is a quite remarkable talent.

Fans — demanding breed that we are — want players to be tough enough to play when carrying injuries (as they did in the olden days, before football was as physically challenging as it now is) and to not 'cry off' with niggles. But if those injuries lead to mistakes — as they will (it stands to reason the player will be impaired) — then we get angry at them for putting the result at jeopardy. If Kirkland was experiencing back spasms at the time of his failure to react to shots, is it understandable that he wouldn't have complained too vehemently, at the risk of losing his place, or seeming uncommitted. Outfield players can find a way back into the team for a variety of reasons, and often in a number of different positions; goalkeepers get much less chance of a recall, unless they are the outright first choice and thus able to walk straight back into the side.

Gordon Strachan, who gave Kirkland his big break at Coventry City, said "Chris has got a huge presence," and noted that but for injuries, he would be the England No.1 by now. Strachan also noted that Kirkland was incredibly skinny when he was 15, and said (tongue-in-cheek, I presume) that the young kid was unable to even kick the ball out of the area. But in time he would come to *command* his area.

In 2003, the then England U21 boss, David Platt, spoke in glowing terms. Like Strachan, he noted Kirkland's 'presence', before going on to say that he is an "extremely dedicated person that wants to become better and better at his trade. He gives you a safety net." Platt's effusiveness continued, "To be honest, I've seen a lot of youth football across the world since I took this job and I think in Chris we have the best young goalkeeper in the world."

The testimonies continue, from all quarters of the game — too many to list — although Kirkland needs to now start proving his quality, rather than have others talk about it. Being free from injury is the only way he can manage this.

Dudek has to remain the favourite to be sold, should Liverpool choose to cash in — as financial needs appear to suggest they must — on one of their goalkeeping assets. As goalkeepers don't tend to reach their best until their early 30s, Kirkland still has plenty of time on his side — while Dudek, approaching 33, is now at a stage where he should be at his peak, and yet still the doubts persist. Selling Kirkland would be a huge gamble, especially as Liverpool's rivals, Chelsea excluded, are desperate for a 'keeper of Kirkland's quality and promise. Kirkland, if he has Benítez' trust — and this appeared to be the case, when fit — can offer a long-term solution to the goalkeeping problems at the club, with Carson as the more-than-able deputy. Kirkland's contract doesn't expire until 2009 — he signed a six-year deal back in 2003 — and as a boyhood fan of the club, who travelled with his father on the supporter's club coach from Leicester to watch the Reds, he is in the only place where he cares to be. Providing he can be cured of his physical ailments, he conceivably has 15 years ahead of him at the top of the game — pretty much what fellow ex-Coventry 'keeper Ogrizovic managed when he left Liverpool at Kirkland's age.

At present both Dudek and Kirkland are of comparable ability, but it would be like choosing to keep Ian Rush ahead of Michael Owen in the mid 1990s: one had no further scope for improvement, while the other could, and would, only get better with experience.

The surprise of 2004/05 was that Scott Carson got to keep goal for Liverpool more times in his first three months at Liverpool than he had for Leeds in a lower division. With Kirkland out long-term, and Dudek suffering some minor strains, the young Yorkshireman got his chance: four times in the Premiership and once in the Champions League. In those five games he did extremely well, bar one howler against Juventus, which, thankfully, didn't prove costly. No one would have wanted such an error, if it ended up eliminating Liverpool, hanging over a young player's head. Even though only 19, he is not afraid to shout at senior defenders when *they* make mistakes — a very Schmeichelesque trait. Caron's progress continues at startling speed. Within a month of that game he received his first England call-up.

If the club retains Kirkland and Carson as its two goalkeepers, then the gloves will be *on* safe hands for many years to come — conceivably even the next 20 years. Reports in the media widely forecast a move for Villarreal's José Reina — another young 'keeper, aged just 22 — so maybe Liverpool will be welcoming a new custodian to the club over the summer.

Chapter sixteen

King Carra: Jamie of all trades, master of one

A very subtle but nonetheless seismic shift took place over the winter of 2004/05. Almost unnoticed, with a stealthiness unassociated with his all-action, vocal performances, Jamie Carragher — man for all positions, but, until Benítez took charge, outright master of none — became the Kop's number one idol. It first became evident around Christmas 2004. Steven Gerrard's position as Local Hero had been tainted by his flirtation with Chelsea and ongoing refusal to rule out leaving Anfield, and suddenly a boyhood Blue was succeeding a boyhood Red as the fans' favourite. Liverpool fans had, all the same, finally *fully* warmed to Carra after years of admiration coloured with nagging doubt, and a tendency to take him for granted. As with Fowler before him, a boyhood Evertonian ended up epitomising the Kop's desire, and, in the No.23 shirt, ran out at Anfield as the fans' favourite.

Bootle-born Carragher had finally transcended the adjectives that had been tied like tethers to his ankles throughout his career — compliments that somehow also seemed to damn with faint praise: *dependable, reliable, versatile.* It made him sound like a mid-range *Skoda*. Suddenly he was *remarkable, colossal, indispensable.* Commentators in the national media began, somewhat belatedly, to take note. He was suddenly named amongst the very best central defenders in the land, while still never having the cachet of someone like Rio Ferdinand, whose exorbitant transfer fees and assorted outrageous hairstyles (and periodic tabloid notoriety) turned him into a 'superstar'; or John Terry, whose regular goals ensured he grabbed headlines for his actions at both ends of the field. Terry won the PFA Player of the Year, with Carragher not even present in the best XI (inexplicably, Rio Ferdinand was chosen as the second centre-back). But the voting for that award takes place a long time before the end of the season; the Football Writers' Footballer of the Year is voted for in the final weeks of the campaign, and this time Carra was recognised, coming third behind Terry and the winner, Frank Lampard.

Carra's winning mentality was never in doubt from the moment he made his debut in 1997 as a raw and somewhat ungainly midfielder, and who, at home to Aston Villa in his next game, misled all Liverpool fans by *scoring a goal* on his first start — something he'd repeat only once in the next 300+ games. Years earlier, Ronnie Moran — who had seen and done it all at Liverpool — suggested Carragher would be best suited to centre-back, but like all young players in that position, mistakes dogged his early career in that role. Gérard Houllier later converted him to full-back, with considerable wisdom. It was in this position that he was spoken of as one of the 'old school', a throwback to days when defenders simply defended: equally prepared to enter into a 50-50 with a skinny winger or a Panzer Tank. But full-back, while highlighting Carra's old-fashioned defensive qualities and never-say-die spirit, also exposed his weaknesses: the absence of a trick or two to go past opposing full-backs when overlapping, and the inability to whip in a decent cross. Even now, everything with Carra involves an exaggerated use of the instep: the side-foot pass is all he knows, as if his legs are not assembled like other players', but instead permanently set into 'block tackle' mode: foot placed at 90° like a golf putter. Attacking moves lost all momentum when the ball reached his feet, as he stopped, looked around, turned back and played a square pass.

As fans we crave exciting full-backs who double-up as wingers. It is only once we are faced with an attacking full-back who cannot actually defend that our cravings for an exponent of the 'basics' returns. But the ideal full-back remains a combination of the two, with the best recent example being Markus Babbel during the Treble season, when — despite not being the flashiest of players — he exuded quality and effectiveness at both ends of the pitch. (Steve Finnan, now Carragher has finally moved infield, has started to show the form that made him so highly rated by his peers, although I know I am not alone in wondering how Rob Jones would be faring had his career not been so prematurely curtailed by injury. Given that he is still only 33, it would be interesting to see Jones, if still fit and playing to the peak of his abilities, in a Benítez team — age not a barrier to making it into the Spaniard's defence, given that he won the 2004 *La Liga* title with a 39-year-old, Amedeo Carboni, at full-back; the Italian featuring in 33 of the 38 league games. Jones was the apotheosis of the modern full-back, and while famously he never scored for the Reds, his attacking instincts were very strong.)

Since moving to centre-back Carra's passing has proven to be surprisingly accurate and incisive: no doubt down to the option of being able to look both left and right — whereas previously, being on the wing meant he could only look infield, or back. He's also proven that he can go past players with a drop of the shoulder or a quick dragback (nothing much more fancy than that — he's not taken to nutmegs or elaborate Ronaldinhoesque flicks over opponents' heads). Much of this is down to forwards' challenges tending to be a cross between a 'token effort' and a hedging of bets, where they gamble on the defender making a mistake. By committing themselves they offer a cool centre-back the chance to turn out of trouble. Carra is especially adroit at this. He seems to play himself into trouble by trying to control the ball (and therefore the situation) in a tight area, and then, without breaking sweat, turn in the opposite direction and, now with time and space, release a pass into midfield. It's a part of his game that is still developing apace, and like Tony Adams before him, he is a supposed clodhopper turned *libero*; the footballing equivalent of ugly duckling turned swan. There can also be no doubt that while Benítez doesn't permit his centre-backs to needlessly over-elaborate with the ball, he does encourage more composure at the back than his predecessor, who was more than happy to see his defenders 'get rid' as early as possible, and as far as possible. In the most recent Mersey derby, Carra showed just how composed he has become. As Everton launched long ball after long ball, Carra was seen strolling around with the ball at his feet as the tackles flew in. He was rightly voted Man of the Match.

Not your average 'road-sweeper'

Erstwhile Southampton manager, Lawrie McMenemy — a man whose south coast side put up a hard-fought challenge to Liverpool for the league title in 1984 — came up with a great analogy about the different types of player you need to win football matches: 'concert violinists' and 'road-sweepers'. The former category, amongst others, includes Dalglish, Barnes, and now Xabi Alonso: those who make the game look effortless, and beautiful to watch. You pay money to hear the music — the harmonious note that chimes — when they strike a football. But they are nothing without the workers who scurry to clean up around them: the road-sweepers.

McMenemy said that whenever a 'road-sweeper' came into his office looking for a pay rise, he'd open the window to the street outside and shout "send up another road-sweeper, will you?"; the clear implication being that these types of players are ten-a-penny, and instantly replaceable. You need a number of them in your side, of course, but there were always plenty going spare; their *identity* wasn't crucial. It also draws to mind Eric Cantona's disparaging description of his (highly decorated) colleague Didier Deschamps as a mere 'water carrier'.

It's fair to say that, going on this analysis, Jamie Carragher is more of a road-sweeper than a concert violinist. You'd certainly never pay to watch him try to make sweet music with a football. It's also true: road-sweepers *are* ten-a-penny. But not road-sweepers like Carra. He is the kind of man that, if an *actual* road-sweeper, would, if not supplied with an adequate broom, get down on his hands and knees to pick up the rubbish with his bare hands, or his teeth. Hell, he'd even head battered old tin cans into his refuse bag.

The credit for Carra's ascent belongs mainly to three people: the player himself, as no one else puts the effort in for him, either in training or in matches; Rafael Benítez, for recognising that the time was right for the player to move to centre-back, and encouraging his development; and Gérard Houllier, whose faith in the player was unshakable, and who, in 2000, foretold of the transformation now taking place; stating that, with more experience, he would make a top class centre-back. "He'll be our Marcel Desailly", said the Frenchman, although it took a Spaniard to prove the point.

Carragher's early days at centre-back — once it was clear he didn't quite have the wherewithal for central midfield — were blighted by the mistakes all young players make in that position, when the inexperience shows, and the slightest slip gets punished. He scored as many own goals against Manchester United in one Anfield game as he has managed to date at the correct end during his Liverpool career. It didn't help that he was surrounded by a collection of fairly incompetent defenders in those early days. In the summer of 1999 Houllier went out and signed two older, more experienced defenders of a similar ilk to Carra: Sami Hyypia and Stephane Henchoz, who went on to form a formidable partnership together over the next few seasons. Carragher shifted to right back, but then, the following summer, Houllier signed Markus Babbel, the highly-accomplished German international, on a free transfer from Bayern Munich. Babbel arrived with a massive reputation, and didn't disappoint. Yet again Carragher's days were listed as numbered, and yet he was reborn at left-back, and had an absolutely inspired time in that position as the team went on to win the cup treble in 2001. Babbel's serious illness — a year spent severely incapacitated with Guillain-Barre Syndrome — meant a return to right-back for Carra until, in 2003, Houllier signed the Irish right-back, Steve Finnan — previously selected by his peers in a Premiership team of the season, and seen as a more complete footballer than his Scouse counterpart. The attack-minded Irishman was not bought as cover, and again conventional wisdom suggested the demise of Carra; but 'JC' was back in the team at left-back — Houllier simply couldn't omit him. The only full-back who could successfully dislodge Carra from the Liverpool side *played for Blackburn*: Lucas Neill, whose reckless high tackle broke Carra's leg in September 2003.

Maybe — and somewhat perversely — we can also thank Lucas Neill. It hurt Carra in more than a physical way. He couldn't stand not being part of the team, and having to watch from the sidelines — this is a man who, by all accounts, eats, drinks, sleeps and breathes football — drove him barmy. There was a detectable difference when he returned later that season; even more hunger in his play, if that was possible, and an improvement in the quality of his distribution, not to mention some scalding long-range efforts on goal, one of which came within inches of winning the Anfield derby. Or maybe it was us — the fans — who came to notice what the team would be like without Carragher.

We didn't like what we saw. Absence made our large, red, collective heart grow fonder.

Eleven Carraghers

Gerrard Houllier once stated that he would "win the league with eleven Carraghers", and the comment has since been turned into a Kop anthem ("We all dream of a team of Carraghers", to the tune of *Yellow Submarine*). While it was surely said simply to highlight the then-underrated and under-appreciated Carra's importance, it is also clearly not true — not least because you need players who average more than one goal every five years, and who have some sort of creative power in the final third. In other words, *you need your concert violinists, too.* But where Houllier was utterly correct is that the kind of mentality Carragher has is what all the best sides need.

Houllier deserves a lot of credit for turning Carra from a typical English kid — one who would famously shame himself and the club at a Christmas party — into a man whose professionalism and dedication marked him out as an inspiration to others.

While the doubts about Carra have largely dissipated, a couple remain. Perhaps it depends on who he is partnered with, as any weaknesses in one central defender can be counteracted by the man playing alongside him. While not sluggish, Carra is also far from the quickest defender around. When there was a chance that he'd start England's first game in Euro 2004, as cover for injured Sol Campbell and suspended Rio Ferdinand (a spot that eventually went to Spurs' much-improved Ledley King), TV stations, with a fear bordering on the hysterical, showed a clip where Thierry Henry gave Carra five yards on the Anfield flank and overtook him in ten. Despite it being slightly misleading, as Carra also had to change direction while Henry had already built up a head of steam, there's also little doubting that Carra is not a defender like Chelsea's William Gallas, who can keep pace with the most jet-heeled attacking talents.

It says a lot that when Djimi Traoré was not in the side, Carragher was the club's quickest defender during 2004/05, and this highlights a major problem with the personnel Benítez inherited. Houllier had tried the tall and pacy Igor Biscan at centre-back the previous season, with mixed results: the big Croat was sensational at times, but looked lost at others, and was ultimately (somewhat harshly) ridiculed whenever he made the slightest mistake, in contrast to the way someone like Rio Ferdinand can cost his team goals and still *do no wrong*. For all Biscan's good games (and there were more good ones than bad), it was clear he lacked the concentration and consistency to play at the heart of the defence at a top club, where pressure is greatest. It was an interesting experiment, but one which ultimately failed. A year later, and Carra was partnering the canny but sluggish Sami Hyypia. If Carra could compensate for Hyypia's statuesque running style (at times the Finn appears like an ice sculpture), it was only a partial compensation. Neither are sprinters. While an advanced reading of the game can compensate on most occasions, nothing can beat the kind of cover Mark Lawrenson so famously provided, where anyone clean through on Liverpool's goal could be caught.

The other weakness with Carragher is that while he is superb in the air, and as brave as a lion, he is not as tall as many centre-backs. If Hyypia is ever replaced by a smaller, quicker player, the Achilles Heel of aerial inadequacy that dogged the club during the 1990s could return. Where Carra's reasonable pace gets Sami out of some tight spots, Sami remains the defender who can deal with 6' 5" strikers. Carragher used to be given a torrid time by Everton's Duncan Ferguson, whereas Hyypia usually won the dual, to the point where Ferguson's elbows would flail with deliberate movements toward his marker's head, as his frustration grew. Perhaps the English game moves ever further away from the big target man, with Shearer and Ferguson close to retirement, and the hugely-effective Niall Quinn having already hung up his boots. The modern game involves almost every team utilising a speed merchant who plays on the shoulder of the last defender, or drops deep and sprints at them. But just when you think it'll be all sophisticated interplay and balls into feet, or perfectly-weighted passes into space, promoted clubs bring their own brand of direct football, or players like Southampton's Peter Crouch emerge as if from some genetic experiment gone horribly awry — 6' 7" of lanky beanpole, but who can cause any defence problems. (At the time of writing, Crouch is being linked with a move to the Reds.) It seems the English game will always involve at least some use of the long ball to the big striker — even Chelsea made good use of it, often bypassing the midfield in heading directly to Didier Drogba. While Drogba struggled to score goals, the tactic, when resorted to, proved extremely effective.

As good as Ayala, as sound as a pound

Perhaps the greatest compliment for Carragher comes from his current club manager. Midway through his first season, Rafael Benítez said of the no.23: "I have worked with some great defenders at Valencia such as Marchena, Pellegrino and Ayala. If you say to me that Ayala was the best then I would say Carragher is not a worse player than Ayala."

Speaking on the *BBC's Football Focus* in March 2005, John Terry, Chelsea's defensive lynchpin, claimed Carragher to have been the best central defender in the Premiership over the course of the season. It has taken time, but word is spreading. Pundits are taking note. Unfortunately, people form quickly-cemented opinions on players, and leave themselves little leeway to reassess, so it takes time for some players to get their dues.

When Carragher himself was interviewed — by Sky TV, prior to the Everton game at Anfield — he was asked if he would ever consider leaving the club. (How often must any player be asked this question?) "You could join a bigger club and win more medals — why stay at Liverpool?" asked Jeff Shreeves. Jamie, having none of that, gave a snort of contempt that shook his pinned-on microphone. "Bigger than Liverpool? Are you kidding? Who's bigger than Liverpool?" he asked with a barely-suppressed smirk, turning the tables on his interviewer. You see, to Jamie Carragher — avid student of the rich history of the club — there remains no English club to have won more league titles, or more European Cups. If Liverpool were now in the footballing backwaters, that would perhaps be slightly less relevant — after all, Nottingham Forest's two European Cups, while momentous achievements that will never be forgotten, will not save them from financial impoverishment and further relegation. But the interview in question was conducted days after Liverpool won through to the quarter-finals of the Champions League. He is aware that Liverpool have won the major honours more often than any other English club.

The final word

A season which started with Jamie Carragher's position once again under threat, ended with the highest possible praise: pronouncements of respect from two players — Johan Cruyff and Paolo Maldini — guaranteed entry into the World's Best Ever XI. The Italian legend was quick to note the impressive role played by Carra in taking Liverpool to the final. After the match, the Dutch legend didn't hold back: "I call Jamie Carragher my Marathon Man. He looks like a marathon runner whose legs are turning to jelly as he's about to cross the finishing line but he finds more energy to get there. The sliding tackle he made after receiving treatment for cramp summed up the character of the team. He was phenomenal."

Any additions to the trophy cabinet over the next half-dozen years will almost certainly be in no small part down to Jamie *"he's Scouse, he's sound"* Carragher.

Chapter seventeen

Champions League knockout stage - Road to Istanbul

Bayer Leverkusen, February and March, 2005

The draw for the knockout stages of the Champions League, while keeping the big guns away from Anfield, still managed to pair Liverpool with old adversaries: Bayer Leverkusen, whose late, late goal eliminated Gérard Houllier's Liverpool at the quarter-final stage in 2002, and who went on to beat the waiting Manchester United in the semi-final.

Bayer Leverkusen, while lacking the stars of three years earlier — Ballack, Lucio, Ze Roberto, all sold to Bayern Munich — were still to be respected. For all the lack of world-class stars, they topped their group ahead of Real Madrid, Roma and Dynamo Kiev. Each of those teams left the Bayer Arena with their tails between their legs, and three goals conceded. Leverkusen had also managed to put four past Bayern Munich in the Bundesliga over the winter months. While not the best on their travels, they were not to be underestimated over two legs. The tie, however, was effectively over before half-time in the first game, with goals by Luis Garcia and John Arne Riise confirming the Reds' authority, as they poured forward time and time again. A Didi Hamann free-kick in the second half put Liverpool 3-0 up, but the formality of the second leg was suddenly erased by Jerzy Dudek's handling error in injury time, which gifted Leverkusen a lifeline. Where Leverkusen would have needed to score four times to eliminate Liverpool, suddenly a 2-0 win would be enough to see the German club through — far from inconceivable.

The tie as a whole, however, belonged to Luis Garcia, who scored crucial goals in both legs — each the kind of finish with which Robbie Fowler made his name. The opener at Anfield, which set the tone, followed an amazing piece of work by Igor Biscan. The big Croat bamboozled two opposition midfielders before sliding an inch-perfect pass through to the little Spaniard, whose first-time shot on the turn, which slid under the body of the onrushing keeper, was reminiscent of many Fowler goals. Any fears that the game in Germany would lead to Liverpool's elimination were put to bed — along with the tie itself — by two sharp close-range finishes from Luis Garcia, one of which diverted Biscan's header past a defender on the line and into the net, the other a delightful near-post flick. Milan Baros added a third, and this time — unlike three years earlier — Leverkusen's late goal was utterly meaningless. No one had predicted a 6-2 aggregate score, but suddenly Leverkusen, given their lack of top-class status, were written off after the event as 'mediocre' opposition (shame no one told Roma and Real Madrid). The same could not be said of Liverpool's next opponents.

Juventus, 6th April, 2005

It was a game that was almost certainly needed, but one which nobody particularly wanted; the timing, however, was particularly apt, as the 20th anniversary of Heysel approached. That a friendly meeting between the two clubs had not previously taken place meant that all the issues of that fateful day in Belgium in May 1985, when 39 people died in the crumbling Brussels stadium, were to be played out for the high stakes of a semi-final place. It only served to add more pressure to the occasion, with a media frenzy surrounding the two games. There were innumerable magazine and newspaper articles, and a selection of television documentaries.

Would Liverpool be 'allowed' to win? Not as in *Would Uefa rig the result?*, but would there be a moral pressure — an obligation — on Liverpool to lose? Or had that scenario been fully played out 20 years earlier, when the Reds were left in no position to emerge victorious from a game the world felt they deserved to fail in (including the referee, who awarded Juventus a penalty for a Gary Gillespie foul five yards outside the box). Although both sets of fans had been culpable that balmy Brussels day, that the loss of life resulted on the Italian side meant Liverpool were inevitably cast as the villains.

As it transpired, Liverpool made a whole host of gestures of remorse ahead of the game in April 2005: a Kop mosaic; a silver plaque; a flag of friendship paraded by Ian Rush, Phil Neal and Juventus' match-winner in 1985, Michel Platini; and a magazine aimed at the Italian supporters. Juve's 'Ultra' fans, the *Drughi*, who were stationed at the base of the Anfield Road stand, turned their back on the offer of 'Memoria e Amicizia' (Remembrance and Friendship), offering only a middle-finger gesture, but many Juve fans responded with applause. Once the pre-match attempts at conciliation were concluded, a line was drawn under the events of 1985 — not to be forgotten, of course, but the chapter could at last be closed.

The game itself started at a ferocious pace, with Milan Baros having a shot on goal within the first ten seconds. It set the tone, to a backdrop of what John Aldridge described as the best atmosphere at Anfield since the Kop went all-seater. Wave after wave of attacks followed, and the shell-shocked Juventus players found themselves 2-0 down before they had much chance to come to terms with the occasion. After ten minutes Sami Hyypia — who'd lost his place in the league to Mauricio Pellegrino — crashed in a superb left-foot volley from Luis Garcia's flick-on, as the big Finn found an ocean of space at the far post. (Had Juve been implementing zonal marking — the system used by Liverpool to defend set pieces, and for which Benítez had been criticised earlier in the season — then they would have had someone stationed in that part of the area, and wouldn't have allowed Hyypia a free shot.) Fifteen minutes later, Anthony Le Tallec flicked a pass to Milan Baros, but the Czech didn't quite read the intentions; the ball ran kindly to Luis Garcia who, 30 yards from goal, let the ball bounce one further time before launching a dipping left-foot shot into the top corner of the net. In the Anfield Road end, £32m-worth of goalkeeper, Gianluigi Buffon, watched helplessly as the ball arced over his head. This was a 'keeper who cost twice as much as Liverpool's entire starting XI. Juventus had now conceded as many goals in 45 minutes as they had in the previous eight Champions League games — and even one of those two goals had been a Real Madrid penalty.

Injuries to Dudek and Kirkland had forced Benítez to field £750,000 rookie, Scott Carson, in goal. The Reds came close on a number of occasions, but Juventus also hit the post through Zlatan Ibrahimovic, and Carson pulled off a superb close-range save with Alessandro Del Piero clean through on goal. The second half saw Liverpool tire, perhaps as a result of the tough league encounter with Bolton three days earlier, while Juventus were fresh, the Italian league programme being postponed while the Pope lay critically ill. The reigning *Serie A* champions and current league leaders showed a lot of class in the second half, and controlled more of the game, but still rarely tested Carson with anything meaningful. Even their goal came from a tame header by Fabio Cannavaro, which Carson inexplicably failed to hold. The two-goal lead and sense of euphoria was suddenly undone by the softest of goals, and the tie swung in Juve's favour.

How could the best performance, and the best win of the season — against as good a team as any in Europe — feel, in some strange way, like a defeat? The nature of the Juventus goal certainly added to the feeling that the Reds were doomed. Had Liverpool come from a goal down to snatch a 2-1 victory, it would have felt like wonderland, but instead doubt clouded the joy at the shrill sound of the final whistle.

It was also the sense that Liverpool would need a conclusive victory to stand any chance in the second leg. Real Madrid had gone to Turin with a 1-0 lead, and as such, with no away goal that could count against them, but they were still eliminated.

No sooner had the game finished than Liverpool's European run was being written off. No one in the media gave the Reds a cat-in-hell's chance at the Stadio Delle Alpi, where the atmosphere was expected to be intensely hostile, and where Juventus — kings of the 1-0 win — needed only their favourite scoreline to eliminate Benítez' team.

Turin, 13th April 2005

Some flags in the Stadio Delle Alpi were less than welcoming to the travelling 3,000 supporters occupying the away section. Others, relating to Hillsborough, were downright offensive. Missiles started raining down on Liverpool fans before the kick off, and only a very small minority retaliated in kind. It wasn't a good start to proceedings. Thankfully once the match got underway the violence dissipated. The Turin police were very complimentary about the behaviour of the travelling Reds, and while the result was important to everyone concerned, the behaviour of the fans was the main issue. There would be no point in winning the game, but being expelled from the competition. As it was, it was the Italians who received more criticism, as indeed they had during the first leg; the Italian media were embarrassed by the rudeness and hostility shown in the face of Liverpool's offer of friendship, especially towards the city's mayor when welcoming them at Liverpool John Lennon Airport.

The build-up to the second leg, in terms of the football, focused on Steven Gerrard, whose groin injury had him pulling out on the Monday. If Liverpool were the one-man team people suggested, then that of course left *no one*. Luckily the players themselves didn't see it that way. However, if Gerrard's injury wasn't enough, he was one of *nine* senior players missing — including players of the calibre of Didi Hamann, Harry Kewell and Fernando Morientes — while Xabi Alonso and Djibril Cissé were passed fit, but nowhere near *match fit*. The odds were stacked decidedly against Liverpool reaching their first European Cup semi-final since 1985.

Where the Reds hadn't been afforded a cat-in-hell's chance, it instead became a game of cat-and-mouse. Only, it wasn't 100% clear who was the malevolent feline and who was the petrified rodent. Liverpool were certainly not being toyed with, as expected, but it was a tense and cagey affair all the same. Zlatan Ibrahimovic missed an easy chance after ten minutes, but it wasn't until the second half that the Italians would have another meaningful attempt at goal. Yet again Cannavaro came close with a far post header, in a replica of his goal at Anfield, this time after Djimi Traoré was inexplicably out-jumped by a player eight inches shorter; the attempt crashed against the post, and Dudek did well to claw the ball to safety. And that was it — the sum of Liverpool's concerns.

It was one of those games where the phrase "take nothing away from Liverpool, but . . . " appeared in every single match report. The *Old Lady of Turin* herself may as well have been playing for Juventus, such was the limited threat Juventus posed to the Reds' defence. But how much of that was down to Benítez' tactics (adjusting to three central defenders, and outwitting Fabio Capello, his former mentor), and his team's performance — especially the towering Hyypia, who found his best form for a couple of years, and the fearsomely committed Carragher — and how much down to Juve's ineptitude? Did Juve simply fail to play well, or did Liverpool *stop them* from so doing? Is it ever possible to fully tell? While the Reds received a lot of credit, there was also the suggestion that Juventus didn't force the issue enough.

The scenes at the final whistle showed how much it meant to the boys in red, with even usually placid, non-demonstrative players like Igor Biscan celebrating like men possessed, crazed glints in their eye.

Chelsea await

How close the comparisons between Jose Mourinho and Rafael Benítez, their paths crossing once again? Last season's two European trophy winners also won their domestic leagues. While Mourinho won the most prestigious cup competition, Benítez won the toughest domestic league. Both men were linked to the Liverpool job last summer, when it became clear they were ready for new challenges. A strange quirk of fate ensued, whereby the two men — who, had they stayed in their old jobs at Porto and Valencia, would have been contesting the European Super Cup at the start of the season — ended up contesting the Carling Cup final and the Champions League semi-final. Just as Arsene Wenger and Alex Ferguson continue to lock horns (for 2nd place in the league, and in the FA Cup final), the new guard — the young Europeans, the Next Generation — continued their own private battle. These will be the four contesting the top four spots next time around.

While Mourinho claimed he was offered the Liverpool job, it remains clear to most Liverpool fans that Rick Parry and David Moores appointed the right man. That is not to say that Mourinho is an inferior manager to Benítez — indeed, the two have been equally impressive in recent years. Both men followed a Uefa Cup victory with Champions League success the following season, although Benítez became the first man in history to do so with two different clubs. Each has won the league title in one of the three major European leagues: Benítez twice, Mourinho once. Mourinho's achievements at Chelsea in 2004/05 were hugely impressive, but he had an abundance of luxuries; Benítez had relatively little money to spend at Valencia and Liverpool.

Perhaps Mourinho originally made the statement to undermine his Spanish counterpart, ahead of the first league clash — to tell Benítez that he was only second choice. The two men, however, seem at least on a par.

Mourinho has done a superb job at Chelsea — for all the obvious help he had from Roman Abramovich, he still made that money, and the quality of players he inherited, count. But it is doubtful he would have been the right man for Liverpool, whose fans are wary of flashiness and ostentation. Bill Shankly shared some of Mourinho's arrogance, and also had a clever way with words, especially with regards to psychology — motivating his own players, and 'psyching out' the opposition. But the two men were not cut from the same cloth. There was a heart and soul about Shanks; Mourinho may indeed care deeply and passionately, but he spends too much time acting cool — trying to look and act the part and cultivate an image. But Shanks *was* the part. Mourinho is not a fake as such, but he appears to have learnt his tricks second-hand. Shanks learned his trade the hard way.

If Mourinho is the modern-day Clough, then perhaps Benítez reminds us of Bob Paisley. Even though Rafa's English isn't perfect, he still often makes more sense than dear old Bob ever did, with his 'doings' and 'gubbins' and 'whatshisnames' littering every sentence. Crucially, each man could make himself understood to his players.

There is a humility, a quiet dedication to the task that sets Benítez apart. He is a football man — anything else is irrelevant. Not for him the TV adverts, his own national television show back home, and the constant preening for the cameras. And Benítez is a *Liverpool* man. He didn't need to hail from Merseyside to fit in with certain aspects of the city's character — the 'down to earth' attitude that made Jamie Carragher quickly give up possession of his first and only leather wallet, as it was too flashy (what was wrong with keeping his money loose in his pockets?) Had Mourinho, as Liverpool manager, stumbled into a bar containing 500 Reds, you sense he would have stood on a table to make himself seen and heard, and asked for the karaoke microphone, before twisting the lyrics of Carly Simon's song to "I'm so vain, I'm sure this song is about me".

When Benítez did so, it was about the fans. This humble man was humbled, and embarrassed, by the attention. But all the same he knew an important bond had been secured.

Chelsea, Stamford Bridge, 27th April, 2005

One of the biggest occasions in English football history — and here Liverpool were once again, slap-bang at its epicentre. While the new millennium hadn't proved much better than the 1990s in terms of the club's average league position, four domestic cup finals in five years was nothing to be sniffed at (one more than the entire previous decade), and on the continent the club had started repairing its damaged reputation in European competition. First the Uefa Cup victory in 2001, then the Champions League quarter-finals a year later; and now, the run to the semi-finals. In those four years, teams like Roma, Barcelona, Borussia Dortmund, Dinamo Kiev and Juventus were vanquished, and the club's Uefa coefficient (a ranking based on the previous five years of European competition) rose to such a point that the club was one of the highest-ranking teams on the continent.

It was a far cry from the 90s. If the club hadn't returned to scale the heights of the 60s, 70s and 80s, it had at least got itself back in the 'big time'.

On the outcome hinged possibly the highest stakes of any all-English clash — with arguably more riding on it than those who annually contest the FA Cup final; league-title play-offs (such as at Anfield in May 1989); or the race for 4th spot in the league, which is now annually billed as a £20m game. (It is if you get to the semi-finals the following season; it can also be worth approximately 50 pence if you fail to negotiate the qualifying tie: be warned, Kenwright and co.)

While English teams have met before in the European Cup (such as the Reds, as holders — yes, Uefa, *holders* — losing to Nottingham Forest in the first round of 1978/79, and Arsenal facing Chelsea in the quarter-finals in 2004) this was the first time two English sides had met in the semi-final. The only bigger game would be two English clubs contesting the final. While games which decide league championships remain massive occasions, there is an extra spice to European occasions; domestic issues being settled on a larger stage, so there is the doubling effect of 'two for the price of one'. However highly Liverpool Football Club values its 18 league titles, the four European Cups mean that bit more: that was always clear in the words of Bob Paisley — as 'old school' as you get — who understood their true significance. (Perhaps the significance of making the 2005 final is a little lessened by the Reds not being the English champions for the previous 15 years, but it remains hugely impressive nonetheless.)

Liverpool rolled back the years to put in an old-style European performance — calm, controlled, measured. In leaving Stamford Bridge with a 0-0 scoreline, Benítez pulled off a wonderful result, but one which essentially left a one-off knockout "winner takes all" second-leg. Chelsea had only managed to manufacture a couple of clear-cut chances, and both were blazed into the stand. Liverpool, meanwhile, forced Petr Cech into meaningful action on two occasions: first, with a smart stop from a right-foot Riise shot, and then, more commendably, a world-class tip around the post from Milan Baros' glancing header. Late on, substitute Djibril Cissé had a couple of chances to run at the stretched Chelsea defence, but he couldn't make the space count.

It was proving to be the perfect evening — lacking only the 'dreamland' of an away goal — when, with just two minutes to go, Xabi Alonso was chasing back to put pressure on Eidur Gudjohnsen. The Icelandic international, sensing Alonso alongside him, tried to barge the Spaniard off his stride. Having failed to successfully do so, the Chelsea striker threw himself to the ground in a heap, winning a free-kick in a dangerous position, and more tellingly, getting Alonso booked, and therefore suspended from the second-leg. Alonso was distraught, having instantly realised the consequences of Gudjohnsen's 'simulation'.

As a result, Liverpool would be lacking their most influential midfielder in six days' time, but fortunately central midfield was the strongest area of the squad (providing Didi Hamann could return from injury). Alongside Alonso in the middle of the park at Stamford Bridge had been a colossus: a powerful all-round talent making tackles, knocking passes and running past people for fun. Only, it was Igor Biscan, not Steven Gerrard. Once again Igor proved that his form was more than a lucky streak. Gerrard was patently off-colour, and many put it down to the 'Chelsea factor', in the same manner his performance in the Carling Cup final was affected by a season of speculation linking him with a move to Stamford Bridge. It was only the following day that the true reason came to light: he had awoken at 2am the morning of the match in agony, with a tooth abscess worsening to the point where he needed emergency dental surgery before the game. The lack of sleep, the anaesthetic and the antibiotics would also have taken their toll on his body and on his mind. Gerrard had done miraculously well just to be out there and playing.

Chelsea, Anfield, 3rd May, 2005

European football at Anfield in the month of May: it had been absent for too long. Skies cobalt blue at 7.45pm — proof that the game really mattered. The atmosphere inside the ground was not so much electric, as *nuclear*. A spine-tingling *You'll Never Walk Alone*. As the post-anthem applause broke out, fusion occurred on the Kop: the heat and light of a thousand suns blinding the Chelsea players. Crowned Premiership Champions three days earlier, following victory at Bolton, this would be a different kind of test for José Mourinho's men. Much had been made in the build-up to the game of the role the Anfield crowd would play. Mourinho, as ever, was confident, explaining that his players had already visited the arena and left with a win — clearly not realising that the noise from the crowd at midday on New Year's Day, when tired and hungover, would bear no resemblance to the most significant European night in 20 years.

It helped that the tie was so delicately balanced. It was too tight to call, and each team had factors working in their favour. Liverpool, at home and backed by the raucous Anfield roar, were without an away goal to act as a buffer. Chelsea needed only a score draw, while the Reds needed any kind of victory. Many predicted Chelsea's miserly defence would hold Liverpool at bay, and enable them to repeat what they had already done home and away against the Reds this season: win by a solitary goal without reply. They had just set the record for 1-0 wins by any Premiership-winning side (ten), and ominously for Liverpool hopes they weren't fussy about where they did it; half of those single-goal wins had come away from Stamford Bridge. However, in recent European matches the Blues had been shipping goals at an alarming rate.

The Londoners were buoyed by the psychological boost of having won their first title in 50 years, but may have celebrated a little too hard; or at least lost a little focus, and relaxed a fraction too much. The Reds, meanwhile, were a colossal 33 points behind them in the league table. Chelsea needed victory to justify the recent £213m investment, but by winning the Premiership (as well as the Carling Cup) they had already outstripped all their achievements since 1955. Liverpool had less pressure and expectation, but had no other chance of silverware, and were below Everton in the race for 4th place. Chelsea had been beaten semi-finalists the year before, so it was suggested that fear of failure would drive them on. It also meant that they knew the pressure of the big occasion. Chelsea had won three of the four previous encounters, but Liverpool were getting closer to victory in each successive game. The Blues had a couple of key players missing due to injury, and had to alter the shape of their attack. Liverpool's squad contained three key players only just returning from long spells on the sidelines — Cissé, Hamann and Kewell — and who were therefore lacking in match sharpness. The Reds were also without the side's key player, Xabi Alonso, following Eidur Gudjohnsen's clear dive in the first leg, not to mention those ineligible for the Champions League. Chelsea's players had been 'though the mill' at the Reebok Stadium the previous Saturday, with Mourinho fielding his strongest side against Bolton in order to take his team to Anfield with confidence sky-high, while Benítez had rested Hyypia, Traore, Baros, Biscan and (for a half, at least) Luis Garcia for the home draw with Middlesborough, while Hamann was returning from a six-week lay-off.

Wherever you looked there was a *pro* here and a *con* there.

If the outcome was too tight to call, the only goal of the game proved even tighter. The move started on the left wing, with Riise cutting inside Lampard 40 yards from goal. Instantly a roar burst from the Kop, even though Chelsea had nine men behind the ball. Riise's pass into Gerrard's feet still suggested little danger, with the Liverpool captain facing his own goal. Milan Baros span in behind the Chelsea back line, and Gerrard flicked a delightful pass straight into his path: the kind of move — pure perfection in its timing and execution — that could dissect any defence. Baros beat the onrushing Cech to the bouncing ball, lifting his foot high to scoop the ball over his international colleague's head. The young Czech 'keeper collided with the young Czech striker. There was a moment's pause, as the Kop howled for the award of the most obvious penalty of the season, but the referee waved 'play on'. The ball fell onto the prone Baros' back, and bounced away from John Terry inside the six yard box. In a moment of sublime anticipation, not only had Luis Garcia moved in from the right wing to back up the play, but he read the awkward bounce and adjusted his feet accordingly, leaping to make contact with the ball at its highest point; waiting for it to fall would have given Terry the chance to clear. It flicked off Terry's thigh, and looped towards the goal-line, where Ricardo Carvalho and William Gallas waited. Upon hitting the turf, it skipped up a little, as the spin hastened its path towards goal, and that was just enough to take the ball over the line as Gallas hooked it away. Or so the referee's assistant thought.

Luis Garcia also played his part in forcing the officials to award the goal: he wheeled away in certain celebration, not looking back until he reached the fans in the Lower Centenary stand. Referees and linesmen often base their decisions on the reaction of the players. The little Spaniard was so certain, it meant he *must* have scored. The Chelsea defenders all paused, and none argued with the referee when he pointed to the centre circle. The crowd's reaction also said it all: *goal*.

However, did the ball actually cross the line? Not a single Liverpool fan cared (then, as now). But of course the post-match focus was on the nature of the goal; virtual replays suggested the whole of the ball was not over the whole of the line, but the freeze-framed television pictures clearly showed Gallas' left foot plumb on the line, and his right foot — with which he made the clearance — subsequently behind the line.

As the move unfolded, the officials had a number of decisions to make. Was Baros offside? (No, his run was perfectly timed.) Was Baros' foot high enough to constitute dangerous play? (Possibly, although he was far quicker to the ball than Cech, and as such, with the 'keeper two yards away, it wasn't obviously dangerous; had Cech been quicker to see the danger, then it would have been a Chelsea free-kick.) Was Cech's challenge worthy of a penalty? (Without doubt, as it was late and reckless, and floored the striker.) Would Cech have been shown the red card? (The referee later confirmed that yes, he would have dismissed the 'keeper.)

Clearly, and understandably, the referee did not want to *have* to send off a player just three minutes into the match, especially as it would have meant a suspension from the final. But that doesn't justify 'fudging' the decision: Cech could still have been dismissed even if the referee allowed play to continue. (The referee later booked Baros for a fractionally late tackle, and yet Carvalho, who was 'on a yellow', escaped censure on three separate occasions: clearly the referee felt an imperative to not book players in danger of missing the final.) The award of a penalty, and having to face ten men for the remaining 87 minutes, would clearly have suited Liverpool, but the two previous penalty attempts had seen Baros miss at West Brom, and Gerrard blaze wide at home to Spurs. In the end, the award of the goal was a form of justice, not least because it followed the *fifth* clear penalty claim of the season for the Reds against their west London adversaries; not a single one was granted. On New Year's Day, at the exact same position on the pitch — underneath the crossbar, in front of the Kop — Tiago had punched a ball from the goal-line. If two wrongs do not make a right, then *five* wrongs deserve some kind of divine retribution.

From then on the game was a tight, tense affair that opened up in the second half as Chelsea poured forward and Liverpool hit on the break, mostly through the three substitutes: Cissé, Núñez and Kewell. On three occasions Cissé came close to sealing the victory: a header from a fine Djimi Traoré cross; a shot from the edge of the area that deflected into the side netting; and, following a poor Gallas header, and instinctive lob that lacked the elevation to beat Cech.

Dudek, meanwhile, had next-to-nothing to do, much like at Stamford Bridge. In the 67th minute the Blues managed their one and only attempt on target over the course of the two legs — a stinging Frank Lampard drive from a free-kick, which the Reds' keeper tipped around the post. Otherwise Mourinho's men huffed and puffed, creating two clear chances in each match, but every one was either high or wide, but at any rate certainly far from handsome. As such, it was hard to see how they felt worthy of a place in the final. It was especially fitting that as the 97th minute approached — the referee inexplicably adding six minutes of injury time, possibly in an attempt to appease Chelsea officials, as there was nothing in the second half to warrant more than half that amount — Eidur Gudjohnsen, the man whose dive had ruled out Alonso, hit a wild close-range shot a yard past the far post. Had it been on target, the immense Jamie Carragher may have cleared, but the relief was palpable. As it was, Carragher collapsed and lay prostrate, clearly in shock, his face buried in the Anfield turf. His footballing life had just flashed before his eyes. Luckily, so too had Gudjohnsen's drive. It was another 'tight' moment, and the margins between success and failure were summed up in that one instant. Had the Icelandic international scored, there was no time left for a Red riposte, and Chelsea would have won on the away goal rule. Liverpool would certainly have felt cheated, given the six minutes added to the end of the game. Gudjohnsen received his comeuppance, as did Mourinho: underestimate the mythical power of those 12,400 people in the Kop at your peril (especially with the spirit and soul of 100,000 others crowded behind that goal, and the history enshrined therein). Diving on the spur of the moment is one thing — a rush of blood, a decision rashly made in the heat of battle — but planned and premeditated diving to deny another professional his place in the next match (as appeared to be the case), can only lead to one thing: cosmic retribution. It's the only kind of justice that is above the influence of money.

Jamie Carragher had just played the game of his life — which was saying something, given the levels he had reached over the course of the season, not least in the previous three Champions League matches. Combining the expert reading of the game of Alan Hansen with the brute force and colossal bravery of Ron Yeats, it was the kind of display that will be talked of in hushed reverence in 20 years' time. It's easy to go overboard in terms of praise, and confuse what constitutes greatness — but it was undeniably the stuff legends are made of. As towering as Sami Hyypia proved, Carragher — five inches shorter than his Finnish defensive partner — seemed twice as tall. Alan Hansen described

Carragher as "ten times" the player he himself had been; a ludicrous overstatement, of course, but refreshing to hear all the same, if only to know that the 'present' was finally allowed to stand shoulder to shoulder with the 'past'. Hansen remains the one centre-half against whom all others in red must measure themselves. But it was hard to believe that even Hansen, in his glorious pomp, ever had a better game than the one Carra pulled from the hat on May 3rd.

When the referee *finally* blew for full-time, in the 97th minute (it felt like the 97,000th), Anfield erupted like Krakatoa: an undulating sea of bright-red lava, bubbling and spewing on the Kop, along the Main and Centenary stands, all the way down to the home section of the Anfield Road end. It was chaos; delirium reigned. The players lost themselves in scenes of wild celebration. Xabi Alonso, dressed in jeans and hooded top, ran onto the pitch and exchanged a massive embrace with Steven Gerrard.

The most extreme reaction was from John Arne Riise, who, in a moment of utter abandon, threw himself into the Kop, and seconds later, threw his kit, John Aldridge-style, to the delirious fans. Thankfully Riise kept his modesty tucked within his grey jockstrap. "I didn't know what I was doing, I just kept giving the fans everything I had on," he later said. "I can't remember if they started calling for me to do it or not, but I had said to the players before the game that if we won I'd strip off and give all my clothes to the fans. It was the greatest night ever. You should have seen the dressing room, it was unbelievable. I could have cried. In fact I was crying one minute and laughing the next — and I wasn't the only one."

Money had been on the agenda too often during the course of 2004/05. But now — as in 2001 — the main focus was on the chance to achieve something monumental. Benítez, while still bemoaning the disappointing league form, went out of his way to note the positives of the European campaign. "The most important thing above everything else is we've recuperated the prestige of the club. Maybe people are seeing Liverpool can rule Europe again," said Benítez. "We can attract players in England, but maybe the biggest impact is in Europe where people will say Liverpool are at the top again. That's important. The result is significant for many others reasons, including the sponsorship situation and the signing of players. This will make it easier for us. Maybe I will now have more money, certainly more than a week ago."

If it came back to money, it's because money could help towards sustainable success, taking the club beyond one-off achievements, however remarkable. But it was the direction in which the club was headed which mattered most. "When you talk about players," the manager said, "they see we're on the way up. Players like Steve Gerrard can see the difference and know where we are going in the future. In Xabi Alonso and Steven Gerrard we have the spine of a team for many years."

AC Milan awaited in the final — and some test they would provide, in what many would later call the greatest European final of all time . . .

Part Three: the future

Chapter eighteen

Tomorrow's men

One of the most common explanations espoused to explain the absence of a league title at Anfield since 1990 is the "lack of local heart", especially with the greater influx of foreign players, as seen across the board at Premiership clubs. (But which hasn't stopped certain other clubs from winning the title.) It is often suggested that the great Liverpool sides always contained a selection of local players who were 'key' to the team: its *heart*, no less. And that is, of course, a complete fallacy. Unless your geography is so poor that you count Glasgow, Edinburgh, Dublin or Jamaica as 'local' to Liverpool, then players like Kenny Dalglish, Graeme Souness, Ronnie Whelan and John Barnes were actually from much further afield. Prior to the 1990s, very few of the Liverpool's *indispensable* players hailed from Merseyside, and even fewer — a paltry amount — came up through the club's own ranks. It was only in the '90s — when the club was no longer at the pinnacle – – that its key men, its far and away best players, were either Scousers, or at least products of the Academy. There is a rather large paradox in there somewhere.

In some ways the club should actually be considered *Scottish*: there can be no doubt that Scotland is the country to have contributed most of the crucial elements in the club's post-war success. Its most inspirational manager — the incomparable Bill Shankly — was from north of the border, and Kenny Dalglish's record when in charge — three league titles, two FA Cups — can be bettered only by Shankly and Bob Paisley. Its best players were also Scottish: Billy Liddel and Dalglish remain the two most revered men ever to wear the red shirt, followed fairly closely by Graeme Souness, arguably the club's finest-ever midfielder, and Alan Hansen, its best-ever defender. Ian St John, Ron Yeats and Steve Nicol were also far from shabby.

In fact, the starting XI for the 1986 FA Cup final — when beating Everton 3-1 — contained not one single Englishman, let alone any Scousers. It didn't stop Hansen from lifting the cup.

How many Liverpool players came through the youth ranks in the 1980s? Sammy Lee made his debut in 1978, and after that you have to go all the way to 1986, when Gary Ablett made his first appearance, to find a Liverpudlian having any kind of run of games — and even then, Ablett was never to go and really establish himself. He also suffered a lot of criticism from fans — arguably more than had he been from outside the city.

Players like David Fairclough and Sammy Lee, despite obvious highs, never quite had the glittering careers at Liverpool that the aforementioned bought-in players experienced. These two, along with Ablett and one or two others since, have perhaps seemed less glamourous, and were possibly taken for granted. Ultimately, there were always far better players at the club, and that was what held them back the most.

Many of the other local players from the halcyon years found their way into the Liverpool side via a circuitous route — the kind you no longer see. Kirkby-born Terry McDermott started out at Bury, and arrived at Liverpool via Newcastle United. Jimmy Case arrived from non-League Liverpool South, for a paltry £500 — a steal at ten times the price. Even Scousers David Johnson and Steve McMahon started their league careers at Everton, and arrived at Liverpool via Ipswich and Aston Villa respectively. Jason McAteer was the last imported Scouser, back in 1995. Prior to Steven Gerrard, Robbie Fowler, Jamie Carragher and Michael Owen, the best players to emerge through the ranks were Ian Callaghan, Tommy Smith, and Phil Thompson, and Thompson was the last of those three to make his debut, in April 1972 — 21 years before Fowler's.

There can be no doubting that local talent remains important to a club like Liverpool, in that it's always better if there are highly accomplished Academy graduates in the team. But it's even better, given the choice, to have a Xabi Alonso than a Jason McAteer (conversely, it's preferable to have a Jason McAteer than an Istvan Kozma). The key remains how good the player is, not where he hails from. Can he play, and does he *care?* World-class foreigners are preferable to local journeymen. There were no Arsenal fans complaining during their unbeaten league season of 2003/04: they were elated to see Thierry Henry tearing down the wings, as opposed to some local product like Perry Groves. Of that side, only Ashley Cole came through the Arsenal youth team, and Sol Campbell was the only other Englishman to start regularly. That players like Henry and Patrick Vieira played with such passion and commitment (and no little skill) was all that counted.

Then, of course, there were the two situations that arose with Chelsea over the course of 2004/05. For all the protestations from fans about how representing their local club means more to players, it was Ashley Cole — and not Henry — who was accused of meeting Chelsea officials behind his club's back. Abramovich's billions meant nothing to Henry, when the Russian made the mercurial Frenchman his primary target upon moving in at Stamford Bridge; Henry was happy at Arsenal, and wanted to play for Arsene Wenger, with whom he shared mutual trust and respect. (Football isn't always about money.) Similarly, it was Gerrard who was sorely tempted by the west London riches on offer in the summer of 2004, and who may yet leave his beloved Reds to join the 'Russian Revolution'. (Of course, at that time there were no *non*-Scouse players at Liverpool that Chelsea were interested in unsettling and prising away — the anticipated £20m offers for Bruno Cheyrou and Salif Diao never materialising.)

In the past, such as in the late 1960s and early 1970s, Liverpool mined clubs in the north for their best young players, rather than promoting from the club's own youth set-up. Steve Heighway arrived from non-league Skelmersdale and made his debut in 1970; Ray Clemence from Scunthorpe United in 1967; Kevin Keegan from the same club four years later; Emlyn Hughes from Blackpool in 1967. Before them, 'Sir' Roger Hunt, from Lancashire, was poached from non-league football.

Once he was in charge, Bob Paisley picked up young players like Ian Rush (18) from Chester, Steve Nicol (19) from Ayr United, and Ronnie Whelan (18) from Home Farm in Dublin. There was no need to produce players of such quality, when they could be found relatively cheaply elswhere. (Having said that, has any manager in the history of football mined smaller clubs for cheap talent as well as Paisley?) Small clubs now hold the big clubs to ransom if they have a jewel on their hands, and those jewels grow ever more rare.

Back then, it was possible to find top quality players at Bury and Scunthorpe, to pluck them from obscurity and, after a spell in the Central League, feed them into the first team. But such a step-up is no longer possible. Such is the quality in the top division, from all over the world, that it is now incredibly rare for a lower league player to jump three divisions. Even if those players exist, it can cost as much to buy a bottom-division left back as it would to buy a full international from France or Spain. (The last great player to be plucked by Liverpool from the relative obscurity of the lower divisions was Rob Jones, in 1991.) These days, Premiership clubs can even be wary of taking players from the division *directly below*; Dean Ashton and Rob Earnshaw being recent examples where only relegation-threatened teams dared to invest in players who are clearly talented, and who know where the back of the net is. Everyone says there's now a bigger gap in quality between the Premiership and the Football League, as evinced by the lack of teams from outside the top flight making it to the latter rounds of the FA Cup, and by the fact that the promoted teams are nearly always the ones facing relegation twelve months later. Gone are the days when a team like Nottingham Forest could be promoted and be Champions of England within a year, and Champions of Europe a year later.

So it's clear: Liverpool football club has had a fair amount of notable local-born players and Academy graduates. But since 1959, rarely more than two or three at the same time. During Gérard Houllier's reign, there were nearly always three: Gerrard, Carragher and Chester-born Owen, who was at the club from the age of nine. More players of their calibre and commitment would have helped the Frenchman achieve his ambitions. They existed, of course: from other parts of England, and all over the world. Often he just didn't buy the right ones.

Bright futures

Young players may not realise it, but they represent something remarkable and unique to football fans. In amongst the mundane drudgery of a faltering campaign, when August's optimism has long-since given way to mid-season resignation, the *promise of a brighter tomorrow* is gold dust. The future is always better (to optimists, at least). Thoughts turn to glamorous summer signings, and the kids in the youth team who are ready to make the step up. A football fan's thoughts are always half turned to the future, as are a manager's. They may claim to take it 'one game at a time', but there has to be a long-term plan, too.

The thing with the kids is that they are yet to fail us. Their ability to succeed or fail at the top level is protected by the fact that they've never had the chance, therefore they can't be proven incapable. So the cry goes up: give them a go, they can't be any worse than *so-and-so*. Of course, they *can* be.

Often it's an experienced international who they are 'supposedly' superior to. And throwing a kid in before he's ready can do more harm than good. You don't want to destroy a player's confidence by asking him to swim when, at that stage of his development, he's only capable of sinking or, at best, treading water.

The club's recent failure to produce a youth team player capable of becoming a fixture in the side — the last was Steven Gerrard, who made his debut in November 1998 — has been the cause of much hand-wringing and consternation. It was no secret that Gérard Houllier and Steve Heighway fell out over what the former saw as a lack of quality emerging from Kirkby, and what the latter saw as the manager's refusal to consider his protégés and instead buy in kids from France. The first team had reached the stage where it needed an injection of quality, and the Academy was offering only 'very good' players — not potentially great ones. Stephen Wright came and went, and appeared to have found his level with Sunderland. Neil Mellor, so prolific in the Reds' reserves, failed to convince while on loan at West Ham, scoring only two goals. Jon Otsemobor had a couple of great games for the first team, but failed to get a look-in when on loan at Bolton, and looked more at home at Crewe. John Welsh, promised 15 games by Houllier during 2003/04, ended up barely featuring.

All of these players have enough about them to suggest fine careers in the game — but that doesn't mean they are set for *great* ones. In squads that contain 20 full internationals, young players at the big clubs need to be exceptional to thrive. And maybe that's the whole point: there is no place in the major sides for players who aren't of the very highest standard.

Of course, that means there is less opportunity to get experience for those in need of it, and in some ways that makes it a catch-22 situation, with loans to other clubs being the only viable solution. At this stage it is worth noting that no youth team graduate released by Liverpool, Arsenal, Manchester United or Chelsea at an early stage of their career has gone on to prove the decision a major mistake. These clubs have let good young players go (usually due to character flaws), but in recent years have not let a single *great* one go. Older players like Beckham, Owen and Fowler moved on either because they themselves wanted to, or because their club felt it had already seen the player's best years, and was time to cash in. You will find a long list of players — Stephen Wright, David Thompson, Keith Gillespie, David Healy, Robbie Savage, Jody Morris, John Harley, Jay Bothroyd, Julian Gray, et al — who were released by the 'big four' early in their careers. None would now get into the first team of the club that let them go; and none have gone on to do so well for themselves that they played for a club that finished higher than their first employer. (Kevin Nolan of Bolton remains the closest Liverpool have come in recent years to passing up on a fine young player, but that was when he was 15, and before he had sufficiently developed.)

Some players will improve after leaving a massive club — transfered as a small fish from a big pond to become a bigger fish in a smaller pond, they thrive under less pressure, or with more responsibility within the team. Big clubs simply don't make mistakes. You get the odd example of a *very young* kid who's told he's not good enough, such as when a teenage Alan Shearer failed to impress on his Newcastle trial. (Although by making him play in goal they were hardly going to see the best of his striking prowess — the stupidity of the English game in years gone by never ceases to amaze.) But when a player has been on a club's books for a number of years, and approaching his twenties, a full assessment will have been made. It's hard to think of a single top international player released by one of the big English clubs since Manchester United, in the early-to-mid-80s, let both David Platt and Peter Beardsley go. By 1990 both were starring for England as the side came within inches of making it to the World Cup final.

Benítez, upon arriving at Liverpool, instantly found a place for Darren Potter and Stephen Warnock; the latter returning from a very successful loan spell at Coventry City, having previously done well on loan to Bradford City. There was no messing about: both were involved in the crucial Champions League qualifier in Austria, against Grazer AK.

Benítez was hailed as someone who puts his faith in youth, but in truth he was not doing anything any other manager would not have done. Let it not be forgotten that Houllier, as soon as he was in sole charge, instantly promoted Steven Gerrard and Stephen Wright from the Academy. A new manager has a clean slate, and so can assess *all* his options in the way an established manager can't (given he will be at a stage of his stewardship when experimentation should be a thing of the past). Benítez was later lauded for using the youngsters in the League Cup, but again, this is nothing Houllier didn't do most seasons. Fringe players like Otsemobor made next to no inroads into Benítez' plans over the duration of 2004/05, although John Welsh, after initially failing to impress the manager, did start to feature a little in the second half of the campaign, notably in the Champions League against Bayer Leverkusen, and when starting league games against Bolton and Crystal Palace. Potter and David Raven were understandably seen only on rare occasions, given the early stage of their development. Warnock and Neil Mellor both featured fairly regularly at certain parts of the season, but mainly because of injuries to more senior players. While both did well, neither was what you could consider a 'youngster'. Where Owen and Gerrard were England internationals as teenagers, Warnock and Mellor were now 22, and still not regulars in their club sides. Still young, of course. But not 'kids' still wet behind the ears. By the age of 22 it should be clear whether or not the player has a future.

Of course, players like Owen and Gerrard don't spring up on an annual basis. And the next great Scouse teenager was an Evertonian — Wayne Rooney — who made the unusual decision to stick with the Blues rather than join the Reds, unlike so many of his predecessors. You cannot 'make' players like Rooney, Owen and Gerrard — there is no secret formula perfected in a laboratory, where a child is taken and experimented on by men in white coats, resulting in a fully-formed talent revealed to the world on a conveyor belt. You can only find them — the diamond in the pit of coal — via your talent scouts, and try to lure them to your club, which often involves rule-bending sweeteners to provide extra incentives, or a phone call from a star player or the club's manager. From that point on, it's about giving them the best advice, looking after them as human beings first and foremost, and allowing their talent the freedom to breathe and blossom.

At the start of 2004/05 all U17 and U19 sides were disbanded as the youth structure in England was restructured, resulting in an U18 league. Liverpool's U18s had a torrid time, and lost nearly every game. But the point of a youth team is not to win trophies, simply to produce great players. (That was not meant to sound easy.) You could have a great team, made up of eleven good players who combine particularly well, but where none of the individuals are capable of making the grade. Or you could have a shocking team containing two truly outstanding kids, and see more benefit to the first team. Obviously a winning mentality at that age helps, and it does tend to be the case that successful youth teams are the ones that throw up the most gems. (See Liverpool's only FA Youth Cup success in 1996, with a team containing Owen, Carragher, Thompson, and Gerrard.) The majority of youth team players don't even get to have careers in the professional game — most drift away from the sport, or ply their trade in non-league football. So anyone who makes it in the top two divisions is more the exception than the rule.

Where FA Youth Cup success has been lacking in recent years, there was some optimism provided in the Carling Cup, when 'Benítez' Babes' progressed to the semi-finals, before a more experienced side surmounted that particular hurdle, 2-0 on aggregate against Watford. David Raven — winner of an award as one of the four most promising youngsters in the land when aged 16, and captain of England at various youth team levels — announced himself onto the scene in the win at White Hart Lane, where a very raw Liverpool side defeated a full-strength Spurs line-up on penalties, after a 1-1 draw. That result remains one of the highlights of the season, as it was totally unexpected. Raven, although nominally a centre-back, made his bow in the right back role, and given his lack of height, that could be the position he makes his own in years to come.

A collection of Liverpool rookies and reserves had earlier beaten Millwall 3-0 at the New Den — an incredibly impressive result, given the hostilities in the crowd, as Liverpool fans were taunted about the 96 deaths at Hillsborough. Millwall internet fora were the starting point of these songs, where, ahead of the game, groups of Lions' fans tried to think up the most sickening songs possible. It was a minority, condemned by fellow Millwall supporters, but still disgusting behaviour. To insult the dead and dearly-missed is as low as you can get. Millwall's Chairman, Theo Paphitis, in claiming that his club was whiter-than-white (no pun intended, given the National Front element among their support) would have been well advised to check various Millwall websites for written proof of the intentions of those attending. The victory at Millwall — set to scenes of crowd trouble reminiscent of the '70s and '80s — was given a gloss by Milan Baros' two late goals, having entered the fray after 70 minutes, but the victory was well-deserved all the same.

One of the players to emerge with most credit from these two games was young American centre-back, Zak Whitbread — another with a very bright future, although whether he will be quite good enough for Liverpool only time can tell.

Change needed

In March 2005, Benítez made known his displeasure with the reserve set-up at Anfield. He explained: "We need to change things and the first idea will be to change the structure of the reserve team. If you don't have a lot of money you need to have good young players for the future with quality in the reserve team and, although we do have good players there, we need more. We have used some of them in the Carling Cup but I want to be able to use reserve players in the Champions League. I want more English players because it would be easier for me. But when you go to buy an English player the price makes it forbidden — they are asking £4m for 15-year-old players! We have a list of young English players but besides their names we have a price and that makes it difficult. If you go to look at young players in Argentina you can maybe sign three for every English one."

The mention of Argentina was no accident. Benítez is a big fan of players from that country. His success at Valencia was built around the spine of Roberto Ayala, Maurico Pellegrino and Pablo Aimar. Spain — given the language, climate and style of football — is still the most popular destination for South American talent heading to Europe. But it is still a market that English teams need to analyse.

"We have reorganised the scouting department and we're finding new scouts for many countries," explained Benítez. "So far we've recruited three new scouts abroad and have changed four or five with regards finding players for the first team. I hope to recruit at least another three. We have someone in South America now, Spain and Portugal. We need to place someone in Africa, although it's not always easy to find the right people. We will recruit more scouts."

It's worth noting that these are all countries famed for skillful, expressive football. *Latinos* and Africans. The club's scouting networks already exist in other areas of the world, so maybe it's simply redressing the balance. Benítez continued: "Sometimes finding a player is about being in the right place at the right time. You always need to see the player more than once, and then you lose time. Maybe it's true sometimes you can tell if a player is good enough within five minutes, but then there is a danger someone will come and offer more money. We can't get involved in auctions."

That is the key — being first to spot the talent, and procuring it before the more wealthy clubs are alerted. Arsenal have frequently beaten wealthier competitors in this respect. Benítez has already showed he knows how to spot — and sign — a *real* player, in the form of Xabi Alonso. But at the cost of £10.5m. Still money well spent, of course. But the key is for him to find players like that (not that they are ten-a-penny) when they are 17 or 18, and yet to sign a professional contract. Benítez's reputation in his homeland will ensure that young Spaniards will want to trust their careers to him. Just as Wenger started out by buying Frenchmen — a teenage Nicolas Anelka, and rescuing Patrick Vieira from the AC Milan reserves when the giant midfielder was just 20 — then Benítez needs to find some young Spanish bargains to set the ball rolling, as he should know that market better than anyone.

Arsenal have developed a sensational youth team: a mix of the very best local talent combined with top quality youngsters brought in from all over the world: players like Cesc Febregas, snaffled away from Barcelona (much to their chagrin), and able to look outstanding in the first team at the age of 17. (The Catalan side also lost 17-year-old defender Gérard Pique to Manchester United.) Wenger's is the blueprint Benítez will need to emulate. Without large investment, Liverpool simply cannot compete with Manchester United and Chelsea, whose wealth is self-generating in the first instance, and a bottomless pit in the second. Benítez's budget will bear more resemblance to Wenger's over the years — the Frenchman having recouped almost as much as he has shelled out, and much of the balancing of their books is down to finding a player like Anelka for £500,000, and selling him for £23m — and doing so *after* he's helped them to a league and FA Cup double. Success at Liverpool will depend largely on the manager's tactical acumen, and how he motivates his team. But also crucial will be the club's ability to source young players from England, and further afield, so there is talent on tap, ready to drip through. It is currently a long way behind Arsenal in that regard.

Has the Academy in Kirkby 'delivered' since it was opened in 1999? Was the initial outlay (and £3m annual running costs) money well spent? That's something that will need a little more time, as the first set of boys — the ones who have had their *entire* footballing education at the complex — are yet to make their way through the system. The benefits will filter through over a number of years. At least that's the theory.

The value of a good youth set-up is evident in the quality produced in the last decade. It is probably as a result of a low point in the 'cycle' that the last six years have seen no one particularly special come through the ranks; just as Manchester United's well has run a little dry. It would be nice to think players of the calibre of Gerrard and Owen are already at the club, in its junior teams, ready to make similar progress. If they are, the club will do well to protect their identities, for fear of "Joe Cole syndrome" — the player shown off to the Upton Park faithful before he was even close to the first team, and starting out under the kind of pressure that only made it harder for him to succeed.

Benítez has already started addressing the shortfall in teenage talent at the club. Paul Harrison, the young English goalkeeper at the club, was deemed not good enough — a real shame, given the boy's father and uncle died in the Hillsborough disaster. It would have been both fitting and poignant if he had been able to make the grade, but a move away from Anfield beckons. In January 2005 Benítez moved to sign 19-year-old Scott Carson, whose deal at Leeds was about to expire, for less than £1m. Younger than Harrison, Carson was already the regular England U21 keeper. Carson represents the kind of outstanding teenage quality the club needs to attract, at a price that represents a real bargain. The best players will always want to play for a club like Liverpool, and a manager like Benítez. The fee is the key.

Great expectations

It is hard to fully understand one particular criticism of Gérard Houllier, where it was suggested he *willfully* omitted Heighway's charges, due to the two men not seeing eye to eye. That would surely be a case of cutting off his nose to spite his face: no manager would risk his job by opting to not play a kid who was patently good enough — the next Owen or Gerrard, for example. If a player is good enough, he will get to play.

But it did become clear that there was not enough dialogue between the head of the first team, and the head of the youths. Some of Houllier's young overseas imports, such as Carl Medjani, who arrived from St Etienne in August 2003, initially appeared no better than players already at the club, such as David Raven, and it seems Heighway felt there was favouritism shown to the French boy. But even Medjani was a fine talent: captain of the France U18 side, and invited to train with Manchester United by Alex Ferguson before Houllier stepped in. He had also been courted by Arsenal and Bayern Munich. Benítez sent the player out on loan to French Second Division side, L'Orient, in the summer of 2004, and he will hopefully return much-improved from the experience. Given Benítez had loaned out a series of Houllier's other signings from French football — older players like Cheyrou, Diouf, Diao and Vignal — with a view to them never returning, it was naturally assumed that Medjani would follow suit. The difference is that Medjani, at just 19, retained the potential to succeed, while the others had received ample opportunity in the Liverpool first team, and ultimately been found wanting.

Houllier was not mistaken in gambling relatively small sums on Gregory Vignal and Djimi Traoré; nor was he wrong to snaffle up Bayern Munich's out-of-contract Alou Diarra. Diarra is often cited as an example of the invisible man, but this is a player who became a full French international in 2004 during his loan spell at Lens — proof that great development in his game was taking place, even if it wasn't overtly visible to those on these shores. This summer he will either return to Liverpool, with two years left on his contract, or be sold — for considerably more than the compensation Liverpool had to pay Bayern.

Although not exactly "cheap" by anyone's standards, it's also hard to argue against the combined £6m paid out for Anthony Le Tallec and Florent Sinama-Pongolle. Players of that outstanding pedigree simply weren't coming through the youth system at Liverpool — two of the best in the world for their age group when Houllier again beat Manchester United and Arsenal, among other top clubs, for the signatures of the 16-year-olds. (One well-publicised signing Houllier lost out on was the then 17-year-old Swiss central defender, Philippe Senderos, who, now aged 19, has already had a very successful run in the Arsenal first team — highly unusual for a teenage centre-back.)

Arsene Wenger, when talking about his young French striker, Jeremie Aliadiere, claimed that the difficult age for player development at a top club is 19-22. By that he meant that the players are too old for the youth team, too good for (or not benefiting by playing in) the reserves, but not yet good enough for the first team — trapped in some kind of nether world, neither here nor there. Loan deals become the only option. And yet the press often see this a sign that a club is prepared to let a player go. It was suggested that Le Tallec's Liverpool career was over when, as a 19-year-old, he was sent for a year at French First Division club, St Etienne (you should know that name well), especially as the player had asked for the move. But Rick Parry told the French club, in no uncertain terms, that there would be no option of a permanent deal at the end of it. However, Le Tallec suffered the same fate as Neil Mellor had at West Ham: namely that their new clubs were under great pressure (St Etienne to get away from the relegation zone, West Ham desperate to make the play-offs), and therefore not in a position to gamble on youth.

The idea of such a loan arrangement is to give the player the experience he needs, including how to deal with the pressure of *meaningful* matches played in front of large crowds (even 15,000 is a massive leap from a few hundred at reserve matches). Reserve football involves a strange mix of players: raw-but-hungry kids (some very young); older pros out of the first-team picture and going through the motions; valuable players looking for fitness after injury; players sent there as a form of punishment (being sent to Coventry with the reserves being an even greater punishment); even trialists, of variable quality. If the first team has a game during the week, the reserve side can be comprised solely of kids; if the first team doesn't have a game for a couple of weeks, it can be full of key players looking to maintain fitness. There is no consistency of selection, and sometimes, especially during the winter, there can be no reserve football at all for months on end. Regular first team football, even at a lower level, can help young players develop at a better rate.

Young players progress at different speeds, and experience accelerated spells of development, like 'growth bursts' of talent and proficiency. (As well as *literal* growth spurts helping or hindering their development.) Those whose physiques are the most impressive at 14 or 15 tend to make the breakthrough at a more tender age, as they are the boys ready to compete with men (give or take the odd exception to the rule, like Michael Owen, whose pace meant he could escape past defenders before they out-muscled him). Players like Norman Whiteside, Mark Hughes, Sol Campbell, Emile Heskey and Wayne Rooney had the physiques of 28-year-olds when they made their high-profile breakthroughs as mere teenagers. But often these are the players who develop the slowest after this point. They may still become great players, and improve, but the playing field levels out when those who develop more slowly eventually catch up. Just look at Shaun Wright-Phillips, who has been tipped to leave Manchester City this summer for a £20m fee. Two or three years ago, no one thought he was anything particularly special at all, but he always had good natural ability with the ball — he was just small and unable to impose himself. Sometimes it takes time to develop, especially for smaller or less-muscular players.

It was never going to be easy for Le Tallec and Sinama-Pongolle in their early years at Liverpool, and not just in terms of getting their names to fit across the back of their shirts. After all the hype, and following two years waiting in anticipation, many fans expected both of them to be fully-formed world-class players as soon as they arrived. After all, these were voted the top two players in a recent U16 World Cup — and, to boot, winners of the *Golden* and *Silver* boots. Disappointment set in early with some fans, despite the occasional encouraging cameo from both players. It didn't help when some TV "experts" were writing them off, or casting doubt about their ability, when they were still just 18. Utterly ludicrous. (What next? A promising six-year-old boy told he'll never make it in the game?)

Sinama-Pongolle's pace and trickery won several penalties in late 2003, and he was denied on a few more occasions, with legitimate appeals waved away. But his finishing was erratic. Le Tallec showed some nice touches, an ability to win headers, and a willingness to tackle, but his problem was *where would he play?* Houllier opted to use him mostly on the right of midfield, where he would be under a little less pressure, but where he could also feel isolated. (Central players tend to thrive on constant touches of the ball, so when they play out wide they're always looking to wander into the action — resulting in the team losing its shape. Wide players are used to standing in space, and waiting.) Le Tallec's best position — where he made his name — was as the 'second striker', playing in the Bergkamp/Dalglish role, looking to use his clever footballing brain to drop deep and pick holes in the opposition defence with penetrating passes, while possessing an ability to get into the box and finish, which was highlighted during the pre-season game against Wrexham in July 2004, when he scored both goals in a 2-1 win. He had also put in some stunning displays for the reserves in that particular role. Good players can play anywhere — for example, at the Ajax Academy Bergkamp learnt the game during stints all across the field, including full-back. But all players have their *best* position, and while Bergkamp has occasionally featured in midfield for Arsenal, Arsene Wenger has yet to deploy him at left back, or in goal.

Le Tallec and Sinama-Pongolle remain incredibly good players for their age — just 20 — a fact that should not be overlooked. Both still have extremely bright futures ahead of them, and almost certainly at Liverpool if they progress steadily. Sinama-Pongolle would already have made his 100th senior professional appearance had a serious knee injury not interrupted his momentum. (He has already played 49 games for Liverpool, although 32 have been as sub.) He had started to find the net with a little regularity in the winter of 2004, scoring the winner against Southampton and a fine half-volley at West Brom, as well as converting the penalty that earned a draw in the Carling Cup at White Hart Lane (and scoring the decisive kick in the ensuing shootout). Most notable was the goal that altered the complexion of the game against Olympiakos, scored a mere minute after his half-time introduction. It was the most important goal scored by any Liverpool player during the season, as it was the one that undeniably altered the course of the game, and the course of Liverpool's season in Europe. Without that goal, the others could not have followed. He also produced one of the most memorable moments of skill: the shimmy that sent Vieira and Lauren the wrong way in the home victory over Arsenal.

Le Tallec is not that far behind, but needs to win back the trust of Benítez, after opting to go to St Etienne on loan. It takes most players a little while to get used to playing at the very top level (especially if they haven't got blistering pace or staggering upper body strength, as is the case with Le Tallec; or are very small, as is the case with Sinama-Pongolle). It's even tougher if the player in question is also having to adapt to a totally new style of football in another country. It is still *football*, of course, but played in a totally different manner. It is like asking a rookie rally driver to jump straight into the cockpit of a Formula One car, and expect him to tear past Michael Schumacher. It's a different kind of driving, in a different situation, and with different challenges.

Reports have emerged in recent months suggesting that Uefa are yet again toying with restrictions on clubs, to thwart those teams who buy in their entire first team squad. In the future, Champions League squads would need to contain a number of homegrown players. Of course, such a ruling will be questioned in the European courts, so there's a fair chance that it won't come into being. But even if it does, 'homegrown' is an umbrella term that would include players like Le Tallec and Sinama-Pongolle — players who have spent significant part of their developmental years at their current club, and could be classified as graduates of the Liverpool youth system. Had the ruling been in place during 2004/05, Liverpool would have been fine with the list of players they registered. Chelsea and Arsenal would not.

Obscurity knocks
Not every 'next big thing' becomes as successful as anticipated. Some end up not even being able to turn heads in a Sunday League game. So many factors come in to play: injuries from which it's impossible to fully recover; burn-out, from overplaying as a kid; falling out of love with the game, and losing the necessary desire and hunger; interference from outside influences, leading to a lack of professionalism; the feeling of having 'made it' simply by signing the first basic professional contract, or believing the hype.

Injuries play a big part in a young player's development. It can be impossible to keep pace with your peers if you are in traction, with your knee requiring a succession of operations. Stephen Warnock and Steven Gerrard were both held back by serious physical problems that made training and playing difficult, and often impossible.

David Mannix was a real star at the age of 13, in a similar way to Gerrard and Owen. But his career came perilously close to being over before it ever really began: a serious knee injury hampering his progress between the age of 16 and 18. Only now is he starting to get some momentum, and is making great strides. Hopefully he's already used up his lifetime of bad luck, and will go on to become a household name, but no one can say for sure. Liverpool have been involved in two of the most famous cases where hugely-promising teenagers have failed to make the grade, and simply disappeared from view. These are cautionary tales.

The first comes with the unforgettable name of Cherno Samba, which, during the year 2000, evoked images of quick Brazilian feet and graceful skill. For a while he appeared on the back pages of the tabloids more than Michael Owen, as Liverpool fought off stiff competition to try and sign the 14-year-old from Millwall. Having spoken to, and visited a number of clubs, Cherno chose Liverpool because "they showed they wanted me the most". After a week-long trial, which went well, Cherno was back at school when he got a call on his mobile. It was Michael Owen. His friends were gobsmacked. Owen, he claims, told him to sign for Liverpool, as the two would form a great partnership. The deal was all ready to go through, but the two clubs could not agree compensation. Millwall, understandably, did not want to lose their hottest prospect on the cheap. Liverpool were worried that as Millwall would not name a price, a tribunal would pluck a figure from the air, and it would be exorbitant. An *impasse* was reached, and a deflated Cherno lost his way, along with his motivation.

Samba, still only 19, is fortunate to have time still on his side, and is trying to rebuild his career, having recently started a four-year 'development contract' with Cadiz, who are doing well in the Spanish second division (and where Harry Kewell spent part of the season training to get fit). He is also currently a member of the England under-20 side. He could yet make the grade: unlike Wayne Harrison.

Harrison, just 17 at the time, was signed by Liverpool in 1985 for a then world record fee for a teenager — £250,000, paid to Oldham Athletic. (To put it into context, Steve McMahon, signed from Aston Villa around the same time, cost only £100,000 more.) But Harrison's dream of representing the club he supported quickly turned as sour as milk left for a week in the summer sun: a double hernia, groin problems, damaged cartilage in his knee and an injured shoulder. Just as things were looking up, a collision with the Bradford City reserves goalkeeper damaged both the medial and cruciate ligaments in his knee. Six years — and 23 football-related operations later — he was told by the new Liverpool boss, Graeme Souness, that the doctors felt he would never be able to play again. They were right.

Jermaine Pennant, signed by Arsenal as a 15-year-old, after the player had already represented Notts County, is another whose application and temperament have — like Samba's — been repeatedly questioned. Clearly it can be tough when players have it all before they are legally allowed to drink or vote, and when common sense is not one of their strong suits — although it's hard to find much sympathy for their plight, especially considering what others, like Harrison, have to endure. It takes more than prodigious talent with a football to succeed. Good luck, and good sense, are two crucial aspects of making it to the top, and staying there.

Golden groups

In the 1990s, Liverpool and Manchester United produced the best homegrown players seen in English football in generations. Before them, in the mid-80s, Arsenal had a collection of kids emerge under George Graham, who became part of the team that won two titles, but with the exception of Tony Adams, none went on to have much impact beyond these shores — Paul Davis, Niall Quinn, Michael Thomas, Paul Merson and the late David 'Rocky' Rocastle were all fine players, but none were ever thought of as world-class. Adams, the most mocked initially, went on to become one of the great leaders.

Although they occur, such clusters of talent remain rare. United's team of 1996 featured the players dubbed "Fergie's Fledglings": David Beckham, Nicky Butt, Paul Scholes, Gary Neville and Ryan Giggs. Within the space of five years, between 1993 and 1998, Liverpool promoted to the first team Robbie Fowler, Michael Owen, Jamie Carragher and Steven Gerrard, as well as lesser talents, Dominic Matteo and David Thompson, who both came very close to England caps. (Matteo later went on to represent Scotland.) The club could quite conceivably go another 50 years without mining such a collection of gold nuggets, especially with Steve McManaman having already made the breakthrough at the turn of 1990. Although all played together in the same side during 1999, the main disappointment for the club was that, unlike their rivals at Manchester United, these players would all peak at different times, and would never appear together in one side *when at their best*.

That would have been something truly special: if in 1999 we'd seen the McManaman of 1997, the Fowler of 1996, the Owen of 2001, the Gerrard of 2004 and the Carragher of 2005, all in tandem; add the Matteo of 2001 — when at Leeds — and the Thompson of 2003 — at Blackburn — and you can really sense the missed opportunities.

A great shame, but such is the nature of homegrown talent. It comes and goes in waves.

Chapter**nineteen**

This is Anfield – *isn't it?*

There is a game that takes place at Anfield at the stroke of midnight every Saturday, at the precise moment the 'day of football' gives way to Sunday morning, the day of rest. Away from the cameras' glare, and not picked up by anyone in the media (even those 'in the know'), the 'secret' weekly occasion doesn't even warrant the wattage of floodlights. The only fans present are those whose physical remains were buried in the ground *within* the ground, and those who never returned from Hillsborough in April 1989: Anfield's eternal spirits. They gather together at the perimeter on all four sides of the pitch, their smiling faces up-lit with a glaucous sheen as each holds a small orb of wax, flames flickering on its wick. The lambent glow of the candles casts enough light for the players to see each other, amid a flurry of dancing shadows as the wind whips down the touchline. Not that these footballers need light: so telepathic, they can find each other with pinpoint precision even in the dark.

On one such night, Bill Shankly, dressed in a white mac, walks over to one group of fans, and says "Y'see, I told ye — it *is* more important than life and death." And then he winks, and turns on his heels.

One team is managed by Shankly, the other by Joe Fagan, each taking it turns to pick a player from those assembled on the touchline, with Bob Paisley invariably the first name called by Shanks. Bob is not the best player, of course, but is on the same wavelength as the boss. Elisha Scott, in thick roll-neck jumper and woollen gloves, keeps goal at the Kop end for his Scottish manager, and ahead of him Emlyn 'Crazy Horse' Hughes charges about the pitch with the energy and elegance of a young foal, complete with bobbing head, but also no little skill, and with a heart as big as the ball itself. Burly Billy Liddell, hair slicked in a centre-parting, receives a pass from Paisley and powers past defenders at pace, cutting inside from the left wing to arrow a shot at goal; Gordon Hodgson tucks away the rebound as it spills from Sam Hardy's grasp. For Fagan's team, Albert Stubbins — who, in 1946, chose Liverpool ahead of Everton on the toss of a coin — reforms his potent strikeforce with Jack Balmer, who, months after Stubbins' post-war arrival, scored hat-tricks in three successive league games, a feat not since repeated in England. The old magic is still there, and despite never being a firm crowd favourite, Balmer scores three yet again, with Stubbins also on the scoresheet. Elsewhere, Jimmy McDougall, Tom Bromilow, Harry Chambers, Jack Parkinson and Phil Taylor pass, move and tackle, their feet not quite touching the ground. And on some Saturdays, such as this one, Matt Busby leaves Manchester to join his old teammates for the craic: football, camaraderie, and the post-match libations in the Sandon. On this night the game ends 4-4, and the ribbing commences before the players even reach the changing rooms.

Anfield is Anfield

For 120 years that exact same rectangle of land in L4 has been home to many of the game's biggest legends, as well as hosting countless more. Liverpool's *Field of Dreams*. It was built, and, true enough, they came. But an era draws ever closer to an end. One of the most famous football stadia in the world — and probably the most revered, judging by the way players from visiting European teams still speak of its aura in awed tones — will close its turnstiles for the last time, and, just a John Arne Riise long-throw away, the club will re-open them onto a new future.

Will Anfield still be *Anfield* when the club relocates a few hundred yards? Still *in* Anfield, of course. And let's not forget: Anfield came into existence when a team — Everton, no less — were unprepared to pay the rent at Anfield. Everton soon vacated Anfield, and now, in the 21st Century, Liverpool are proposing to make the opposite move, returning to the very roots of football in that part of Merseyside. And they will be doing so unaccompanied by the Toffees.

For a while, it looked as if the government, courtesy of sports minister, Richard Caborn, were going to coerce both clubs into sharing a new ground; or rather, Everton moving in on Liverpool's plans, once their own fell flat. Pressure wasn't confined to Westminster. Liverpool City Council leader Mike Storey told *BBC Radio Five Live:* "I guess that sadly a groundshare won't happen and in years to come we will regret it." The Northwest Development Agency also inserted its over-sized oar, and refused to remove it, preferring to prod, and then prod some more. In September 2003, Bryan Gray, chairman of the NWDA, said: "The Northwest Development Agency, together with Liverpool City Council, have asked Liverpool Football Club and Everton Football Club to discuss the economic development and regeneration benefits of building a new, world-class football stadium in Liverpool." It wouldn't be the last time they'd ask.

Ground-sharing may exist on the continent, but then so does a tendency to eat shelled slug-like mollusks, the legs of pond amphibians, and the eyes of sheep. That doesn't mean the English, for all our culinary crimes, would accept such delicacies served in the local chippy. What works in Milan would not work in England. Football culture can be gently altered over a period of time, but it cannot reversed overnight. A Liverpool Council spokesman said in December 2004: "It's disappointing that both sides have been unable to reach agreement." The spokesman added: "However, the existing plan for a new Anfield is part of a major regeneration of the Anfield and Breckfield area. We fully intend to deliver that because of the economic benefits it will bring to an area which badly needs them."

Had the folly been further pursued, the project would never get off the ground, and in 2020 both sides would still be gridlocked in disagreement. There's no point something making financial sense if *no one likes it,* and everyone ends up giving it a wide berth. If that was the case, everyone would be driving Skodas.

So will the new stadium be called Anfield? What's in a name, anyway? Well, quite a lot, obviously. A rose might indeed smell as sweet by any other name, but if it was called 'sewage' you wouldn't buy your fiancée a dozen for Valentine's Day. (Of course, you might buy some for your mother-in-law.) Arsenal's jaw-dropping £100m deal for their new Emirates Stadium at Ashburton (which also included eight years' shirt sponsorship) did not so much raise eyebrows as, to quote Rick Parry, prove a real "eye-opener". Selling the stadium's name has been likened to selling the club's soul. Perhaps it is. On the other hand, £100m is almost *ten* Xabi Alonsos. Draw your own conclusions on the way forward on that particular issue, but sparks are sure to fly.

Build it, and they will come.

When the time comes, the men gathered for the midnight kickabouts will put down the football, and Shanks, Paisley, Fagan, Tom Saunders, Reuben Bennett, Liddell, Stubbins, *et al*, will each lift a brick, a seat, a square of turf and — not alone — they will walk, as the protectors of Liverpool's heritage, to Stanley Park, to lay a new foundation. We won't see it — at least not in this lifetime, this dimension — but they will reconstruct the stadium and the Boot Room, and will continue to play their game as before. The move will be strange, not to mention emotional. It will take some getting used to, for all concerned.

This is Anfield. This is the playground of ghosts, the home to memories and history. Whatever happens, Anfield cannot die. A stadium can be torn down and quickly forgotten, but Anfield exists beyond mere bricks and mortar.

Whatever its form, wherever its grass, Anfield's *spirit* will live on.

After all — this is Liverpool Football Club.

Chapter twenty

Part Four:
Champions of Europe, 2005

Magical Mystery Tour

For the majority of the 40,000 Liverpool fans who made the trip to Istanbul, the journey was to prove an apt metaphor for the final that later unfolded: an extended ordeal, toil and effort running into overtime, all of which looked like coming at extreme financial expense — but one which, ultimately, was worth every ounce of energy, and richly rewarding.

For us fans, simply getting to the game appeared to pose more of a concern than the threat posed by AC Milan. Flights to Istanbul were thin on the ground, with prices hiked up to the £1,000 mark to cash in on the event. Like the match itself, the Reds had to do it the hard way: be it getting to the country — many travelled via Bulgaria, Greece, Latvia, Albania and Romania — or getting to the Atatürk Stadium, which was inconveniently positioned in the middle of nowhere, with just one gridlocked access road open to Liverpool supporters. Milan fans, meanwhile, were allocated the airport which was closest to the ground, and which also happened to be far larger than the one made available to all Reds. It was never going to be easy, seeing as Liverpool took three times as many fans as Milan. But if it was possible, you simply had to be there.

To put my own journey into context, in 1999 I was diagnosed with Myalgic Encephalomyelitis (M.E.). The condition — one which very few people understand, and which still needs a helping hand with regard to raising awareness — had gone undiagnosed for several years, and was getting progressively worse. At the age of 27 I had to give up all forms of sport, and in the last couple of years, from once being an 'every game' regular at Anfield, the frequency of my attendance has now been forcibly reduced to a more sporadic pattern. I say this not to elicit sympathy, as that is of no use to me or anyone else, but to highlight the lengths people such as myself, and many others, go to in order to follow their club. While my illness makes getting around harder than is ideal, I am also fortunate enough to be neither bed-ridden nor wheelchair-bound. In Taksim Square several Reds *were* in wheelchairs, highlighting that whatever it took, you could not let the chance pass you by. Other sacrifices were less easy to detect: but many will have been made by the travelling hordes, and many far greater than mine.

In truth I had not the slightest intention of going to the final, until an incredibly generous friend made a promise that he'd pay for my trip if we beat Chelsea. He was already in possession of tickets via the Uefa ballot. How could I say no? I knew the journey would be tough, given that even going to Anfield could be exhausting, but it would be the 'old gang' — those of us who sat together in the Lower Centenary for all those years — reunited for a road trip that would take us from Sofia to Istanbul, having flown to Rome, and from Rome to Bulgaria. But as I suggested, nothing would be straightforward. A day before we were due to depart we discovered that our minibus would not be allowed into Turkey, and it became clear to me that the alternatives would put too much stress on my immune system, which was already impaired. Strings were pulled, swaps were made, and I ended up on a flight out of Luton early on the morning of the game. On Monday 23rd it looked like my hopes of getting to Istanbul had been permanently dashed; by lunchtime on the 25th I was touching down at Atatürk Airport.

The buzz

Those who travelled in support of Liverpool converged at Taksim Square. The standing area at the top of a parade of shops provided the location to unfurl flags and banners. Below, a crowd of thousands gathered around the bus stops and taxi ranks, spilling onto the road and back around towards the park. Cans of beer were bought from entrepreneurial Turks and a football was repeatedly kicked aimlessly high into the sky; it only needed the presence of Duncan Ferguson to make it feel like watching Everton's desperate attempts to find an equaliser at Anfield in March. As I attempted to inch through the throng, to rendezvous with my 'gang' (who had had the journey from hell to get there — 'welcome to hell', indeed), this ball came sailing down with ice on it, striking a policeman square on the shoulder. Everyone paused, and the surrounding area fell silent, as the policeman stood with the ball in his hand, holding it as if it were the weapon of a crime. Completely deadpan, he then drew back his foot and toe-punted a drop-kick that ricocheted off a tree and hit a bus. Everyone was having a great time, and nothing — apart from raucous renditions from the travelling Kop's repertoire — could disturb the peace. (What a contrast to Heysel, almost 20 years earlier to the day, that there was not one single arrest among the thousands of travelling Reds.)

The sun was shining, there wasn't a cloud in sight, and this small part of Istanbul felt like the centre of the universe. And so began the mass exodus, as everyone commenced their quest to make it to the other side of the city, and the venue for a certain football match.

My party jumped aboard one of the hundreds of specially laid-on buses from Taksim Square to the stadium. It was a remarkable two hours. Reds were crammed in like the London tube at rush hour. To a man we incessantly sang "Ra-Ra-Ra-Rafa Benitez . . .", as we stomped our feet and drummed on the metal plates above the window. The noise carried out to the waving Turks lining the streets and applauding from the high-rise blocks, and to those honking horns in passing cars. It was like the semi-final atmosphere from Anfield, generated by 50 (maybe 150!) Reds packed onto one ageing bus. I was sat next to the only Turk onboard — an elderly man who had decided to take the ride, to experience something unique. Every time anyone put a cigarette to their lips he was offering his lighter; bizarrely, he sat the entire journey with an unlit cigarette in his mouth, and refused the Liverpudlian offers to return the compliment. He only removed it when trying to sing "Xabi Alonso, Garcia and Nunez", while waving regally to the crowds as if he was the luckiest man alive. We were royalty, greeted by the people of Istanbul as the bus wove through the streets. (Again, how different to years gone by?) Progress was steady, until we got to within a couple of miles of the stadium — from which point it was gridlock: bus, taxi, bus, taxi, bus, taxi, *ad infinitum*. Only those on mopeds could make their way through. Oh, and those haring at 70mph the wrong way down the dual carriageway.

There was a party taking place atop the bus in the lane next to ours: John Power, the lead singer of the Scouse band Cast (and before that a guitarist in the legendary La's), was dancing with four or five others, and jumping from bus roof to bus roof, even on the rare occasion when the vehicles were edging along at 10mph. Eventually everyone lost patience at being stuck in a virtual car park. Bus by bus, fans deserted their inert vehicles and began walking the last two, three, four or five miles, across a barren lunar landscape in the middle of nowhere, toward the party taking place outside the ground in the distance, which was lit by what was either the stadium or, some pondered, a crashed spaceship. A red river ran down the hill, to the sea of red, dancing and singing in the Atatürk car park. It was a pilgrimage — a kind of worship not made by fans of the club for two decades.

Having been urged to make it to the ground early, we had all skipped eating since lunchtime. Food and drink would be available at the stadium, we were told. They weren't. Unless, of course, you had access to the hospitality tent: the *Champions League Village*. How typical of Uefa to take care of all the dignitaries, but ignore the genuine fans. All there was to greet the rest of us was a stage with disco lights and a parade of festering chemical toilets. The weather had turned: it quickly clouded over, and the evening air had a distinct chill. In the circumstances, it was amazing that the travelling Liverpool fans were in such a good mood. And spirits stayed high — until the first minute of the match put a dampener on proceedings.

The most remarkable comeback of all time
The Golden anniversary of the world's greatest club competition: 50 years of high drama topped, on 25th May 2005, by the 'final of all finals'. As with the 2001 Uefa Cup final, Liverpool were tipped to bore the world; now, as then, they thrilled it beyond expectation, beyond *belief*. Except this time it meant a whole lot more: a bigger competition, better opposition, a more remarkable set of events. No team had ever come back from three goals behind in the previous half-century of the tournament's finals. And then came Liverpool: how fitting that the Reds should get to keep the trophy, courtesy of their fifth success in 28 years, given the nature of the victory. The turnaround from 3-0 down was enough in itself to merit a permanent housing of the trophy at Anfield.

Too often in football adjectives are cheapened by their use following relatively meaningless endeavours. As a result, there is nothing that can accurately convey the scale of a truly remarkable, fantastic, wonderful, spectacular, inspiring, unbelievable, bewildering, stunning, monumental, momentous and "incRedible" achievement. The only more remarkable comeback imaginable, would be to see the 2006 Grand National at Aintree won by Lord Lucan on Shergar, with Elvis Presley riding pillion.

Possibly the greatest individual talent the world has ever seen was in no doubt as to who deserved to win. Diego Maradona has never been especially fond of the English, and was surely at the final to support the Italians, having spent many years in that country. However, he left a convert. "Liverpool showed that miracles exist. They proved that football is the most beautiful sport of them all. After this game, my English team is going to be Liverpool. I came across some of their fans beforehand and they told me they were going to win, but that they would be made to suffer. It's just the way it happened. Liverpool are the best team in the world for what they have done in this Champions League. They deserved the Cup."

He was not finished. "Even the Brazil team that won the 1970 World Cup could not have staged a comeback with Milan leading 3-0."

Johan Cruyff, himself widely regarded as holding a place in the top five players of all time, said: "There's not one club in the world so united with the fans. I sat there watching the Liverpool fans and they sent shivers down my spine. A mass of 40,000 people became one force behind their team."

That is the power of the night: enchanting the game's legends and enticing a new generation of fans. Perhaps they will be called 'glory hunters' by many of their peers, but young boys and girls all over the world will now have a special place for Liverpool in their hearts, if their hearts have not already been won over by another club. As great as Chelsea's league success proved — a new highest points tally, and beating, by one, Liverpool's 1979 record for fewest goals conceded (in four less games, mind) — it had no single moment to match this night in Istanbul; nothing to quite capture the imagination. As happy as Chelsea fans will have been, none will have experienced the utter delirium of May 25th 2005. No amount of money could buy the drama and excitement tied up in winning *number five*.

Overcoming power and money was the key: the two most expensively-assembled squads in the world were vanquished, in the semi-final and the final; Fiat-backed Juventus, in the quarter-final, were not constructed on a shoestring budget either. Milan's owner, the Italian Prime Minister Silvio Berlusconi, who has bankrolled his side to an extreme degree, proved a laughably bad loser, but his bitter words only make Liverpool's victory all the sweeter: "Milan played much better throughout. We created move after move while they didn't create one move worthy of the name. What a shame."

What a shame indeed . . . Perhaps he missed the three fine moves which led to Liverpool's goals? He was right to some degree: over the course of 120 minutes, Milan played the better football. No one can dispute that. But who had the greater character? Football isn't just about creating the most impressive moves. Milan's defence had kept nine clean sheets in the competition *en route* to the final. In 180 minutes, Manchester United could not breach that famed rearguard once. Liverpool did not breach it three times courtesy of luck.

The best victories are never the 6-0s; they are the ones where the odds are overcome, and at half time in the Atatürk Stadium those odds were 360-1 against Liverpool emerging victorious. The better the opponent, the more impressive the comeback. But in order to make a remarkable comeback, you need first to make an almighty mess of things. From darkness comes the light, and those first 45 minutes were *black*.

It's all gone "Pete Tong"

Fifty-two seconds. That was all it took for the party to be well and truly 'pooped' by Milan. As the rhyming slang goes: it all went Pete Tong. The Istanbul evening — which had grown increasingly dark and sinister as black clouds gathered in bullying formations, with kick-off looming — was proving ominous. Liverpool were out of their league, and, it was easy to conclude, on their way out of the Champions League — for both 2005 *and* 2006.

The game had barely started when Paolo Maldini received Pirlo's free-kick and struck his shot into the ground. It looped up and arced over Jerzy Dudek's despairing dive. Was it down to Liverpool's zonal marking, or the fortunate result of a skewed cross and a miss-hit shot?

The Reds responded with a gutsy few minutes: Riise hit a phenomenal volley that cannoned back off Jaap Stam, and then Hyypia rose to head towards goal, but Dida was equal to his effort. Milan, with Kaká, Shevchenko and Crespo pouring forward, looked dangerous on the break, and 'Sheva' had a goal ruled offside — a warning of what was to follow. Liverpool players were still asking for a penalty — Nesta going to ground in front of Luis Garcia, and in so doing, unintentionally blocking the ball with his arm — as Milan strode upfield, Kaká sending Shevchenko through down the inside-right channel. The Ukranian's pull-back looked scuffed, but it evaded Hyypia and Carragher. Chelsea's Hernan Crespo, on a season-long loan to the Italians, scooped the ball home from inside the six-yard box.

Within minutes, it got worse. Another stunning break, with Kaká's sublime through-ball curling around Carragher's despairing lunge, and Crespo was in again, this time dismissively dinking the ball past Dudek.

We only sing when we're being humiliated

Half-time provided the reason why Liverpool Football Club is so special. A thrashing — a meltdown — was on the cards. It was painful. Losing a game of football is hard at any time. But when you've allowed yourself to dream the impossible dream, and in so doing, made an arduous and expensive journey to where Europe ends and Asia begins, as 40,000 Reds had, it *hurts*. At half-time, perhaps one or two Reds started their journey home. The other 99.9% stayed on, and began a chorus of "we're gonna win 4-3". It was brave, it was slightly amusing, but it was not sung with any great belief. Those around me in the East stand — which was a 'neutral' section containing only a handful of Milanese and thousands of Reds — were signing along, half-heartedly, as texts arrived on their mobile phones suggesting "you're gonna lose 7-0". At the time it was hard to disagree.

It's easy to think of football purely in terms of that rectangle of grass and what takes place within its white lines, but it's so much more than that; if not exactly life and death, then it can end up representing whatever you want it to.

Inspiration in life can be rare, and at times we are all guilty of taking our football club for granted. In this era when the professional game has been tainted by violence, sex scandals, drink and drug abuse, not to mention the mercenary greed of players and their leeching agents, it was nice to be reminded of the power of sport; indeed, the *point* of sport. It exists to teach us about ourselves, and about life. Everything is contained within the game of football, providing you are prepared to look for it. It is what it means to us — not to anyone else — that matters.

If we cannot learn lessons by participating in the game itself, we experience it vicariously through the exploits of those we choose to worship. But sometimes the lines blur, and a true symbiosis occurs. If it's obvious to say that the crowd in Istanbul could not have won without the players (the eleven best players plucked from the crowd, even including the likes of Bolton's Kevin Nolan, ex-Middlesborough star Craig Hignett, and various retired Reds, would not have beaten Milan), then for once it was no exaggeration to say that the players could not have won without the support of the travelling Kop. Just as it had against Juventus and Chelsea in the previous rounds, the noise from the stands affected the outcome of the match.

The first five minutes of the interval saw little activity from the Liverpool fans: a collective too stunned to do anything other than stare at the night sky. And then it all changed. *Everything.* The atmosphere, the belief. The reason? One song. *You'll Never Walk Alone* means more — so much more — than any other football song. It can be sung in victory, as the final whistle approaches — as it so often is. It has also been sung at funerals for the lost souls who supported the club, including those who died in so doing at Hillsborough. Its meaning would transcend any comparable terrace anthem if there existed any other anthems to compare. But none do. Its words have not been altered to fit around the club or its exploits on the pitch: they remain true to those penned by Oscar Hammerstein.

At 10.40 Istanbul time the Reds in the crowd rose, one by one, to add their voice to the choral harmony that, despite the soulless arena designed to let sound escape into the night air, reminded the team — and reminded all the fellow fans — that everyone should keep their head held high. There was nothing to be afraid of any longer: the storm had passed, and of course, after the storm comes the golden sky.

Above all else: hope.

In your heart.

The effect was so strong, it inspired the players as they sat shell-shocked in the dressing room (or possibly lay prostrate, hoping a hole would swallow them), preparing for the second half, or possibly hoping it never arrived. The muffled sound of the crowd drifting down the players' tunnel lifted them off the ground. Maybe it didn't have them pounding the walls screaming "We can win this! This Milan side are there for the taking!", but it registered all the same.

If the crowd weren't giving up, how could they? If 40,000 people made such a sacrifice, surely there was no option on giving up?

It was hard to avoid imagining how it looked and sounded to the AC Milan fans: how many of them may have paid their money at least partly to hear the legendary rendition? (Especially after their *Fossa dei Leoni* so amazingly sang it in 1989, following the Hillsborough tragedy.) Liverpool fans singing *You'll Never Walk Alone* is one of those things opposing fans — especially in Europe — feel a great need to experience. It is like those who paid to hear Sinatra, in his prime, singing My Way. There will be much talk about the downside of vacating the current Anfield, but *You'll Never Walk Alone* travels with the Kop, wherever that Kop may be. *You'll Never Walk Alone,* it is fair to say, is Liverpool Football Club. It is its philosophy, its belief system. That one song is all you need to know.

It was a very powerful experience, as a fan, to hear the familiar song sung — and to be part of the choir — in *such* footballing adversity. It summed up everything that is good about supporting your team; and in my case, it summed up why Liverpool Football Club is so special. A circle of discovery and inspiration between the players and the fans was completed by the team in the second-half. Believe, and it might just happen . . .

And so it began: the comeback. All credit to the players, for their miraculous contribution. But it started in the North, East and West stands at the Atatürk Stadium, and enveloped the whole of Istanbul. Without that song, the Liverpool players — described as "dead and buried" — would, like zombies in ancient myths, have needed to force their way up through the very turf as they fought to exhume themselves.

Dead and buried?

Far from it . . .

The tactical battle

Rafael Benítez received a lot of criticism for his decision to deploy Harry Kewell behind Milan Baros: not just for selecting Kewell, who many felt didn't deserve his place, but as an overall tactical *idea*. It did not necessarily tally with the perceived wisdom before the game as to where Milan's weaknesses lie. In the build up to the match, several pundits pointed out the success PSV Eindhoven had in utilising the space between Milan's midfield and its ageing defence. Andy Gray, for one, said the best way to beat Milan was to get at them, and attack them with pace. Teams who had been timid and defensive — such as Manchester United in the 'Round of 16' — were beaten without the Italians even having to break sweat.

Benítez had never forgotten the first time he saw Kewell: how the Aussie had tortured Jaap Stam at Old Trafford in 1999, when playing for Leeds as a striker. Here was the chance to hope he could do the same once again, while being able to drop into midfield to make the most of any gaps. It made sense, especially as Kewell had finally looked fit and sharp in training.

"One small thing can change everything," said Benítez. "Like when people ask me did I pick the wrong team at the start — I say why? Because if you have Harry Kewell fit, maybe it would be different. If you don't concede a goal, it would be different for sure. That's football. *Football is football,*" he added, quoting Real Madrid's erstwhile Yugoslav manager, Vujadin Boskov, whose limited grasp of Spanish led to him coining the phrase as shorthand for "anything can happen".

Tactics play a crucial role in any major game, especially if you are the less-talented side. Milan's teamsheet is intimidating to say the least, a collection of players on the wishlist of any European manager. Some of Liverpool's players, it is fair to say, are not even on Benítez' wishlist. But when you concede a goal in less than a minute against the best collection of players in world football (Milan possess the attacking stars to rival Real Madrid, and the defensive giants the Spaniards lack), it is a blow to the confidence and a blow to the gameplan. Football is football. The tactics had yet to even come into play before the Reds were chasing the game against the big favourites. Milan's confidence was as boosted as Liverpool's was shattered. Kewell was looking sprightly and determined until succumbing to yet another serious muscle injury. The Australian received jeers from the Liverpool end and some vitriolic criticism in the papers, and yet in those opening 20 minutes no Liverpool player looked worthy of the shirt: eleven men in red were shell-shocked. Kewell left the pitch at 1-0, not 3-0. Before his abductor muscle snapped, his movement had been bright and lively, but by then the entire Liverpool side had lost their composure, and he wasn't able to get into the game — the same as all his teammates. Fortunately, just as in Cardiff, his replacement scored Liverpool's second goal when chasing three — only this time it actually counted for something.

It did not need a scapegoat — in many ways it was no one's fault. Milan were buoyed by an early goal, and from then on their imperious class was impossible for Liverpool to live with. They became an unstoppable force, and although his omission was seen as key, it's hard to imagine Didi Hamann making much difference while Milan were so pumped up. (It took half-time for Milan to take their eye off the ball.) It was like a boxer having a fixed idea on how to face Mike Tyson in his prime, but Tyson finding a crushing blow with his very first punch; once hit squarely on the chin, you are entitled to walk for a while on wobbling legs, if not collapse outright. A predator then moves in for the kill, and that is precisely what Milan did; their mistake was to believe the match was over at half-time.

It didn't help that the occasion got the better of some Liverpool players. It's easy to be critical of players like Djimi Traoré for nervous displays, but this was the biggest game by far in the lives of the starting XI. These are human beings, not androids.

(As I watched the elaborate pre-match entertainment conclude, and took in the wild array of colours, sights and sounds that greeted the players as they strode out, I couldn't help but worry for their nerves: it didn't *look* like any other game I'd ever been to. It had a sense of occasion dripping onto every inch of the pitch. Even the running track that surrounded the advertising boards — usually so conducive to a subdued atmosphere — confirmed it as a major event: only Olympic venues seem to have them these days. And if an Olympic venue is used for a football match, it means it's of great import.)

Many of those playing in red had experienced cup finals — after all, this was the sixth the club had reached since the turn of 2001 — but none had been as momentous as this. Only Didi Hamann, on the Liverpool bench, had played in a game as big — or indeed, in his case, even bigger: the 2002 World Cup final. Vladimir Smicer, another sub, had played in the final of Euro 96, but it's harder to judge the importance of that particular competition. Milan were a team who had been there before. Seven of them had won it at Old Trafford in 2003. Paolo Maldini was in his *seventh* European Cup final; Clarence Seedorf held a record, having already won the competition three times with three different clubs. Others had played in World Cup finals — and won.

The introduction of Didi Hamann at half-time was rightly hailed as a masterstroke, as the German held the space in which Kaká had previously been running riot, but the change would have meant nothing had Milan kept their professionalism. Any team that celebrates at half-time has lost its focus. The tactical switch was so much more than swapping personnel: the key was the switch to a three man defence, and how Hamann's introduction liberated others. Gerrard now had the freedom to get forward, but it was no great folly to start him alongside Alonso in the midfield. Why wasn't Alonso keeping tabs on Kaká in the first half, or Gerrard — who could match the Brazilian stride-for-stride — chasing back to snap into those famous lunging tackles? There were two central midfielders in red, and yet neither was anywhere near the back four. The entire team was being overrun. In the first half the game seemed to pass Gerrard by. The weight of the world was on his shoulders. Many experts had called it a 'waste of talent' whenever he was employed behind the main striker, and here he was, in what people claimed to be his best position, helplessly watching the game take place around him.

"Game well and truly over"

Andy Gray, commentating on Sky Sports, wasn't alone in thinking Liverpool were dead and buried. ITV were also reading Liverpool the Last Rites. Perhaps the events of the second half — when it transpired that the game was anything but over — can be traced back to west London: not to Chelsea, but to Fulham. That October day in 2004 proved Liverpool could come back from the brink of defeat (after introducing a canny midfielder at half-time), and was used as an inspiration for the even more remarkable Olympiakos recovery in December; which, in turn, will have given the players at least a glimmer of hope, even if Milan were an entirely different proposition to the Greeks.

Half-time was when Benítez earned his corn, and confirmed his status as a master tactician. Any Plan A can go wrong if circumstances dictate, but unlike his predecessor Gérard Houllier, Benítez always has a Plan B, as well as plans C—Z if required. "It was very difficult to go into that dressing room and see the players with their heads down," Benítez later admitted. "We talked about different things. We had worked very hard for ten days and we needed to fight to the end. You have to keep believing in yourself.

"We had fought hard to be in the final. I was thinking about what to say and what to change. I needed to change the system and we needed to be more aggressive. I had to give confidence to the players. The first thing I did was explain the plan to Didi. I wasn't thinking about winning then, only about scoring. If we did that then Milan's reaction could be very different. They were afraid and everything changed when we scored. I was last in the dressing room. I didn't hear Milan celebrate but Alex Miller did. He told the players they were celebrating winning the cup. That was a good thing for us."

Milan celebrated at half-time, and had the air of men strolling onto the pitch ready only to complete a cakewalk. They weren't prepared to finish the game — for them, it was already over. Liverpool were actually better served by Crespo's (cheeky) third than Milan. At 2-0 the Italians would have still taken the second half seriously; as it was, they were smoking metaphorical cigars. (How beautiful, then, that it should have been Vladimir Smicer who was in Taksim Square six hours later, smoking what he described as the 'biggest cigar of his life'.)

Benítez' assistant Paco Ayesteran said of *El Jefe*: "We were three nil down and had made three mistakes, but to solve the problem showed his capability. I have never seen him nervous because when you are nervous you cannot think clearly, but to change the system was the key. Rafa is someone who thinks very quickly but it is difficult to think quickly and think right. That shows his talent. We couldn't change things in the first half because of the problems with Harry's injury but he came up with a great solution at half time. Didi started winning the second ball and that became a great help."

Liverpool finally got their passing game going. It wasn't perhaps the inspired pass-and-move of the well-drilled Italian aristocrats, but it was effective nonetheless. Riise was released down the left, and while his first attempt at a cross was blocked by Gennaro Gattuso, the second sailed into the heart of the area. Steven Gerrard, now allowed the freedom to get forward into the box, rose majestically to force home a difficult header, using every last bit of sinew to generate the sufficient power on what was only a hanging cross. Game on . . .

Gerrard, who won the Man of the Match award, finished the game at right-back, as Benítez reshuffled his pack for the final time, to ward off the threat of the tricky Brazilian substitute, Serginho. It was a complete mismatch: Gerrard won every single tackle, until the winger gave up taking him on and resorted to crossing as early as possible.

English spirit

If Liverpool lacked the world-class talent abundant in the ranks of the Serie A side, they did not lack heart, or English spirit. That was slightly ironic, given there were only two

Englishmen in the team, the lowest ever number of home nationals in a European Cup-winning side. The special never-say-die character (that pundits like Alan Hansen had earlier suggested was so sadly lacking in the foreigners signed by Houllier and Benítez) was all too evident: if Steven Gerrard was the catalyst for the remarkable turnaround, and Jamie Carragher's cramp-defying extra time efforts typical of the man's gigantic season, then what of the other twelve involved — none of whom were British?

Kewell tried to play on with a torn muscle: utterly impossible for any player, and yet he still got stick. The Australian aside, there was only the injured Steve Finnan (Irish born, but a man who learned his trade in England) who failed to make a significant contribution, having only played that miserable first 45 minutes. Sami Hyypia recovered from an awful first half, where his lack of pace was cruelly exposed, to look as commanding as ever; Xabi Alonso never stopped looking for the ball, and used it with typical intelligence; Luis Garcia never stopped running into space, and neither did Milan Baros, who had a thankless task against the twin peaks of Jaap Stam and Alessandro Nesta (the same applied to Djibril Cissé); John Arne Riise used every ounce of his considerable stamina; and Didi Hamann never let his omission from the original line-up affect his coolness. Each of Liverpool's four penalty takers was from the continent (Gerrard would have taken the fifth), as was the goalkeeper.

Perhaps the three biggest plaudits, in terms of character, need to go to the three most-questioned foreigners who featured in the final. First, Vladimir Smicer, who knew he was playing his last game for the club. He has always loved being at Liverpool, but had been told by Benítez that his contract would not be renewed. Since arriving in 1999 he had put in some sensational displays. The problem was that they were far too few and far between; possibly as, for most of the time, he was deployed in a wide area when it was behind the main striker where he excelled. Whenever he found his true form he fell victim to another niggling injury. His performance as a right winger after replacing Kewell, and then, later in the game, as an orthodox central midfielder (having swapped positions with Gerrard), was superb, and his swerving strike for the second goal, and cool penalty in the shoot-out (at a stage when Liverpool were in danger of throwing away a two goal advantage), resulted in the perfect going-away present. He'll never be remembered as a Liverpool legend, of course, but for all the criticism from his doubters over the previous six years, he has played a full part in *achieving* something legendary. In twenty years' time, people will smile at the thought of Vladimir Smicer, and his two key contributions towards lifting the trophy. He had earned the right to kiss the badge in a fond farewell.

Next was Traoré, who had rebuilt his career — and his reputation — over 50-odd games during the season, but with several pieces of poor play looked like undoing all his good work in the game that mattered most. His lunging goal-line clearance from Shevchenko towards the end of normal time was as important as any of the three goals that hauled Liverpool back into the game.

Finally, Jerzy Dudek, who revived memories of his remarkable debut season for the Reds. If arguments will always persist about the best save of all time (although Gordon Banks' dive to thwart Pele in the 1970 World Cup is still widely regarded as unsurpassable), then can there have been any better 'double save' than that which the Pole mustered in the 117th minute, to deny a bemused and bewildered Andriy Shevchenko? The first stop came from a downward header that reared up on its way to the back of the net; Dudek clawed it away before it crossed the line, but as miraculous as the save was, he could do no more than present the Ukranian — Europe's deadliest marksman — with a gaping goal from four yards out. If Shevchenko was the assassin supreme, then the enduring image was one of a cold-blooded execution: Dudek helpless on his knees as, from point-blank range, the Milan no.7 pulled the trigger, to put him out of his misery — and us with him. The shot fired, the crowd gasped, but instead of the ball rippling the net, it ricocheted off Dudek's arm and flew over the bar. It looked like 'Sheva' had missed the 'unmissable', but Dudek had moved to block the shot, and somehow — how, exactly, he didn't seem to know, and Shevchenko certainly didn't have a clue — got enough on the ball to make the deflection meaningful. Nine hundred and ninety-nine times out of a 1000, both keeper and ball would have ended up in the back of the net. This time, they didn't. Was this destiny?

In interviews following the final, Milan players all said they knew at that point that they just could not win; Liverpool players, meanwhile, felt assured they could not lose.

Completing the impossible

When you need three goals to draw level, it's hard to evaluate which is the most crucial. Clearly without the first you cannot score the second, and so on. So each matters equally. But if you had to choose one that had a greater effect than the others, it was arguably Smicer's. Steven Gerrard's strike may have got Liverpool back into the game, but at the time it looked like little more than a consolation. Milan were always going to rock briefly as a result, but it wouldn't be long before a side of such experience regained its composure, and reasserted its authority.

As it transpired, they hardly touched the ball in the next ninety seconds. It may have come their way when an offside flag was raised to Milan Baros' run, but the referee didn't blow his whistle. When they eventually did get the ball back it was in the form of a restart from conceding another goal. The ball was worked from left to right via Alonso and Hamann, until it ended up at Smicer's feet. The Czech let fly with a swerving drive from which Baros did well to pull his hand out of the way. Suddenly Gerrard's goal wasn't a consolation: it was a platform. If Gerrard's header was the slight seismic tremor, the light shaking of the ground, then Smicer's was the confirmation that an earthquake was under way. The second goal, following so quickly upon the first, shook Milan in a way Gerrard's had not; Gerrard's had worried them, of course, but Milan retained a two-goal cushion. Smicer's goal eradicated the Italians' sense of control. Smicer's goal caused outright panic. Once that one went in, the Reds had 30 minutes to score the equaliser — and at the rate goals were going in, that was enough time for twenty.

The nature of the goal helped too: a semi-speculative shot from distance that the keeper might well have saved. That it beat Dida, who could only palm it into the net, just made it seem like it would be Liverpool's night. Milan's superstars suddenly contemplated how awful it would be to throw away this game — even worse than the Serie A title they had recently conceded to Juventus. It was only a matter of three further minutes before the comeback was complete. The ball was worked once more from right to left, this time to Jamie Carragher on the halfway line. He strode forward with great purpose, and with admirable composure sent a firm low pass into Milan Baros' feet. The Liverpool no.5 flicked a delightful touch to Gerrard who was powering into the area. (While Baros would yet again fail to score, he made a telling touch in the build up to a goal, as he had with the winner against Chelsea in the semi-final. He played his part.) Gerrard, with the goal at his mercy, felt his heels clipped by the cynical Gattuso, who also gave the Liverpool no.8 a shove for good measure: quickly followed by an attempt to assume the look of an angelic child. The referee had no hesitation in pointing to the spot. Gattuso escaped a red card (in fact, he wasn't even booked) by virtue of not *technically* being the last man, with Cafu alongside him, but this was an interpretation that made a mockery of the rule. While Cafu was in line with Gerrard, the Brazilian stood no chance of tackling the Liverpool captain, who was well inside the area, and in the centre of the goal, with the ball at his feet. As such, Cafu was out of the equation. The only two men who could intervene were Dida on his goal-line, and Gattuso; and as such, Gattuso should have walked.

The arguments over the penalty, and whether or not the Italian midfielder should have been dismissed, did not help Xabi Alonso's composure as he waited like a condemned man on death row, alternately licking his lips and frowning nervously. The young Spaniard strode forward, and struck a clean penalty hard and low into the corner, but Dida dived quickly to his right to pull off a superb save. As the ball spilled back into play, it was a three-way race for the rebound. Alonso, Luis Garcia and the Milan defender, Alessandro Nesta all sprinted towards the six yard box; the Liverpool no.14 got there first, having the presence of mind to strike home (left-footed, this time) high into the roof of the net. He barely had time to turn around before Baros was hauling him to the ground and his wide-eyed delight disappeared under a pile of red shirts.

History repeating itself

The final would be decided by a penalty shoot-out, just as it had been in 1984. Jamie Carragher could be seen gesticulating wildly to Jerzy Dudek, making it clear that the Polish 'keeper had to do whatever he could to put off the Milanese penalty takers, reminding the No.1 of the legendary antics of Bruce Grobbelaar 21 years earlier. And it worked. Dudek explained his shoot-out antics: "Before the penalties Jamie Carragher came up to me like he was crazy, as he always is. He grabbed me and said 'Jerzy! Jerzy! Jerzy! Remember Bruce!' I just said to him 'Okay Carra, take it easy'. I've seen the videos."

The shoot-out was essentially won for Liverpool with Milan's first kick. Serginho, who had been successful with the equivalent spot-kick two years earlier, found himself totally unnerved, not just by the cacophony of boos and whistles from the majority of fans, but also by Dudek on his goal-line. The Pole did not yet resort to the 'wobbly legs' routine Carra advised (that was to come, of course), but for a while he did wave his hands like a hyperactive semaphorist. Even that was fairly meaningless. What counted was this: as soon as Serginho looked up after spotting the ball, Dudek took a large stride to his left. Dudek was effectively saying "If you've decided to put the ball this side, you now have to change your mind", and the one thing a player is told never to do, is change his mind. Just as Serginho was preparing to slot the ball into the open side of the net, Dudek moved across to his right. It wasn't chaotic jumping around, where a 'keeper only ends up putting himself off; it was considered, purposeful. The Brazilian, confused and nervous, chose to blast the ball. It may well have hit a Milan fan in the South Stand.

Next for the long walk was Didi Hamann, who had missed in the shoot-out against Birmingham in the 2001 League Cup final. This time he made no mistake, planting a firm shot to Dida's right. For the first time on the night Liverpool were ahead. More remarkably, in the aftermath it came to light that the German had finished the match, and taken his kick, with a broken bone in his foot. Liverpool's injury jinx struck again, but this time it came too late to harm the Reds' campaign. (Had the break been more serious, and Hamann been forced off on a stretcher, then heaven knows what would have happened.)

Next, Dudek saved from Andrea Pirlo, whose downcast demeanour was undoubtedly not aided by Dudek's frantically windmilling arms. "One or two Milan players changed their habits," said Benítez, "and Jerzy did a really good job when he went to the other side and saved."

Up stepped Djibril Cissé. The referee made him re-spot the ball, and usually such a pause is fatal to a player's concentration and composure. But the Frenchman, as we all now know, is made of tougher stuff than most. He must also have felt that destiny was on his side before he strolled up to the ball and coolly slotted it past Dida. Tomasson scored his, Riise missed — his placed, not powered, penalty well-saved down by the post

— and suddenly Milan found their scoring boots. Kaká ignored Dudek's gyrations and lifted his high past the Pole. Smicer's penalty was as good as any, and the most pressured of any the Liverpool team had taken, and so it was suddenly left to Andriy Shevchenko to keep Milan's hopes alive. Surely he would succeed: after all, hadn't he won his team the Cup two years ago, in exactly this situation? As he waited his eyes seemed hollow: was he haunted by his improbable failure to score at the death? Dudek appeared to have dived out of the way of the ball, as the Ukranian sent his kick centrally, but the Pole stuck out a trailing hand...

And that was it.

Liverpool were Champions of Europe.

Simple . . .

What a way to say farewell

All three of Liverpool's scorers against AC Milan, including Cissé and Hamann in the shoot-out, missed a large chunk of the season through serious injury. It was fair to say that, at last, they were receiving their pay-back.

Even the players who will be shown the door will have no real complaints; they won't be happy to be leaving, of course, but if they have to, what better way to go out? If it may seem unduly harsh to release or sell players who have played their part in a momentous success, then sentimentality cannot be allowed to get in the way of essential team rebuilding. Some who are tipped to be shown the door will remain as valuable squad players; others will perhaps only play once at Anfield next season, in the visiting team. While Benítez will now have money to spend, he cannot restructure the whole squad. Great players rarely come cheap, and making wholesale changes presents new problems: gelling a side, and settling new players quickly. Where Benítez had three years in many fans' eyes to make Liverpool challengers for the title, the problem now is that expectations have been raised.

And so the cycle of success breeding expectation continues: the club's past — now, its present — craves repetition in the future.

Benítez was not going to fudge the issue of releasing those for whom he can find no great use. "You have to speak to them face-to-face because the worst thing is not to tell the truth, to keep people in your squad when they are not playing so that they lose confidence." All players will respect such respectful treatment. The other benefit of freshening the squad is that it will ward off complacency. Anyone considering resting on his laurels will be history.

Where now?

So will Istanbul prove to be a one-off success, or the springboard to further glory? It seems highly unlikely that Liverpool can dominate the game in the way they once did, given the strength of Chelsea, Arsenal and Manchester United, but the Reds now have a chance to make it a regular four-horse race for the major honours.

Winning the trophy will present problems for next season. Being in the Champions League (should Uefa finally come to its senses), along with the World Club Championship in Japan in December 2005, will make progressing in the Premiership harder. The Reds are now there to be beaten: a notable scalp, more so than ever, for which scalp is more to be coveted than that of the Champions of Europe?

The benefits, however, should far outstrip the drawbacks. The confidence that victory will breed will be impossible to measure: but it *will* be significant. The team has learned to believe, and perhaps no amount of adversity can stop the Reds when their backs are against the wall. Olympiacos and, more crucially, AC Milan, will be part of Benítez' team talks for the rest of his time at Anfield. You can tell players not to give up hope; but nothing can beat reminding them that they have done it before, in the most miraculous comeback of all time.

The joyous celebrations after the match, and the homecoming tour through the city — where up to one million fans lined the streets — will have further strengthened the team bonding, and improved the spirit within the ranks. On the 25th May, a team came of age. The manager now has the money to improve the squad. The world's top players will have been captivated by the team's showing in Turkey, but also by the special support of the fans. Forget money alone; players would love to represent a club that receives that much support from its followers. Liverpool has always been a special football club — we knew that. But across the continent, younger players may never have realised; older ones may have forgotten. Beating AC Milan was the most timely reminder possible.

Liverpool will earn an estimated £30 million from their European Cup win in Istanbul — but this doesn't take into account the immeasurable knock-on effect on the club's general appeal over the forthcoming years, where more shirts will be sold, more merchandise will be bought, and so on. Christmas stockings from Woolton to Warsaw, even as we speak, await their copy of *'Du-Du-Du The Dudek: Dance Your Way To Fitness The Jerzy Way!'* Over the course of the competition, Liverpool earned £20.2 million in performance bonuses (which included £4.5m for winning the final) and their share of the media revenues. Taking into account gate receipts and sponsorship bonuses, the club's total earnings from participation in the Champions League will rise to about £30 million, according to Deloitte's sports business group. One obvious benefit will be the £10m guaranteed for reaching the group stage of next season's competition — the most likely outcome, despite Uefa's mixed messages.

Meanwhile, Carlsberg, who had been dying to claim that Liverpool were 'probably the best team in the world' since its association with the club began in 1992, could finally smile to themselves. Having come close to giving up interest in the Reds, the Danish brewer agreed to extend its £5 million-a-year shirt sponsorship deal for another two seasons.

As fans, we care about trophies, not about how much money our club has in its coffers. But the two go hand-in-hand to a degree. You don't need the *most* money, as Liverpool proved, but you do need some. And the more you have then the more — if in the right hands — that can be done with it. And in Rafa Benítez, all Liverpool fans can rest assured on that score.

Postscript

Where does inspiration on the football field end, and 'real life' begin? Does one bleed into the other?

I'd say yes. And this is how . . .

In some ways the end was only the beginning for me. Getting home would prove to be one the toughest challenges of my life — certainly the most physically gruelling. It started with the horrific journey by bus to the airport which took more than three hours — great for the first hour as the celebrations rang out, before everyone grew weary, or completely passed out. Next was the total chaos of the airport, where Turkey turned us into tramps: coupons for food in the marquee feeling like the procedure at a soup kitchen, and as the sun came up, fighting for cardboard boxes on which we could lie in the gutter outside the terminal, as, in dirty, smelly clothes, we all sought to get back to England. Sleep was a gamble, as no one knew when their flight would be called. At 5am a dazed Veggard Heggem wandered past on his own. Finally at 6am everyone was allowed into the terminal. Not that any planes were about to take off.

At 9am I managed to get my first sixty minutes of sleep in 30 hours, passing out on the dirty terminal floor, and at 10am I was woken: people were going to "storm" passport control. None of the flights to Luton had been called in the eight hours since the first was scheduled to leave, while only a handful of flights had departed to the north of England. In the end the airport staff said to just get onboard the plane on the tarmac, no matter which Luton flight you were booked in on: planes were treated as buses, in that if you could get onboard, it was yours. As we were driven by coach to our Boeing 737 we saw a group of Reds run down the steps of a parked-up Airbus and sprint to an adjacent plane on the tarmac. It resembled a game of Musical Airplanes. Any way you could get out of Turkey, you were going to take it.

All the while, the reminder from the fans at half-time, and the players in the second-half: don't give up.

My ordeal was not over. Back in England, and totally exhausted, I encountered roads as chaotic as those in Istanbul. What should have been a two hour drive north took three times as long: a car transporter had caught fire and melted the motorway. It was then that recalling the efforts of the Reds meant most — to keep me going, to keep me sane. I envisaged Steven Gerrard's extra-time tackles on Serginho, and Jamie Carragher's cramp-defying efforts to keep Milan at bay. Most of all, I pictured Djibril Cissé side-footing his penalty past Dida, and his ecstatic celebration. When his career was left in what appeared to be tatters by that horrific double leg break in October, writing this book had not even been considered. If Cissé felt a special sense of destiny on his side, then I could but think that luck, fate, destiny or simply good timing had played its part in this project. It was suddenly going to resemble a work of fiction; trouble was, surely no one would believe it? The final chapter would read as 'magic realism'.

I had a book to get home to finish, a deadline to meet. Rafael Benítez and the boys had given me an ending worth any possible price I would have to pay. As I sat in yet another traffic jam, the events in Liverpool, broadcast on the radio, kept me company: one million Reds lining the streets to greet a victorious team returning home.

Again and again I said it to myself: Liverpool Football Club, Champions of Europe. Liverpool Football Club, *Champions of Europe*.

And no, it hadn't all been a dream . . .

have a **hand** in raising awareness...
wear your colours

ninety**six**

the ninety**six** wristband

£1*

*Please include an extra **£1** for postage and packaging
if you're in the UK and **£2** if you're outside the UK

The Hillsborough Justice Campaign
PO Box 1089
178 Walton Breck Road, Liverpool L69 4WR
Telephone: 0151 260 5262   **Email:** info@hillsboroughjustice.org.uk
http://www.contrast.org/hillsborough